GIANTS, GOBLINS, AND GOVERNMENT
A MYTHO-HISTORICAL ACCOUNT OF THE ISLE OF MAN

WITH WORKS BY
ARTHUR WILLIAM MOORE

Giants, Goblins, and Government
A Mytho-Historical Account
of the Isle of Man

WITH WORKS BY
ARTHUR WILLIAM MOORE

EDITED WITH AN INTRODUCTION BY
A. E. CONGDON

WHITLOCK PUBLISHING
ALFRED, NEW YORK

The Story of the Isle of Man by A. W. Moore, first pubished by T. Fisher Unwin of London in 1901.

The Folk-Lore of the Isle of Man by A. W. Moore, first published by Brown & Son of Douglas, and D. Nutt of London in 1891.

First Whitlock Publishing Edition 2019

Whitlock Publishing
www.whitlockpublishing.com

ISBN: 978-1-943115-31-0

TABLE OF CONTENTS

INTRODUCTION i

THE LIFE AND TIMES OF ARTHUR WILLIAM MOORE.....xii

A TIMELINE ON THE HISTORY OF THE ISLE OF MAN ... xiv

NOTE ON THE TEXTS AND ACKNOWLEDGEMENTS xix

THE STORY OF THE ISLE OF MAN 1

THE FOLK-LORE OF THE ISLE OF MAN 131

SUGGESTED FURTHER READING 399

INTRODUCTION

"WHITHERSOEVER YOU THROW IT, IT WILL STAND."

—ISLE OF MAN MOTTO

Fionn mac Cumhaill, or Finn McCool, the legendary warrior of Ireland, stands at fifty-four feet tall. Protector of his land and people, Finn is determined to defeat his most fearsome enemy, the Scottish giant Benandonner. After building the Giant's Causeway out of six-sided cobblestones, Finn shouts across the Northern Channel, challenging Benandonner to come to him. However, even though Finn is tall himself, he underestimates the size of his enemy and flees back home to his wife, Oonagh, admitting he picked a fight he shouldn't have.

A quick thinker, Oonagh disguises Finn as a child, covers him with sheets, and places a bonnet on his head. Tucked in a cradle, Finn hides. When Benandonner arrives, Oonagh convinces him to wait for Finn, who, she explains, is away hunting deer in Kerry County. She points out Finn's spear, a fir tree with a pointed stone at the top, and his shield, a piece of building-oak the size of four chariot wheels. Anticipating Finn's return, Oonagh cooks his favorite meal: griddlecake. She cooks two; the first she gives to Benandonner, who

i

is unaware she pressed a piece of iron inside. Devouring the cake, Benandonner breaks three front teeth. Oonagh tosses the second griddlecake to Finn, who peeks out from under his bonnet and sheets and devours the iron-free cake effortlessly.

Benandonner is fooled, believing if Finn's baby can eat a griddlecake without injury, his father must be fearsome. He flees back to Scotland, destroying the causeway behind him. Unable to chase Benandonner further, Finn grabs a chunk of Ireland and aims for the fleeing giant. He misses, but the clod of earth lands in the Irish Sea and becomes the Isle of Man. The hole he leaves in Ireland fills with water and becomes Lough Neagh.

HOW THE ISLAND BECAME THE ISLE OF MAN

From the rugged coastline of Baldrine, one can look out across the Irish Sea towards the United Kingdom. The Isle of Man, a British crown-dependency, lies almost equidistant between Ireland, Scotland, England, and Wales. Geographically, the Isle of Man is three-and-a-half times the size of Washington D.C.: two-hundred-and-twenty-one square miles. It measures about thirty-three miles long and fourteen miles at its widest point. Its highest peak, Snaefell Mountain, offers panoramic views of the six kingdoms on a clear day: England, Ireland, Scotland, Wales, Heaven, and the Isle of Man itself. About ninety-thousand Manxmen and women call this small island with its rocky coasts, medieval castles, and hills home.

Early history indicates the first tribes to inhabit the island were Celts who more than likely came from Ireland as the current Manx Gaelic closely resembles Irish Gaelic. But, because of the island's location, it was easily susceptible to raiders, and soon enough, Scandinavian neighbors from the West began to arrive. Between 800 and 815 AD, Vikings adventured to the Isle of Man mainly to plunder. The island's central location in the middle of the Irish Sea proved advantageous to the Vikings whose sailing route between Scandinavia and Ireland passed by the island. It soon became the base for trading between Ireland and Scandinavia. A few years later, around 850, the Vikings settled on the island, leading to the rule of the Kings of Dublin. These Norsemen were of the Kingdom of Dublin, having expanded their territory to Ireland in the ninth century.

The Earls of Orkney soon claimed rule over the island in 990, but their control lasted only eighty-nine years when Godred Crovan, a Norse-Gaelic strong-arm, dubbed the Isle of Man the Kingdom of Mann and the Isles in 1079. Under this new name, Crovan's kingdom consisted of the Hebrides, the islands of the Firth of Clyde, and the Isle of Man. Viking rule eventually came to an end when Magnus VI ceded the Isle of Man, along with the Hebrides and those of the Firth of Clyde, to Scotland with the Treaty of Perth in 1266.

For the coming century, the Isle of Man would change hands numerous times. As part of his conquest of Wales, King Edward I of England sent Walter de Huntercombe, an English military commander during the Wars of Scottish Independence, to take possession of the Isle of Man in 1290. The island remained with the English until 1313 when Robert the Bruce, King of the Scots, claimed the island. Decades later, the island was granted to William de Montacute, English nobleman and servant to King Edward III. In 1392, de Montacute's son sold the Isle of Man and its sovereignty to William le Scrope. Le Scrope's rule didn't last long, for King Henry IV had him beheaded in 1399. From then on, despite a few Manx rebellions, the Isle of Man has remained under the protection of Britain.

The island is not a sovereign state. Like the Bailiwicks of Guernsey and Jersey, the Isle of Man is an island territory possessed by Great Britain. However, the island is self-governing and operates with its own legislature, Tynwald. The isle proudly showcases its rich heritage, from the Celts to the Vikings to the British.

THE DEATH AND RESURRECTION OF MANX GAELIC

In 2009, UNESCO declared Manx Gaelic extinct in its *Atlas of the World's Languages in Danger*. However, this was not the first time the island saw its native language start to disappear. In the nineteenth century, the Isle of Man became a popular destination for tourists, especially those from Great Britain. When tourism in the isle hit its peak, nearly six hundred thousand annual visitors would come to the shores of the island. In order to profit from this flourishing industry, Manxmen had to learn English, and British English began to overshadow the native tongue of the island. By 1901, only nine percent of the people on the island spoke Manx, and over the next two decades, those figures dropped to one percent. Generationally, households would have Manx speaking grandparents, bilingual parents, and children who only spoke English. Fortunately, this rapid decline inspired ambitious Manxmen focused on preserving their language and the culture of their island. This first revival proved helpful, and the twentieth century found more Manxmen working to keep the island's culture alive.

Ned Maddrell, a fisherman from the Isle of Man, was the last surviving native speaker of Manx from the first revival; he passed away at the age of ninety-seven in 1974. Today, there are more than eighteen hundred readers, writers, and speakers of the language. This new generation of speakers, mostly students who learn in schools teaching with Manx, have encouraged parents and older citizens who have shied away from their native language to learn it once again, connecting them to the island's culture. This second revival shows the efforts of the Manx to keep hold of their distinctive roots.

The author of the works in this book, Arthur William (A. W.) Moore, promoted the study of Manx language and history. One of the revivalists in the nineteenth century, he learned the language at a time when it began to face extinction and the island's literature was despised by the influx of British citizens. The British found the Isle of Man's language and literature to be dirty and a sign of lower-class citizenry. He preserved and translated numerous Manx writings, and the same year he was elected a justice of the peace, Moore published his sketch of the history of the Manx language through the Natural History and Antiquarian Society of the island. With the help of Sir John Rhys, Moore worked to edit *The Book of Common Prayer in Manx Gaelic* in 1893, the earliest and longest manuscript in the language. As part of the history Moore sought to preserve, he also focused on the music, lore, and traditions of the island. 1899 saw the founding of the Manx Language Society, pioneered by Moore himself. The group worked toward maintaining the dying language of the island.

A. W. MOORE: DISTINGUISHED MANXMAN

On February 6th, 1853, Moore was born in Cronkbourne, a town in Braddan parish of the sheading of Middle in the Isle of Man. His parents were William Fine Moore and Hannah Christian Curwen, and he had four brothers and five sisters. At the age of fourteen, Moore moved on to Rugby School, a co-educational boarding school, and shortly thereafter, he passed on to Trinity College in Cambridge, where he graduated with a Bachelor of Arts in 1876 and with a Master of Arts in 1879. Along with his academic accomplishments, Moore also earned his "blue" for his participation in Rugby, an award for those competing at the highest level of the sport. In 1877, he was elected a justice of the peace, and then became a member of the House of Keys, the Isle of Man's parliament, in 1881.

Upon his father's death in 1895, Moore inherited the family business, the Tromode Sailcloth Mills. He successfully ran the business until he was forty-two when the competing steamship industry forced the Mills to close. With no company to oversee, he was able to devote his time fully to the Isle of Man, focusing on the welfare of the island and its people. In

1898, he was elected speaker of the House of Keys, a position which he held until his death. Excelling in politics as well as antiquities, he earned the reputation of being the chief authority of all things Manx, and in 1907, he petitioned for the reformation of the Manx Constitution.

1890 saw the start of Moore's extensive writing career. In the fifteen years that followed, he would publish ten books and one article: *The Surnames and Place Names of the Isle of Man* in 1890, *The Folk-Lore of the Isle of Man* and *Manx Carols* in 1891, *The Diocese of Sodor and Man* in 1893, "Further Notes on Manx Folklore" in 1895, *Manx Ballads and Music* in 1896, *The History of the Isle of Man* in 1900, *Manx Worthies* in 1901, *Bishop Hildesley's Letters* and *Douglas 100 Years Ago* in 1904, and *Extracts from the Records of the Isle of Man* in 1905. Moore's books helped Manxmen understand their nation's history and culture and reminded them the island was a proud and independent nation.

Because he was an expert in Manx language, literature, and history, Moore was also the official translator of the *Acts of Tynwald* and was Vice President of the Celtic Association. At the eisteddfod (a Welsh festival of literature, performance, and music) held in Cardiff in 1899, he was granted the degree of Druid, a high-ranking professional in Celtic cultures.

On the 12th of November, 1909, Moore peacefully passed away in Douglas, the capital of the Isle of Man. Because he was such a distinguished Manxman, a bust sculpted by Taubman resides in the chamber of the House of Keys.

Chosen from Moore's long list of works, the two titles in this book, *The Folk-Lore of the Isle of Man* and *The Story of the Isle of Man*, published in 1891 and 1901 respectively, paint a picture of the early beginnings and beliefs of the island. As Moore dedicated his adulthood to preserving the culture of the island, he sought to educate every Manx citizen. *The Story of the Isle of Man*, printed after his two volume account of

The History of the Isle of Man, informs schoolchildren. Moore's historical account seeks to teach Manx children of their roots and instill a deep appreciation for their native land, from the Norsemen to Moore's contemporaries.

The Story of the Isle of Man introduces readers to the themes of nationalism, creation, and progress. Beginning with the geological origins of the island, Moore posits the fundamental influences from several different nations. Throughout the work, Moore plots out the progress of the island as it shifted from the indigenous peoples, to the Norsemen, and then to the British. Ending with a complete map of the formation of the Isle of Man, readers of any age will gain new knowledge of the nation, a full understanding of its history and culture, and an appreciation for the little island in the Irish Sea.

The Folk-Lore of the Isle of Man recounts the island's mythology. Many of the stories Moore includes are supernatural, as they deal with witchcraft and charms, hobgoblins, and mermaids, to name a few. Some stories are historical, some deal with festivities and holidays associated with the seasons, and Moore includes peculiar laws and customs previously enforced on the island. For example, prostitutes found mothering illegitimate children and continuously gallivanting through town were tied to a boat and dragged in the sea. Bishop Thomas Wilson, overseeing the diocese of Sodor and Man, enforced this law only once, in the case of Katherine Kinred. Leading a scandalous life and souring the Christian name, Kinred was dragged out to sea at the height of the market crowd to serve as an example. *The Story of the Isle of Man* provides an extensive background of the beginnings of the island, and *The Folk-Lore of the Isle of Man* does as well. However, Moore intends to map out the legends and beliefs permeating the island that serve to instruct and amuse readers. Before Moore, few had undertaken the arduous task of translating and collecting the Manx Gaelic stories, but Moore credits those historians whose stories he includes.

THE ISLE OF MAN TODAY

Pastel pink and red-brick buildings line the coast and the harbors of the Isle of Man. The roads of every major city form a labyrinth between government buildings, harbors, and shops. As the roads lead away from the coast towards the innermost hills and valleys, houses become few and far between. Not many country roads wind and curve through the island, but they offer scenic views of grazing cows and tunnels of overgrown trees and ivy. The roads that stretch along the coast offer warm sunsets and sights of the billowing waves of the Irish Sea. Some of the Isle of Man's busiest towns sit on the coast.

Peel, the island's hotspot for the fishing industry lies on the west side of the island. Many Manxmen find employment in the fish and shellfish trade. In this town, one can learn about the art of kippering, the process of splitting a whole herring butterfly fashion and curing it. Moore's Kipper Yard, the last of the traditional Manx kipper yards (with no relation to A. W. Moore), offers demonstrations of the curing process for adventurous tourists. Peel Castle, built by the Vikings in the eleventh century, can be found here as well. From the shores of the ruins, one can easily spot basking sharks that find their way to the coastline to mate, give birth, and feed on plankton.

Ramsey, another coastal town in the northeastern part of the island, is surrounded by land that reflects the interesting mix of the landscape of the Isle of Man: sandy coasts in Ramsey, wooded glens to the south-east, and a swamp, Ballaugh Curragh, to the north. Farmland also surrounds Ramsey to support the island's agricultural industry. Seventy-five percent of the island's acreage allows for cattle, sheep, and vegetable production. Many family farms and other businesses—including abattoirs, the creamery, and the flour mill—are able to stay operational due to the island's agricultural industry.

E-gambling websites from around the world, like The Stars Group in Canada and PokerStars of Costa Rica, relocated to the

Isle of Man because of the island's low-tax economy. In sharp contrast to the island's rustic and agricultural landscape, the Isle of Man became home to a private space-flight company, Excalibur Almaz, in 2005. The company was interested in crewed expeditions, tourism on the moon, and if plans were successful, they would have charged one-hundred and fifty million dollars per seat, a guaranteed boost to the economy. Lack of funds led program officials to turn the unmanned spacecrafts into educational exhibits.

Due to the variety of cultural influences, tourists and Manxmen alike can experience a myriad of different festivities. One can compete in or spectate the Viking Long Boat races at Peel Harbor, started in 1963, and the Tin Bath races, started in 1971. The latter dares participants to race around Middle Harbor in Castletown in tin bathtubs. Both events garner large crowds. Tynwald Day, held on the fifth of July at St. John's, is a national holiday which celebrates the island's parliament. The event takes place at a four-tiered open-air site where members of the House of Keys and the Legislative Branch promulgate new laws and receive petitions for redress. The ceremony concludes with a formal sitting at the Royal Chapel. Throughout the ceremony, the Manx keep close to the traditions set in place by the Norse Vikings of the thirteenth century. Each year craft and food vendors, as well as entertainers, make for an exciting experience.

As for Celtic celebrations, one can participate in the Hop-tu-Naa. This event occurs on the thirty-first of October, and it is known to predate Halloween and mark the end of summer according to the Celtic calendar. Hop-tu-Naa differs significantly from the British tradition of Halloween: Manx children carry lanterns carved from turnips and sing the "Hop-tu-Naa" song. Yn Chruinnaght, another event, celebrates the Isle of Man's Celtic roots and relationship with the other five Celtic countries. Offering a variety of music, art, dance, crafts, and most importantly, language, any individual with an appreciation for anything Celtic is welcome to partake in the jollity.

One of the most exciting tourist attractions of the island is its annual Tourist Trophy (TT) races. Spectators from around the globe—especially the British, as their public roads were not permitted to be closed and the Isle of Man has no national speed limit—make the trek to witness the brave motorcycle drivers who careen around the Snaefell Mountain course, which is currently 37.73 miles long. Reaching top speeds of one-hundred and thirty-five miles per hour, competitors take a mere sixteen minutes to complete one lap. The race is notoriously dangerous, and the number of fatalities is staggering. The two-hundred and fifty-eight competitor fatalities and fifteen casualties that include race officials, bystanders, and spectators, attest to the risk of attending and participating in the TT races. Nevertheless, forty-five thousand people traveled to the Isle of Man in 2016 to watch the daredevil motorcyclists, contributing an estimated twenty-four million pounds to the economy.

Just as Moore's *The Story of the Isle of Man* shows an ever-changing island as it transitioned from Viking dominance in the ninth century to Manx Home Rule in the nineteenth century, the island has continued to evolve since Moore's death. Manx nationalism was at its highest in the 1960s, spawning the Mec Vannin and Manx National parties. Bunscoill Ghaelgagh, a primary school, was established in 2001 and offers classes taught solely in Manx. It is currently the only school in the world that teaches in Manx. The community thrives with its offshore financial center, tourist industry, and TT races. Ten centuries filled with raids, rebellions, restorations, and revestments left the island a conglomerate of Nordic, Celtic, Christian, and English influences. Even though the island does operate as a British Crown dependency, the small island and its people offer a different kind of experience separate from its protector.

-A. E. CONGDON, 2019

THE LIFE AND TIMES OF
ARTHUR WILLIAM MOORE

1853: Arthur William (A. W.) Moore is born in Cronk-bourne, Braddan. One of ten children, Moore is born to William Fine Moore and Hannah Curwen.

1867: Enters Rugby school under Dr. Frederick Temple. Shortly thereafter, he passes onto Trinity College in Cambridge.

1876: Graduates from Trinity College with a Bachelor of the Arts.

1879: Graduates from Trinity College with a Master of the Arts.

1881: Elected member of the House of Keys.

1883: President of the Isle of Man Agriculture Society.

1885-7: Editor of *The Manx Note Book* periodical.

1888: Member of the Council of Education.

1890: *The Surnames and Place Names of the Isle of Man* is published.

1891: *Folk-Lore of the Isle of Man* is published; *Manx Carols* is published.

1893: Moore, along with Sir John Rhys, edits *The Book of Common Prayer* in Manx Gaelic; *The Diocese of Sodor and Man* is published.

1895: "Further Notes on Manx Folklore" is published in *The Antiquary.*

1896: *Manx Ballads and Music* is published.

1898: Elected speaker of the House of Keys.

1899: Member of the Harbour Board; Founds the Manx Language Society and becomes its first president.

1900: *History of the Isle of Man* is published.

1901: *Manx Worthies* is published.

1902: Receives King Edward VII on the island; created C.V.O.

1904: *Bishop Hildesley's Letters* is published; *Douglass 100 Years Ago* is published.

1905: *Extracts from the Records of the Isle of Man* is published.

1907: Authors petition aimed at reforming the Manx Constitution.

1909: Dies November 12th, in Woodbourne, Douglass.

A TIMELINE ON THE HISTORY OF THE ISLE OF MAN

850-890: The first Norse settlers arrive in Man.

900: The Round Tower is built at Peel Castle; The Vikings build a fort on St. Patrick's Isle.

1050: The Manx bishopric is established.

1079: Godred Crovan becomes the King of Man and the Isles.

1095: Godred Crovan dies.

1100: St. Michael's chapel is built.

1134: King Olaf founds Rushen Abbey and grants the land to the Sauvignac monks of Furness Abbey.

1190: Castle Rushen is built.

1228: The Battle of Tynwald.

1229: St. Germain's Cathedral begins construction which completes in 1247.

1237: King Olaf dies.

1257: *The Chronicles of Man* are written at Rushen Abbey.

1266: The Treaty of Perth transfers the Isle of Man under Scottish rule from Norway.

1275: The Scottish defeat the Manx at the Battle of Ronaldsway.

1313: Robert the Bruce captures Castle Rushen.

1316: Richard de Mandeville raids and defeats the Manx at the Battle of South Barrule.

1373: The Franciscan Friary is established at Bemaken, Ballabeg.

1395: Le Scrope, the King of Man, uses the Three Legs emblem as a signatory to the Anglo-French Treaty.

1405: King Henry IV grants the island to Sir John Stanley.

1417: The first document in the *Statute Book* refers to the Keys of Man and the Isles; a series of important Tynwald Courts take place and establish the Stanley regime, which ends in 1430.

1485: Thomas Stanley II is ennobled as the first Earl of Derby.

1504: The title 'King of Man' is waived for 'Lord of Man.'

1540: Edward Stanley dissolves Rushen Abbey and the Nunnery.

1594: Queen Elizabeth I takes control of the Isle of Man.

1608: Illiam Dhone (William Christian) is born.

1610: Bishop Phillips prints the Prayer Book in Manx.

1612: William I, 5th Earl, and Countess Elizabeth resume the Stanley Rule.

1627: James Stanley, 7th Earl of Derby, becomes the Lord of Man.

1651: James Stanley is captured and executed in Bolton; Illiam Dhone leads the rebellion in Man; the island is taken over for the Commonwealth.

1656: Illiam Dhone becomes the Governor of the Isle of Man.

1660: The Derby rule is restored.

1663: Illiam Dhone is executed.

1672: Charles, the 8th Earl of Derby, introduces compulsory elementary education.

1709: Derby coinage is introduced.

1765: Running trade is suppressed by the U.K. Act of Revestment and the Mischief Act.

1775: Philip Moore edits the Manx Bible, which is then published.

1780: Dr. John Kelly's *Manx Grammar* is published.

1788: Dennison's Theatre opens on Fort Street in Douglas.

1792: The first Manx newspaper is established, *Manks Mercury and Briscoe's Advertiser*.

1803: *Mona's Herald* begins publication.

1821: Riots break out in Peel as Manx and English ports are closed against the importation of foreign corn, meal, or flour.

1825: Economic difficulties of Manx farmers result in potato riots in Arbory and Rushen; they march on Bishopscourt.

1829: Manx Giant Arthur Caley is born; he stands at seven feet, six inches tall.

1847: Queen Victoria and Prince Albert visit the Isle of Man.

1854: The world's largest waterwheel, the Lady Isabella, is built at Laxey.

1858: The Manx society is founded.

1866: The Isle of Man Customs and Harbours Act is passed at Westminster, restoring control of finances and internal administration to the Manx government.

1871: The steam railway is completed between Douglas and Peel.

1873: The Douglas-Peel railway line opens.

1877: The steam railway between Ramsey and St. Johns completes construction.

1879: The Isle of Man Natural History and Antiquarian Society is founded.

1881: Women's suffrage is introduced.

1886: The steam railway between Foxdale and St. John's completes construction.

1890: The Barque Thorne shipwrecks on the rocks of Onchan Head.

1891: The Douglas Prison is built on Victoria Road; it replaces the prison at Castle Rushen.

1892: The Ramsey Swing Bridge is built and installed by Cleveland Bridge and Engineering.

1894: The Manx Electric Railway is inaugurated between Douglass and Groudle.

1895: A Giant Irish deer is excavated near St. John's.

NOTE ON THE TEXTS

In *The Folk-Lore of the Isle of Man*, I removed the initials at the start of each chapter and the pictures at the end of each chapter. In *The Story of the Isle of Man*, I removed the picture titled "Maughold Cross with 'Three-Legs'" because of the poor quality of the image. I also moved the captions for the pictures to the bottom of the page so they are easier to read. In both books, I removed extraneous periods after Roman numerals, and I edited footnotes that referred page numbers in the original publications. Other than making a few minor corrections, the text of both books has been preserved to match the first editions.

ACKNOWLEDGEMENTS

I would like to thank Dr. Allen Grove and Haley Ruffner for their guidance and assistance with writing my introduction and formatting this volume.

I would also like to thank my parents and my grandmother for their endless support.

THE

STORY OF THE ISLE OF MAN

TABLE OF CONTENTS

INTRODUCTION I

CHAPTER I - THE LEGENDS...5

CHAPTER II - THE LEGENDS EXPLAINED 8

    PART I - OUR LAND AND ITS EARLIEST
INHABITANTS...8

    PART II - S. PATRICK AND S. COLUMBA.................12

CHAPTER III - THE NORSEMEN...................................16

    PART I - CONQUEST AND SETTLEMENT 16

    PART II - GOVERNMENT, ETC.. 20

    PART III - THEIR CHURCH 24

CHAPTER IV - THE HOUSE OF GODRED CROVAN..........29

    PART I - GODRED I TO REGINALD I,
1079—1187...29

    PART II - FROM REGINALD I TO THE END OF NORSE
RULE, 1187—1266 33

CHAPTER V - THE "THREE-LEGS" OF MAN....................36

CHAPTER VI - SCOTTISH AND ENGLISH RULE 39

CHAPTER VII - THE HOUSE OF STANLEY......................43

    PART I - THE STANLEYS FROM 1405 TO 1627........43

    PART II - THE REFORMATION 47

    PART III - THE GOVERNMENT..............................50

    PART IV - OUR FOREFATHERS BETWEEN 1405 AND
1660...53

    PART V - THE GREAT STANLEY, 1627—1651........56

CHAPTER VII - THE HOUSE OF STANLEY (1405—
1736) CONTINUED..61

PART VI - EDWARD AND WILLIAM CHRISTIAN........61

PART VII - THE LAST STANLEYS,
1160—1736..65

PART VIII - THE MANX MAGNA CARTA AND BILL OF
RIGHTS..68

PART IX - BISHOP WILSON 72

PART X - JOHN STEVENSON AND WILLIAM
WALKER..78

CHAPTER VIII - THE HOUSE OF ATHOLL.......................84

PART I - THE REVESTMENT 84

PART II - THE MANX BIBLE 87

PART III - THE FOURTH DUKE 90

PART IV - MANX SOLDIERS AND SAILORS...............94

PART V - THE PEOPLE 97

CHAPTER IX - RECENT HISTORY 100

PART I - POLITICAL REFORM 100

PART II - SOCIAL REFORM 104

PART III - INDUSTRIAL REFORM 107

PART IV - HEROES OF THE LIFEBOAT 110

CHAPTER X - SOME MANX WORTHIES........................115

CONCLUSION - OUR HERITAGE..................................119

APPENDIX A - GEOGRAPHY..122

APPENDIX B - CELTIC PLACE-NAMES AND SURNAMES..125

APPENDIX C - NORSE PLACE-NAMES AND SURNAMES..126

LIST OF ILLUSTRATIONS

S. PATRICK'S ISLAND 15

CROSS AT KIRK MICHAEL... 22

RUINS OF RUSHEN ABBEY... 25

S. GERMAN'S CATHEDRAL AND PEEL CASTLE.................. 28

CASTLE RUSHEN 41

JAMES, 7TH EARL OF DERBY 59

BISHOP WILSON 74

BALLAUGH OLD CHURCH 77

CAPTAIN QUILLIAM, R. N. 91

LORD LOCH 102

THE TOWER OF REFUGE 111

THE REV T. E. BROWN... 118

THE
STORY OF THE ISLE OF MAN

INTRODUCTION

WHAT I INTEND TO DO IN THIS BOOK is to tell you something about the history of the Isle of Man, or *Ellan Vannin,* as it is called by Manx-speaking people. I shall try to show you how in ages long past one race of people after another came across the sea to settle in our island; how in time the descendants of these various races became one people, the ancestors of the present inhabitants; how Manxmen used to live in former times; and what have been the most important changes in government, religion, laws, and social conditions, which our country has undergone, and by whom these changes were brought to pass.

Although the history of which I am going to speak is only the history of a little island, and not that of a great nation like England or France, it is, nevertheless, very important to us Manx people, because this little island is our own country. If we study it in a right spirit, it will help us to fulfil our duty more thoroughly, to be better and more useful men and women. It will teach us to feel grateful to those men of former times

1

whose labours have won for us the freedom and the prosperity which we now enjoy; it will help us to value these blessings which were obtained for us by so great efforts and sacrifices; and it will show us how we too may do something to make our country a happier and better place for those who will live in it when we have passed away.

Before I begin to talk about the history of our island, it is necessary to explain some words which I shall often have to use. These words are *State*, *Laws*, *Government*, *Legislative*, *Executive*, *Constitution*, *Sovereign*, *Taxes*, *Excise*, *Customs*, *and Revenue*. When we speak of a *State*, we mean the people of a country, formed into a sort of society to protect and help one another, and to manage those affairs which belong to the people as a whole. England, France, Germany, and the other nations of Europe, are States. Our own little island kingdom is also a State, though it has the same *Sovereign* as a larger State, the United Kingdom of Great Britain and Ireland. Every society (your own family, for instance) has to have some rules which the people who belong to it are obliged to obey. The rules of the State, which its members (or *citizens*, as we call them) are required to obey, are called *Laws*.

The person, or set of persons, to whom the chief authority in a State is granted, is called the *Government*. The duty of the Government is to take care that the laws are obeyed, and, when it is necessary, to make new laws. The power which the Government has of making laws is called *Legislative* power; the power by which it carries the laws into effect is called its *Executive* power.

Government takes different forms in different kinds of States. The three forms which we shall mainly have to consider in the following pages are:—

(I) *A Despotic Government,* in which one person has the sole control;

(II) *An Oligarchical Government*, where a few persons have the control;

(III) *A Constitutional Government*, in which one person is the head, who is, however, guided and limited in his actions by a body of customs and laws, which have gradually sprung up, called the *Constitution*.

The great principle of a Constitutional Government is that the person at its head, called the *Sovereign*, obtains the obedience of the people, on the condition that he is himself obedient to the Constitution.

As members of this State you have duties towards it. I will not, however, speak of them now,[1] but will confine myself to telling you about some of your rights, or, in other words, what duties the State owes to you.

It has to defend you from enemies abroad and at home. For the first purpose, it has the Army and Navy,[2] and, for the second, the judges and police, with court-houses and prisons. It has also to make roads and keep them in order, to build school-houses, provide teachers, to support the aged and deserving poor, and those who have lost their minds, whom we call lunatics, to send your letters and telegrams all over the world, to make breakwaters, piers, &c. But soldiers and sailors, judges and policemen, and the makers of warships, breakwaters, piers, and all kinds of public buildings have to be paid for. How, then, is the necessary money to be obtained? by *Taxes*. What are Taxes? they are payments made by all in proportion to their means, and they are, or should be, for the good of all. They are of two kinds, direct and indirect. I can best explain the difference between them by giving instances of each. Let us take direct taxes first: Suppose that the School Board of a

1 See Conclusion.

2 The Isle of Man is defended by the Army and Navy of Great Britain and Ireland; and the Post Office of that Kingdom attends to its letters and telegrams.

parish has to obtain money to carry on its school; to do this it levies a rate upon every householder in the parish according to the value of his house; and this tax, or *rate*, has to be paid to the collector who is sent to receive it. Other direct taxes are paid in a similar proportion according to a man's house or income. A tax has to be paid, too, for leave, or licence, to carry a gun, to keep a dog and so forth.

As to indirect taxes, every time you drink a cup of tea or a glass of beer you pay an indirect tax. Let us see how this is. Indirect taxes, or *duties*, are of two kinds. The first, called *Excise*, is paid on articles, such as beer, which are made in your own country. The second, called *Customs*, is on articles which are imported, or brought in, from other countries. The maker, or importer, as the case may be, pays the tax, and he then raises the price he sells at high enough to repay him for the cost and trouble of the tax. Whoever, therefore, uses those articles pays the tax on them in proportion to the amount of them which he uses. The money thus obtained by taxes forms the *Income*, or *Revenue*, of the State.

You have now learned something about the duties of the State towards you; and I trust that, when you have read this book through you will also have learned, not only how well our little State has performed these duties, but how right and necessary it is that you, in your turn, should do your duty to it.

CHAPTER I

THE LEGENDS

"Bold words affirmed, in days when faith was strong
And doubts and scruples seldom teased the brain,
That no adventurer's bark had power to gain
These shores if he approached them bent on wrong:
For suddenly, up-conjured from the main,
Mists rose to hide the land: that search—though long
And eager—might be still pursued in vain."

WORDSWORTH

ONLY WAY OF LEARNING ABOUT EARLY HISTORY. — For more than eleven hundred years after the birth of Christ, there were no written accounts of events in our island. The only way, therefore, in which we can learn what took place here is by means of the stories, or legends, which passed on from one generation to another, and have come down to our own time. But this way is at best an imperfect and uncertain one, because, as you know quite well, a story, when it has been repeated by even a few people, becomes very different at the end from what it was at the beginning. In the old days, when there were very few books, men were paid for telling stories, and it is probable that the more wonderful their stories were, the more money they got. You know, too, how much more likely it is that an interesting story will be remembered than an uninteresting one, even if the interesting story be false and the other true.

SUPPOSED ORIGIN OF THE ISLE OF MAN AND ITS NAME. — Many of the stories which have come down to us are evidently false, but others have some truth in them, and we are often able, as I shall try to explain later, to find out what parts of them are true and what are false. And now, let us come to the stories. Some of them, as was natural, were told with the object of explaining things that people were most anxious to know. One of these was how the Isle of Man came to be where it is. The explanation the story-tellers gave of this was that Finn MacCoole—a very favourite hero of Manx legends—having defeated a Scottish giant in the North of Ireland, was running after him, and when he found that he was unable to catch him, he thrust his hands into the ground, tore up the rocks and clay and threw them after him. But he missed the giant, and the rocks and clay fell into the midst of the Irish Sea and formed the Isle of Man, while the place they were torn out of became Lough Neagh. I don't think I need say whether this story is true or not!

The next thing that people wanted to know was how the island got its name and who lived in it. To the first question the answer was that it got its name from an Irish hero called *Manannan-Beg-Mac-y-Leirr*, "Little-Manannan-son-of-the-Sea," who was its king, and also a great magician. We are told that:

> "It was not with his sword he kept her,
> Nor with his arrows, nor his bow;
> But when he would see the ships sailing
> He hid her right round with a fog.
> He'd set a man upon a hill,
> You'd think there were a hundred there;
> And thus did wild Manannan guard
> That island with all its booty."

THE FAIRIES. — To the second question the answer was that the first inhabitants of the island were little and slenderly formed people called fairies, who wore green and blue clothes, with red caps. Their weapons were only arrows headed with flints, but they were so helped by the knowledge of magic possessed by their king, Manannan, and by their priests, or druids, that it took many years to conquer them. When they were beaten, they retired into the green mounds, so common in the island, and their conquerors, who were a race of giants, continued to fear them because of their magical powers. So sure were our forefathers of the truth of this that they thought it necessary to prevent the fairies from being angry and doing harm by calling them "the good people" and by putting out food and water for them at night. According to another story, the fairies and their king were still living among their conquerors when holy men came from Ireland and drove them out. This story has been preserved in the following ancient ballad:

"Then came Patrick into their midst;
He was a saint full of virtue;
He sent Manannan on the wave,
Away with all his bad servants.
And of all those that were evil,
To them he showed but little grace;
Those that were of the conjuror's race
He destroyed and put to death."

The ballad then proceeds to relate how S. Patrick and others converted the people to Christianity:

"He blessed the land from end to end,
And ne'er left a poor person there,
That was bigger than a child, who
Refused to be a Christian.
Patrick then blessed S. German,
And left him the bishop in it,
To strengthen the faith more and more,
And little chapels made he there.
Then came Maughold from the West,
And he came on shore at the Head,
And built a church and yard around.
Connaghyn the next came in,
And then arrived Marown the third."

These are a few of the stories which take the place of history, or the record of actual events.

CHAPTER II

Part I.— Our Land and its Earliest Inhabitants.

"It's clad in purple mist, my land,
In regal robe it is apparelled,
A crown is set upon its head,
And on its breast a golden band—
Land, ho! land."

T. E. BROWN

G EOLOGY. — We know now that the Isle of Man was not hurled by Finn MacCoole into the midst of the Irish Sea, but that it was built up by millions of years ago from mud and sand at the bottom of the ocean.

This mud and sand became hardened into slaty rocks, and then mighty forces squeezed these rocks together and raised them up in a great mass far above the water. Out of this mass, mountains, hills and headlands were carved by the long-continued action of the rivers and the sea. At times, our island has been part of a continent, and, at other times, it has been surrounded by the sea as at present, because the level of the land has been, and is, constantly rising and falling under the action of forces inside the earth, though so slowly that you could only notice any change after thousands of years. These forces have burst forth occasionally in terrible volcanoes, and between Scarlet Point and Poolvash we can see where lava, or molten rock, has poured out, and where showers of volcanic ashes have fallen at some long distant period. After many ages, when the island had grown into nearly its present shape, there came a period of bitter cold. Everything was covered with great masses of ice, which ground and smoothed the rough edges of the rocks. From the gravel, sand and clay, which remained behind when this ice melted, a large part of the lowlands was formed. Soon after the ice age, the great Irish elk, whose bones are found in the mud of peaty hollows, lived here. A skeleton of one of these animals is to be seen at Castle Rushen. These hollows once formed shallow lakes, which have been gradually drained or filled up with mud and peat, bringing the island finally to its present condition.[1]

Thus was our beautiful land with its green hills, its winding glens, and its grand, rocky coast gradually formed.

We have seen that, according to the legends, it was named after Manannan, and that its first inhabitants were little people, with flint-headed arrows, who were conquered by a bigger people. It is, however, much more likely that Manannan, if there ever was such a man, took his name from Man, than Man its name from him, but what Man means no one knows, though many guesses have been made about it.

DESCRIPTION OF THE STONE-AGE PEOPLE. — But, as regards the first inhabitants of Man, we know that, not only are people in the island at the present day who are comparatively short and have long heads, dark complexions, and black eyes and hair, which are the marks of the men and women of the "stone-age," as they are called because they did not possess metal weapons, but that numerous flint arrow-heads and weapons made of stone have been found here; and, as to the fighting between the stone-age people and the bigger men, known as *Celts*, in Man, we can only say, that, since they fought in Ireland, it is probable that they fought here too.

1 For Geography, &c., see Appendix A.

WHO ARE THE CELTS? — Who, then, are these Celts? They are a people who were gradually driven westwards by the Romans and Germans, and settled in the British Islands at some unknown time before the birth of Christ. Not only were they bigger, but they had broader heads and fairer complexions than the stone-age people they conquered, and they had, at first, weapons made of a mixture of copper and tin, called bronze.

Tokens of the work of the Celts, who are the ancestors of most of us, are found in many of the great mounds, or barrows, still so common here, and in the stone circles which, like the barrows, were burial places. The Celts are divided into two distinct branches, one, the Gaelic, to which the Irish, the Scots, and the Manx belong, and the other, the Cymric, or Brythonic, of which the Welsh and the Bretons, or inhabitants of Brittany, are members.

The three nations who speak Gaelic can easily talk to each other, though their languages vary a little, and so can the Welsh and the Bretons; but the Gaelic and the Cymric nations cannot understand each other. So similar is our language, as well as the greater number of our place-names and surnames,[1] and of our customs and traditions, to the Irish and Scottish, especially to the former, that, though we have no written records of our history during the Celtic period, we are able, by studying what is known of Ireland and Scotland at that time, not only to show, beyond doubt, that Man was occupied by a Celtic people, but to form a very good idea of the way in which these people lived and managed their affairs.

THE WAY IN WHICH THE MANX CELTS LIVED AND WERE GOVERNED. — We know, for reasons which need not be mentioned here, that the Manx held their land in common, as other Celtic people did. History tells us that the property of the Irish and Scottish Celts consisted mostly of cattle, sheep,

1 See Appendix B.

and pigs, that they lived on the simplest food and wore the kilt, and that they were ruled by chiefs, who, though they were elected by them, had almost unlimited power over them. We cannot, then, be far wrong in supposing that their brother Celts in Man lived under similar conditions. Imagine the Manx Celtic chief, or king, sitting on some sacred hill—quite possibly our present Tynwald Hill at S. John's, though it was not then known by that name—and talking to his nobles about the laws and judgements he intended to put in force, before declaring them to the freemen standing round the hill. These freemen said "yes" or "no"when their opinion was asked, while the poor slaves, of whom there were probably a great number, were not allowed to say anything.

The "yes" or "no"of the freemen might have been either a form or not; perhaps it was more often the former than the latter. Indeed, the king probably thought of this meeting with his people, which took place once a year only, merely as a convenient way of making his will known to them, and that the freemen thought of it as the one occasion on which they had the right to make complaints. These complaints were then settled by the king in the presence of all, with the help of judges and wise men chosen from among the freemen.

A fair was held at the same time, and there were also recitations of poetry, telling of stories, musical contests, horse races, wrestling, &c.

Till the end of the eighth century our island seems to have been ruled by the Celts alone, since there is no trace of the Romans having come to it, or of the Anglo-Saxons, who followed them, having done more than make raids upon its people.

DATES

Romans in Britain — A.D. 80 — 450.

Anglo-Saxons arrive in Britain — A.D. 449.

CHAPTER II (*continued*)

Part 2. – S. Patrick and S. Columba.

"Blessed be the unconscious shore on which ye tread,
And blest the silver cross, which ye, instead
Of martial banner, in procession bear."

WORDSWORTH

IT IS PROBABLE that, for at least four centuries after the coming of Christ, the people of Man continued to be heathen. They seem to have worshipped the sun and moon, fire, earth, water, animals, trees, and stones, and they were afraid of evil spirits doing harm to them. They had priests who were clever enough to persuade them that they could prevent these spirits from being angry with them by offering sacrifices of animals, and, perhaps, even of human beings. By means of such pretended powers the priests came to have great influence over the people, till, according to one of our legends, they, with Manannan at their head, were destroyed by S. Patrick, who then taught the Celts to be Christians.

S. PATRICK. — Let me now tell you something about S. Patrick. By birth a native of North Britain, he was stolen from the Clyde by Irish pirates when a child. His captors took him to the north of Ireland, where a chief employed him in herding cattle. After six years of this work, he escaped, but was again captured by pirates, who this time carried him to Gaul, or the country which we now call France. By the kindness of some Christian merchants there, he was restored to his father, who had him well taught at schools in Gaul. He was then consecrated "Bishop of the Irish," and landed in Ireland, where he at once began to teach the people and to baptize their children. So successful was he, that at the time of his death Ireland had become a Christian country. It is not known whether he came to our shores or not, but though our legends say that he did, it seems more probable that he did not. There is, however, little reason to doubt that the legends are right in stating that some of his disciples came to Man, because not only do we find parishes and churches here named after him, but after these disciples as well. Thus there is S. Patrick's island at Peel, while S. Bridget gave her name to the parish of Bride.

s. COLUMBA. — The next great saint from Ireland who was connected with Man was Columba, or *Columb-keeilley*, "Dove of the Church," as he was called by Manx people. It is said that he copied the Psalms from a book which belonged to his master, S. Finian, writing them, like all books in those days, on skins. After the copy was made, S. Finian claimed it, and the King of Ulster, who was asked to settle the question, decided it in favour of S. Finian, being guided by the proverb that "Mine is the calf which is born of my cow." S. Columba was so angry at this decision that he determined to leave Ireland. He accordingly sailed away, with twelve of his disciples, in a frail boat made of wicker-work and covered with ox-hides, and they landed on the little rocky island of Iona, off the west coast of Scotland. On this island they built a church and a monastery, and very soon numbers of people went there to be taught the Christian faith. After a time more holy men from Ireland joined S. Columba, who sent them forth to teach the truth in other lands. So great was their success that they converted many of the English as well as the Scottish people, and many also on the continent of Europe. It is certain that they must have included Man in their wanderings, and, in-deed, like S. Patrick's disciples and their followers, they have left their names here. Perhaps, however, an even more striking proof of the esteem in which S. Columba was held by the Manx people is the fact that they have used his name, till quite recently, as a charm against fairies.

THE KEEILLS AND THE CULDEES. — It was at this time that the numerous tiny churches,[1] or *keeills* as they are called in Manx, the remains of which are to be seen in all our parish-es, were built and occupied by pious men, who were named Culdees, or Servants of God. They never married, but lived alone, praying with, teaching, and preaching to the people. Near these little buildings, which are chiefly made of sods, are usually found wells, which were used by the Culdees both for drinking-water and for baptizing children.

---

1 These are the "little chapels" which, according to our legends, were built by S. German. (See Ch. I).

S. PATRICK'S ISLAND

CHAPTER III

THE NORSEMEN

Part I. — Conquest and Settlement

"On his shield sleeps the Viking, his hand on his sword,
And his tent is the starry blue sky."

FRITHIOF SAGA

THE VIKINGS. — By the end of the eighth century the Norwegian and Danish rovers, called *Vikings*, had begun their wanderings, in search of plunder, not only to Man, but to all the British Islands and to western and southern Europe.

The best way, perhaps, to show you what sort of men these Vikings were is to give some extracts from their rules:—No man should run before a man of like power and like arms. Every man should avenge the other as his brother. None should show fear of anything. Everything captured in warfare should be shared in common. No man should take women and children prisoners, or should bind a wound till the same hour next day. No man should have less strength than two ordinary men, or should put an awning on his ship or furl its sail for the wind.

Fearless sailors, fierce, brave, and warlike, they believed that open plundering was honourable, but that to steal secretly was dishonourable.

Such, according to the *sagas*, or poetical tales of their deeds, were the Vikings of old. Their highway was the sea, and they lived, for the most part, on board their ships; indeed, the true Viking was supposed never to sleep under a roof. These ships, which were about 150 feet long, had high bows, carved in the shape of dragons or other strange creatures, and high sterns; between the bow and the stern they were low, so that the oars by which they were rowed in calm weather might reach the water. They had one great square sail, probably something like those on our "nickeys," which was hoisted when there was a wind. They sailed very fast, and their flat bottoms made it easy to run them up on such shores as that between Kirk Michael and Ramsey.

NORSE PLACE-NAMES AND SURNAMES. — How frequently they came to the coasts of Man is shown by the names they gave to its bays and creeks. Some fifty years after their first coming, which was about the year 800, they began to settle in Man, and of this, too, the names of many of our farms, &c., give ample proof.[1]

THE NORSE KINGS. — According to tradition, the first Norse King of Man was called Gorree, or Orry. It is said that when he landed at the Lhane, in Jurby, he was asked where he came from, and that, pointing to the Milky Way, he replied, "that is the road to my country." Hence the Manx name for the Milky Way is "the great road of King Gorree." All that we really know, however, is that, for nearly a century after the settlement, Man was ruled by kings who lived sometimes in Dublin, sometimes in Northumbria, as the country on the east of England, north of the river Humber and south of the Firth of Forth was called, and sometimes in Man itself. Then

1 For these names, see Appendix C.

it came for a short time under the Norse rulers of Limerick. Towards the end of the tenth century, it fell into the hands of the Earls of Orkney, and finally, into the hands of the Kings of Dublin again. Only once, during this period, do we hear of a King of Norway seeking to conquer his former subjects who had founded kingdoms in the British Islands. This was towards the end of the ninth century, when the famous Harold Fairhair placed Man and the Scottish Islands under his rule, which, however, did not last long.

GODRED CROVAN CONQUERS MAN. — At length came Godred Crovan, son of Harald the Black of Iceland, whose descendants were to rule Man for nearly two hundred years. He had been with Harald, King of Norway, when he was defeated by Harold, King of England, at the battle of Stamford Bridge. After that defeat he fled to Man, where he was kindly treated by its king, Godred Mac Sytric. Notwithstanding this, he some years later attacked the Manx. In his first battle against them he was beaten. On the second occasion the same fate befell him, but, the third time, he fared better. Having collected a number of followers, he came by night to Ramsey, and hid three hundred of them in the trees on Skyehill above Milntown. At daylight the Manxmen drew up in order of battle and rushed at Godred and the main body of his soldiers. When they were fighting together, the men who had been on Skyehill attacked the Manx in the rear. This threw them into great confusion, and since, at the same time, the tide had risen in the Sulby river and cut off their retreat, they begged Godred to spare their lives. Godred, who had been brought up among the Manx people and was sorry for them, granted their request, and called back his men from pursuing them.

The next day he asked his men whether they would like to divide the island between them, or to plunder it and go to their homes. Like true Vikings, the greater number of them chose plundering. To those who stopped with him he granted the southern part of the island, and to the surviving Manxmen he gave the northern part of it.

BATTLES.

Stamford Bridge, 1066; *Skyehill,* 1079.

DEFINITIONS.

Vikings. — Bands of Scandinavian warriors, who, during the ninth and tenth centuries, harried the British Isles and Normandy.

Norsemen. — Northmen; the inhabitants of the ancient Scandinavian kingdom now divided into Sweden, Norway and Denmark. The Northmen who came to Man were chiefly from Norway.

CHAPTER III (*continued*)

Part 2. – Government, &c

"Once on top of Tynwald's formal mound
(Still marked with green turf circled narrowing
Stage above stage) would sit this Island's king,
The laws to promulgate, enrobed and crowned;
While, compassing the little mount around,
Degrees and orders stood, each under each."

WORDSWORTH

I HAVE BEEN TRYING TO TELL YOU ABOUT THE NORSEMEN and their conquest of, and settlement in, Man, and I now want to say something about the way in which they lived and to describe their method of government. Our knowledge of these things is chiefly gained from the annals of Iceland and Norway.

HOW THE NORSEMEN LIVED. — They lived in houses with open hearths in the centre of the floor, from which the smoke escaped through a hole in the roof, and they slept on beds made of straw, which were placed round the walls. The men wore grey woolen trousers with socks knitted to them, a linen shirt, a woollen tunic, a coat of mail, and a cloak thrown over their shoulders. Their shoes, like the Manx *carranes*, or sandals, were made of raw hides. Except that they wore a longer tunic and were without the coat of mail, the women's dress was very like that of the men.

THEIR OCCUPATIONS, &C. — The chief occupations of the men, when not on *viking* expeditions, were trade and fishing; and the women milked the cows and spun and wove flax and wool. Athletic sports were their chief amusement. In the long winter evenings they spent their time in telling tales, in asking riddles, in harp playing, and in games of chess and draughts. They were, till Godred Crovan's time at least, freeholders, that is to say, they held their land from the king on condition of giving him their services in war, and they did not pay any rent. This land was probably in many cases farmed for them by the conquered Celts, who were at first slaves. Such an arrangement left most of the Norse conquerors free for occupations on the sea, which they liked much better than the land. They were active traders, doing business, not only with England, Scotland and Ireland, but with Iceland and the south of Europe. The merchandize from the north consisted, for the most part, of fish, hides, and furs, while white woollen and linen cloths, corn, honey and wine were taken back in exchange. They had, however, at least one occupation on land in which they excelled. Of this the beautiful carvings on the old crosses which we have in our churchyards afford ample proof. Many of these crosses have sentences cut upon them in Norse letters, or *runes*, which, like the inscriptions on our modern tombstones, contain the names of those by whose graves they once stood.

THEIR GOVERNMENT. — Now let us see how the Norsemen in Man were governed.

They managed their local affairs in little parliaments, or *things*, as they called them. There was probably one of these in each *sheading*. There was also a great *Thing* for the whole island, which came to be called the *Tynwald*, or Parliament Field, because it was held in the open air. It met once or twice a year to settle such matters as were too important to be dealt with by the small *things*, to have disputes decided by the king and his judges, to hear the

CROSS AT KIRK MICHAEL

old laws proclaimed and to make any new laws that might be needed.

On the hill at S. John's, where Tynwald was, and is now, held, sat the king with, as our Book of Laws tells us, his face to the east, his sword held upright before him, and his churchmen and other chief men sitting near him, while the people stood round the hill. If the king wished to learn anything about the laws of the land, or to have any difficult questions decided, he referred to his *deemsters*; in those days there were no written laws; men trusted entirely to their memory, and it was especially the duty of the deemsters to preserve the memory of these "breast laws" as they were called, and to give the king advice thereupon; usually he directed them to summon the wisest and worthiest men from among the people to aid them in giving advice. No law could be passed without the consent, not only of the wise men thus selected, but of the whole free people, and this fact forms the most important distinction between the Norse Parliament and the Celtic, in which, as we have seen, the consent of the people was not necessary.

Such is the free Constitution which our Norse ancestors have handed down to us.

DEFINTIONS.

Sheading. — Ship-shire, so called because it formerly had to provide a certain number of war-ships for the king.

Deemsters. — Those who steer or guide the *deem* or judgement.

CHAPTER III (*continued*)

Part 3. – *Their Church (? 1000—1266)*

THE VIKINGS AT FIRST HEATHEN. — The Vikings, who were heathen and merciless in their treatment of the Christians, killed the good Culdees they found in Man and put an end to Christianity there. It was probably not before the beginning of the eleventh century that the people of Man again became Christians, Indeed, there is no trustworthy information about their religion, until Rushen Abbey or Monastery, the ruins of which are still to be seen near Ballasalla, was founded. This abbey, which was connected with the great English Abbey of Furness, belonged to the order of Cistercians, or White Monks, who were so named from the white clothes they wore. It received large grants of land from the Manx kings, and was therefore both wealthy and powerful; its monks were not subject to the Bishop of Man, but only to their abbot, as the head of an abbey is called, and to the Pope.

DIOCESE OF SODOR AND MAN. — In A.D. 1154, we hear, for the first time, of the Diocese of Sodor and Man, as our diocese is still called. It consisted of the southern islands of Scotland, extending from the Hebrides to Arran, and Man, and it was then placed under the Archbishop of Drontheim,

RUINS OF RUSHEN ABBEY

in Norway. The name *Sodor* is derived from two Norse words meaning southern isles, so that Sodor and Man means "The Southern Isles and Man," and it is, in fact, the Church name for the kingdom which was then called "Man and the Isles." Though the connexion of the kingdom of Man with the Isles, or Sodor, came to an end in A.D. 1266, the diocese continued to be under the rule of the distant Norwegian archbishop till the fifteenth century.

WIMUND. — During this period two very remarkable men, Wimund and Symon, were bishops of the diocese. Wimund, who is famous as a warrior, not as a bishop, was the son of a peasant. Beginning his career as a chorister at Furness Abbey, he became a monk there, and was sent to the Abbey of Rushen when it was founded. He so pleased the Manx people by his cleverness, eloquence, and pleasant manners, and they were so impressed by his great height, that they made him their bishop. He did not, however, stop long in Man. He is next found claiming a great earldom in Scotland, and, after ravaging the south-western part of that kingdom with fire and sword, he, with the help of the Thane, or Lord, or Argyll, whose daughter he had married, compelled the Scottish king to surrender the southern part of Scotland to him. But he ruled his subjects with such severity that they seized and blinded him and shut him up in a monastery, where he died.

SYMON. — The other bishop, Symon, a good and learned man, did much for the welfare of the diocese. He held a great meeting of the clergy at Kirk Braddan, where laws were passed to govern the Church, and he built part of our Cathedral, or head-church, of S. German, on S. Patrick's Island, where he lies buried.

THE BISHOPS, &C. — The bishops' power, which at first was very small compared with that of the Abbot of Rushen, had, by Symon's time greatly increased. They had obtained a large amount of land from the Kings of the island, and, like the Abbots of Rushen, and of the other abbeys who had lands here, they were Barons of the Isle, that is to say, they were lords and did homage to the king for their property, instead of paying him rent for it. Like other lords, too, they held a court on their own land, and had power to condemn those who lived on it to death if they committed any crime.

Some time before the end of this period the island had been divided into parishes, under the charge of clergy, over whom the bishop, and not the Abbot of Rushen, had authority.

DATES.

Rushen Abbey founded, 1134; *its church completed,* 1257.

Symon, bishop, 1226 — 1244.

DEFINITIONS.

Norse. — The language spoken by the inhabitants of ancient Scandinavia and Iceland.

Diocese. — A territory under the authority of a bishop.

S. GERMAN'S CATHEDRAL AND PEEL CASTLE

CHAPTER IV

THE HOUSE OF GODRED CROVAN (1079 — 1266).

Part I.—Godred I to Reginald I (1079 — 1187).

". . . Till there came to them King Gorree,
With his strong ships and his kingly power."

MANX BALLAD

GODRED I (CROVAN). — Under Godred Crovan and his successors a rather more settled state of affairs existed. Godred was quite a powerful king, who ruled Dublin and the greater part of the province of Leinster in Ireland, as well as Man and many of the Scottish Islands. Moreover, the Scots on the mainland were so afraid of him that, when he said that he would not allow them to build any large vessels, they did not dare to disobey him. Such a man would be well remembered, and the stories of his great prowess would, in course of time, become legends of more than human might. It is therefore not unreasonable to suppose that he is the original of the mythical hero King Gorree, or Orry.

MAN AND THE ISLES. — One very important fact to be borne in mind about the period between 1079 and 1266 is that the King of Man was also chief of a number of islands, including the Hebrides, which extend along the western coast of Scotland. This kingdom, which had the sea as its highway—

and in those days when there were no roads it was possible to travel more quickly by sea than by land—was called "Man and the Isles." It was under the suzerainty, or supreme rule, of Norway. It is true that the Norwegian king did not often interfere in the affairs of the island kingdom; still, even so, it may appear strange that so distant a country should ever have ruled over us in any way. But you must remember that Norway was then a very much more powerful country than it is now, and that it had dominion, not only over Man and the western isles of Scotland, but over the Orkneys and Shetlands and part of the north of the Scottish mainland. It may also appear strange that neither England, Scotland, nor Ireland should have disputed the Norwegian supremacy over Man; but the two latter were weakened by constant divisions and wars, while the former, under its Norman rulers, had, at first, enough to do in defending its Continental possessions.

EXPLOITS OF MAGNUS. — After Godred's death there came a time of war and trouble. In 1098 a battle between the northern and southern Manx, called the battle of Santwat, in which the former were victorious, took place near Peel. Just after this event, Magnus, King of Norway, arrived in Man, and he not only subdued it and all the western islands, but so terrified the King of Ireland that he agreed to carry Magnus's shoes on his shoulders on Christmas Day as a token of submission to him.

OLAF I. — It was not till Godred's son, Olaf I was placed on the throne of Man and the Isles that there was peace, because Olaf kept on such friendly terms with the Kings of England, Ireland, and Scotland, that no one ventured to disturb his kingdom till he had grown old and feeble. Then came three of his nephews from Dublin with a number of soldiers, and demanded that he should deliver half the kingdom to them. Olaf said that he would meet them at Ramsey and talk about this. On the appointed day both parties came there and sat down in order, the king and his followers on one side, and the nephews and theirs on the other. Reginald, one of the nephews, on being summoned to approach the king, turned as if to salute him, raised his gleaming battle-axe on high and cut off Olaf's head at a single blow. After this act of treachery the nephews divided Man between them. But they did not long retain their ill-gotten possession.

GODRED II. — Godred II, son of Olaf, returned from Norway, where he had been doing homage to his suzerain, put the murderers to death, and succeeded his father as king. Soon afterwards, the people of Dublin having asked him to reign over them, he went there with a number of ships and a large army. When Murchadh, King of Ireland, heard of this, he collected a number of men and hastened to Dublin to drive out Godred. On their approach to the city, Godred and his followers, with all the citizens of Dublin, rushed upon them and assailed them with such a shower of arrows that they were compelled to fly. Godred continued to be King of Dublin for a short time, and, finding himself secure on his throne, began to act tyrannically towards his nobles. They consequently rebelled against him, and with the aid of Somerled, the ruler of Argyll, in Scotland, fought a battle against him, which resulted in Somerled gaining possession of some of the isles which belonged to the kingdom of Man and the Isles. He did not take the most northern isles, the Hebrides, but some of the isles which lay between them and Man, so that Godred's kingdom was divided into two parts. A few years later began the conquest of the east coast of Ireland by England, which thus, for the first time, became the most powerful kingdom in the Irish Sea. In this way a new and important influence was brought to bear upon Man.

CHIEF REIGNS.

Godred I. (Crovan), 1079 — 1095; *Olaf I.*, 1113 — 1153; *Godred II.*, 1153 — 1187.

DATES.

Division of the Kingdom of the Isles, 1156; *English conquest of Ireland begins*, 1170.

DEFINITION.

Doing homage. — The submission of a vassal (or dependent) to a lord; literally, to become the man (Latin *homo*) of a lord.

CHAPTER IV (*continued*)

Part 2. — *From Reginald I to the end of Norse Rule (1187— 1266).*

REGINALD I. — Godred was succeeded by Reginald, his eldest son. A great part of Reginald's reign was spent in quarrelling with his younger brother, Olaf, and his authority was thus greatly weakened, so that he found it all the more necessary to keep on good terms with the powerful kings around him, especially with the King of England. He therefore did homage to King John, and, fearing lest his suzerain, the King of Norway, should be offended by this act, he offered him the same proof of his allegiance. On hearing of this King John was so angered that he devastated Man, and compelled Reginald to do homage again. For many years there had been a civil war in Norway, so that the kings of that country had not been able to exert their authority over Man and the Isles. But before the end of Reginald's reign King Hakon IV succeeded to an undivided rule, and Norway soon became powerful again. This led to King Reginald doing homage to King Henry III of England, and, following the example of King John, he secretly promised the Pope that he would hold Man as a fief from him, hoping thus to gain his protection. All Reginald's precautions, however, could not secure his throne; he was deprived of half of his kingdom by Olaf, and at last he lost his life also in a battle against him at Tynwald. Many were slain in this battle; and the southern part of the island was soon afterwards so terribly devastated by pirates that scarcely a single inhabitant was left.

OLAF II. — The reign of Olaf II. is mainly a record of fighting, which ended in his regaining most of the islands which Godred had lost.

HARALD. — His son Harald's reign was a prosperous one. Though dethroned at the beginning of it by the King of Norway, he afterwards succeeded in keeping on friendly terms not only with him, but with the Kings of England and Scotland. But his life was to have a sad ending. When on the way home from Norway with his newly-married wife, the daughter of the king of that country, they, and all with them, were shipwrecked and drowned. His brother, Reginald II, who succeeded him, was assassinated after a reign of twenty-four days.

A USURPER. — A connexion of the Manx kings, also called Harald, usurped the throne, but soon after wards Magnus, Olaf's youngest son, with his father in-law John, who was ruler of some of the Scottish isles, came to Man. They put in at Ronaldsway, and John sent messengers to the Manx people, saying, "Thus and thus does John, King of the Isles, command you." But they were so angry with John calling himself "King of the Isles," that they would not listen to what the messengers had to say. A battle, which was fought on S. Michael's Island, followed, and the invaders were utterly routed by the Manx. When, however, Magnus appeared a few months later, without his father-in-law, he was joyfully received by the Manx, who chose him as their king.

MAGNUS. — It was during the reign of this Magnus that the Scottish kings, whose country had for some time past been increasing in power and importance, carried out their plan of conquering the islands off their coast, some of which belonged to the King of Man, and some to the descendants of Somerled. They had in vain tried to gain their end by bar gaining with King Hakon of Norway, so King Alexander III attacked the Hebrides. To protect these islands King Hakon arrived off the Scottish coast with a large fleet, and, after a hard-fought battle at Largs on the Firth of Clyde, he was defeated, and fled to the Orkneys, where he died during the winter. Magnus, who had not been with the part of Hakon's fleet that was defeated at Largs, then went to Man. Alexander set out with the idea of following him to that island, but when Magnus heard of this he was so frightened that he begged for a truce. On this being granted, he met King Alexander at Dumfries, and did homage to him, promising to furnish him with ten war-galleys whenever he needed them.

Magnus, who was now King of Man only, died in December, 1265, and in 1266 the King of Norway formally ceded the whole of the Kingdom of Man and the Isles to Scotland.

CHIEF REIGNS.

Reginald I., 1187 — 1226; *Olaf II.*, 1226 — 1237; *Harald*, 1237 — 1248; *Magnus*, 1252 — 1265.

DATES.

John devastated Man, 1210; *Civil War in Norway*, 1154 — 1217; *Battle of Tynwald*, 1228; *Battle of S. Michael's Island*, 1250; *Battle of Largs*, 1263.

DEFINITIONS.

Allegiance. — The duty of a vassal to a lord.

Fief. — Land held by a vassal on doing homage and swearing allegiance.

CHAPTER V

THE "THREE-LEGS" OF MAN

THE FIRST THING CONNECTED WITH THE ISLE OF MAN that meets the eyes of most of the visitors who come to our shores is the gilded "Three-Legs" on the paddle-boxes of our steamers. They naturally want to know what this device means, and from whence it comes. I do not suppose that many of you could give a correct answer to these questions. Indeed, I am not sure that I can do so, but I will try.

THE "THREE-LEGS" A SUN SYMBOL. — The "Three Legs" was probably originally a sign or symbol of the sun which was worshipped by the heathen. But why, you will ask, did they worship the sun? And I answer, because the sun is at once the most awful, the most mysterious, and the most beneficent object visible to man. It is the source of light and warmth, and when it sets, darkness and cold soon follow. They saw, too, that when the sun shone, their corn grew and flourished; they therefore came to think of it as the origin of all life. No wonder, then, that they worshipped it. The sun, as you know, was once supposed to move round the earth, and to show this motion it was represented as being like a wheel with spokes. After a time the rim of the wheel, except the three little bits of it which are now feet, was left out, and the spokes gradually became legs.

IT PROBABLY CAME FROM SICILY. — The symbol thus described is found on coins more than two thousand years old, belonging to the island of Sicily, in the Mediterranean. I have told you that the Vikings were great wanderers, and it is well known that Sicily was a favourite island of theirs, and that it belonged to their descendants for centuries. What is more natural than that the Vikings, who had been plundering in Sicily in the winter, should bring the "Three-Legs" with them when they paid their summer visit to Man? There is, however, only one representation of it dating from the days when the descendants of the Vikings ruled in Man, and that is on our grand old sword of state, which was formerly carried before the King of Man on Tynwald Day. The "Legs" on this sword, which belongs to the early part of the thirteenth century, are not naked like those of Sicily, but are covered with armour, and have spurs on their heels. This change, however, seeing that all warriors in those days in the north of Europe wore armour, is only a natural one. We know that the seal of King Harald of Man in 1245 bears the device of a ship, with the Latin motto *Rex Manniæ et Insularum*, "King of Man and the Isles," but this does not prove that our Norse kings did not use the "Three-Legs" also. The most interesting of the early representations of the "Three-Legs" after 1266 is on a beautiful pillar cross near Maughold churchyard, which belongs to the latter part of the fourteenth century.

ITS MOTTO SYMBOLICAL OF OUR HISTORY. — The motto which now surrounds the "Three-Legs"—*Quocunque Jeceris Stabit*, that is, "Whichever way you throw it, it will stand"—is probably comparatively modern. It refers to the fact that the "Legs" will stand in whatever position they are placed, and it is symbolical both of the character of Manx history and of Manxmen, though I do not suppose that it was intended to be so. Is it not wonderful how, though we have been under the rule of several nations, our ancient laws and the framework of our government have stood practically unchanged? And as to the character of Manxmen, do not the lives of those who have gone out from Mona's Isle to other countries give us some reason for saying that, wherever you place a Manxman, he will stand? This means that in consequence of being a good and upright citizen, a Manxman will prosper wherever he goes. Some unknown poet has expressed this idea as follows:—

> "However through the world he's tost,
> However disappointed, crost,
> Reverses, losses, fortune's frown,
> No chance or change can keep him down,
> Upset him any way you will,
> Upon his legs you find him still;
> For ever active, brisk, and spunky,
> Stabit: Jeceris: quo: cunque."

Yet another lesson may be learned from our "arms," and that is, that "union is strength."

> "Three legs armed;
>   Armed in self-defence
> Centrally united;
>   Security from thence."

These words were written below the "Three Legs" in the old building at Castletown, where the House of Keys formerly met.

CHAPTER VI

SCOTTISH AND ENGLISH RULE (1266 — 1405).

STRUGGLES BETWEEN SCOTS AND MANX, AND SCOTS AND ENGLISH. — It is certain that by the end of the last period the Norsemen and Celts in Man had become practically one people, speaking much the same Celtic or Gaelic language as at the present day. You have heard how they came under the rule of the Kings of Scotland; this rule was not established without delay and difficulty. King Alexander had to send an army to Man to compel it to submit to him; but the Manx, under the leadership of Godred, son of Magnus, again revolted, and another army had to be sent, which defeated them at Ronaldsway. In 1290 Edward I, King of England, who had recently conquered Wales, and whose realms therefore surrounded Man, not only on the east and west, but on the south, took possession of the island, and it remained in English hands till 1313, when Castle Rushen was taken by King Robert Bruce of Scotland. We cannot be sure whether any of the Castle Rushen we see now was standing in Bruce's time, but part of it, as well as of Peel Castle, was probably built before the end of this period. For many years after 1313 Man was sometimes held by the

English and sometimes by the Scots, who were constantly fighting with each other.

MAN FINALLY UNDER ENGLISH RULE AFTER 1346. — At last, after the defeat of the Scots at the battle of Neville's Cross, English rule was firmly established. In 1333 King Edward III had granted the island to Sir William de Montacute. His son and namesake, who had succeeded his father as King of Man, sold it to Sir William le Scroop, and he, unfortunately for himself, took the side of Richard II against Henry Bolingbroke. In consequence of this, the latter, when he came to the throne as King Henry IV, caused him to be beheaded, and gave his kingdom to Henry Percy, Earl of Northumberland. Percy, in his turn, got into trouble with the king, who granted the island to Sir John Stanley, on condition of his doing homage and giving two falcons at the coronation of each King of England.

MISERABLE STATE OF MAN. — Almost all we hear about the Manx people during this period leads us to think that they must have been in a very miserable state. Thus at one time the island was said to be "desolate and full of wretchedness"; at another, it was plundered of everything worth carrying off by a body of Irish freebooters, who had defeated the Manx in a battle on the slopes of South Barrule; and finally we are told that its people had to buy corn in Ireland to save themselves from starvation. So poor were they that they could not afford to make any more of the beautiful crosses which were so common in the previous period. Their rulers, some of whose names we have mentioned, changed so often that they were not likely to have been much interested in the island, which they seem to have scarcely visited. Indeed, it is probable that they contented themselves with taking all they could out of it, while doing as little as possible for it.

THE MONKS AND THE CHURCH. — The monks of Rushen, on the contrary, were always on the island, and, as their

CASTLE RUSHEN

revenue increased, so did their power and influence with the people, to whom they seem to have been both kind and charitable. These monks probably reached the highest point of their power at the end of this period. The bishops, too, obtained increased power and authority, though their property was very small as compared with that of the abbeys. Mark, the first bishop appointed by King Alexander, was greedy in exacting money from the people, who at last lost all patience and expelled him from the island. When the Pope heard of this, he placed them under an interdict, that is to say, he would not allow the monks and clergy to baptize, marry, or bury the people, or perform any spiritual office for them. This frightened them so much that they agreed, if it were removed, not only to receive Bishop Mark back, but to pay a tax of one penny on every house with a fireplace, a tax which, under the name of "the smoke penny," has continued almost to the present day.

It was during this time that two Manxmen, William Russell and John Donkan, were bishops. They are the only two Manxmen who have been bishops of this diocese. Both, especially the latter, were able men.

CHIEF REIGNS.

Alexander III., 1266 — 1286; *William de Montacute I.*, 1333 — 1344; *William de Montacute II.*, 1344 — 1392; *William le Scroop*, 1392 — 1399; *Henry Percy*, 1399 — 1405.

BATTLES.

Ronaldsway, 1275; *South Barrule*, 1316; *Neville's Cross*, 1346.

CHAPTER VII

THE HOUSE OF STANLEY (1405 — 1736).

Part I. — The Stanleys from 1405 to 1627.

"The war, that for a space did fail,
Now trebly thundering swelled the gale,
And—'Stanley!' was the cry,—
A light on Marmion's visage spread,
And fired his glazing eye:
With dying hand, above his head
He shook the fragment of his blade,
And shouted—'Victory!'—
''Charge, Chester, charge! On Stanley, on!
Were the last words of Marmion."

THESE LINES, TAKEN FROM SIR WALTER SCOTT'S "Marmion," refer to the exploits of Sir Edward Stanley at the famous battle of Flodden, and may serve as an introduction to the account of this noble family which ruled over Man for more than three hundred years.

SIR JOHN STANLEY I. — Sir John Stanley, the first member of the family who was King of Man, never came to the island. A curious story is told about his wife's father, Sir Thomas Latham. Sir Thomas' father and mother were childless, and it is said that, one day when they were walking together, they saw a little baby boy in an eagle's nest. They adopted this boy, who became the Sir Thomas Latham just mentioned. His only child, Isabel, was married to Sir John Stanley, who took as a crest the picture of an eagle with a child in its nest, which you have, perhaps, seen on Manx coins.

SIR JOHN STANLEY II. — Sir John Stanley's son, who bore the same name, took a great interest in our island. He saw at once that he would never be its real ruler till he had curbed the power of the barons. To this end he forbade them to give shelter—sanctuary as it was called—to such of his tenants as had committed crimes and had fled to them for protection from justice, and he caused a law to be passed that, if any of them did so, they should lose their property; and, at the same time, he summoned them to do fealty to him at Tynwald. Some of them obeyed the summons, but others did not, and were punished by being deprived of their lands.

There were at this time two revolts against his governors; these he put down, but, lest the same danger should arise again, he increased the authority of the governor by ordering that any offence against him should be punished in just the same way as if it were against the king. It was in his time, too, that trial by jury was substituted for trial by battle—that is to say, instead of people settling their disputes by fighting each other, their neighbours were called in to decide between them peaceably. This great reform was passed at "A Court of all the Commons of Man," held at the old Tynwald Hill, at Baldwin, in Braddan. Another useful reform was his order that the laws, which had hitherto depended on the memory of the deemsters, should be written down.

Sir John Stanley was a wise, though despotic, ruler, and he conferred many benefits on the island. But few of the Stanleys who succeeded him, up to the time of the Great Stanley, ever came here, and if they did so, it was only for a very brief time.

THOMAS STANLEY, FIRST EARL OF DERBY. — His grandson was the well-known Thomas, Lord Stanley, who, after the battle of Bosworth Field, which ended the "Wars of the Roses," placed the crown of the dead Richard III on the head of Henry Tudor, and proclaimed him king as Henry VII Stanley was then made Earl of Derby by the grateful king, who was his stepson. Thomas' grandson, also called Thomas, the second Earl of Derby, gave up the title of "King of Man," and took that of "Lord of Man," because he thought the title of a "great lord" was more honourable than that of a "petty king."

POSITION OF THE MANX PEOPLE. — Let us now see what these great lords got from the island which belonged to them. Its people were their tenants and paid them rents, mostly in kind, i.e., in corn, sheep, oxen, or labour. These tenants had to labour on certain fixed days in repairing the lord's forts and houses, and they had to supply the soldiers in the garrisons with corn, and turf for burning. They also paid small taxes for the liberty of fishing for herrings, for importing and exporting goods, also for grinding corn at the lord's mills. Of all these taxes the only one which was complained of was the last. Not only were the tenants compelled to go to the mills to have their corn ground, but if the mills got out of repair, they were bound to help in making them good again without getting any pay. This they thought very unfair, and to avoid going to them they made hand-mills, or "querns," which were seized and destroyed by the lord's order whenever they could be found.

THE MILITIA. — Besides paying taxes, the tenants between twenty and sixty years of age had to serve as soldiers. Every parish and town had its company of foot-militia, who were obliged to see that watch was kept on the hills, both by day and by night, for any enemy that might approach the island.

Each militiaman had to provide himself with a bow and arrows, a sword and a buckler, and he was called out once a month to be drilled. There were also a few horse-militia in each parish. Neither the foot nor the horse-militia were paid. There were, however, some paid soldiers—usually about a hundred—who were employed as policemen and as garrisons of the various forts, the most important of which were the castles of Peel and Rushen.

CHIEF REIGNS.

John I (Knight), 1405 — 1414; *John II* (Knight), 1414 — 1432; *Thomas I.* (Baron), 1432 — 1460; *Thomas II* (1st Earl), 1460 — 1504; *Thomas III* (2nd Earl), 1504 — 1521; *Edward* (3rd Earl), 1521 — 1572; *Henry* (4th Earl), 1572 — 1593; *Ferdinando* (5th Earl), 1593 — 1594; *William I* (6th Earl), 1610 — 1627.

DEFINITION.

Militia. — A body of soldiers for home service.

CHAPTER VII (*continued*)

Part 2. — *The Reformation.*

THE REFORMATION. — Manx history is almost silent about the great religious change which is called the Reformation. The monks of Rushen and of the other religious houses were indeed turned out of their monasteries in 1540, their possessions given to others, and the authority of the Pope set aside; but it is probable that the old form of religion lasted for some time longer, and that any changes in it were made very gradually. One happy result of so slow and gradual a change was that in Man there were none of those terrible persecutions which disgraced the reigns of several English sovereigns.

LAWS OF THE REFORMED CHURCH. — The laws of the reformed Church were not written down till 1610. Some of the punishments inflicted by these laws are very curious. For instance, those who said unkind things about their neighbours had to wear a bridle, and to stand while wearing it at the market cross[1] of the nearest town for several hours on the market day. After the culprit had been exposed to public view for some time, the bridle was taken off, and he had to say three times, "Tongue, thou hast lied."

---

1 There was formerly a stone cross in the market-place of each of the four towns.

Another punishment was inflicted by means of the stocks, a wooden machine in which the arms and legs were fastened. Unfortunate people who were suspected of being sorcerers or witches were also severely punished under these laws. But if tradition is to be believed, their fate had been much worse in the days of the unreformed Church. It is said that they were either burned alive, or rolled down from the top of the mountain called *Slieau Whuallian*, near S. John's, in barrels having spikes inside them, or thrown into the *Curragh Glass*, "Green Bog," a pool near Greeba Mountain. There is, however, no trace of any such punishments in our records, where the punishments usually mentioned are penance and imprisonment. Penance was performed by standing clad in a white sheet, either at the cross on a market day, or in the churchyard during service time. Imprisonment was then a more dreadful punishment than it is now, because the prisoners were confined in a damp, dark, underground vault in Peel Castle, instead of in dry and airy rooms, as at the present day. The worst sins were punished by excommunication, that is, by being deprived of all the privileges of Church membership. An excommunicated person could not even be buried in a churchyard. These laws were put in force by courts presided over by the bishop, the archdeacon and the vicars-general, and fell into disuse only about a hundred years ago. Such a system was suited to rude and primitive times, but when people became more civilized and independent, they would not submit to it, and so it gradually disappeared.

PURITANICAL IDEAS. — About the time that these laws were written down the Manx people seem to have begun to pick up ideas similar to those of the Puritans in England, and, a little later, we find them declaring that they would have no bishop and pay no tithes to the clergy. For a time, indeed, there was no bishop. Till 1651, this was because Earl James did not appoint one, and, afterwards, because Man was under the rule of the Puritan, Lord Fairfax, who did not approve of bishops. In other matters, however, excepting that the Prayer-book was not allowed to be used, the Church was but little interfered with.

DATE.

Vacancy in bishopric, 1644 — 1660.

DEFINITION.

Tithe. — A tenth part; the tenth part of the yearly produce paid to the clergy.

CHAPTER VII (*continued*)

Part 3. — *The Government.*[1]

THE GOVERNOR AND THE OFFICERS. — During the whole of the time that the Stanleys ruled in Man their government was practically a despotism. They delegated most of their power to a governor, and to help him in the executive part of the government, which was then much the most important, they appointed certain officers. The chief of these was the comptroller, who had the control of the revenue. The clerk-of-the-rolls made entries of accounts and wrote down the laws, decisions of the judges, &c, in the rolls or records. The receiver received the revenue and paid salaries, and the water-bailiff collected the customs' duties. There was also an attorney-general who advised the governor in legal matters and looked after the lord's interests generally. It will be seen from the names of most of these officers—"Household officers" as they were called—that their most important duties were in connexion with the lord's revenue. The Isle of Man was in fact the lord's farm or estate, and the governor and the officers were his bailiffs, who had to manage it for him to the best possible advantage.

---

1 In reading this *Part* reference should be made to the Introduction.

THE LAW COURTS. — They had also to preserve order and administer the law. For these purposes they, or some of them, were constituted a court, called the "Staff of Government"; and to carry out their orders, they had a captain in each town, a coroner, with his deputy the lockman, in each sheading, and a moar, who collected the lord's rents in each parish. But as they were usually Englishmen and therefore ignorant of the Manx laws, they often called in the deemsters, who were then elected by the people, and were Manxmen, to help them. When they had to try criminals, they summoned not only the deemsters but the bishop, with his vicars-general, and twenty-four representatives of the people, who were known by the name of The Keys, together with a jury.[2] For a long time this was the only court, except those of the deemsters, who dealt with less important matters, but when the population increased and there was more work to do, the different law courts we have at the present day gradually came into existence.

THE LEGISLATURE. — Now let us see what the legislative government of the island under the Stanleys was like.

The body which made new laws was usually composed of exactly the same members as the court just mentioned (without the jury), but when it sat as a legislative body it was called the Tynwald Court.

You have seen that, during the time of Norse rule no important decision was come to, or law passed, without, not only the consent of the selected wise men, but that of the whole free people. It is evident that this right had fallen into disuse during the troublous epoch between 1266 and 1405, since the deemsters told Sir John Stanley II that The Keys, as the wise men had come to be called—probably from their office of unlocking or explaining the law— could not exist without the lord's consent, and that they could only be called together

---

2 The court thus formed, which was the chief criminal court of the island, was afterwards called "The Court of General Goal Delivery."

when he wanted their opinion on a point of law. But nevertheless, the right of the people to have a share in making the laws was not entirely done away with. They were certainly consulted in the second Sir John Stanley's days, when a "Court of all the Commons of Man" passed a law establishing trial by jury, and when they chose six men out of every sheading to represent their views. For 150 years after this no more new laws were passed, but then a new law had to be considered, and the Keys therefore protested that it was necessary that for this purpose they should be elected by the people and not chosen by the lord. This protest, however, had no effect, since we find that even when a new law had to be made, the Keys were almost always chosen by the governor. Moreover, most of the few new laws took the form of orders given by the lord. The Keys, however, generally made good their claim to have their share in law-making, though they did not gain much by it, because the governors were wont to turn out such of them as would not do what they were told. During the reign of Lord Fairfax, the curious plan of the Keys selecting their own members was adopted. When there was a vacancy they selected two names, and one of these was chosen by the governor. In this way the ancient right of popular election disappeared till it was restored in 1866.

DATES.

Trial by jury established, 1429; *Keys began to elect their own members,* 1659.

CHAPTER VII (*continued*)

Part 4. — *Our Forefathers between 1405 and 1660.*

THEIR DWELLINGS AND WAY OF LIVING. — Our knowledge of the life of our forefathers is exceedingly scanty until we come to the fifteenth century; but during that century there were written some descriptions, which are still preserved, of the dwellings and way of living of the people. The houses of the poorest people were very wretched, being mere hovels with walls made of stones and clay, and with roofs thatched with heather or broom. They usually contained one room only, and in this lived pigs and poultry as well as human beings. They had no chimney, and the smoke, which came from a fire made of peat, made its way out by the door or a hole in the roof. The homes of the farmers and the townspeople were rather better, containing, as a rule, two floors, the upper of which was reached by a ladder placed outside the house. The food of all but the richest people consisted of fish, oatmeal porridge and oat-cake, and their drink of water and buttermilk, with, perhaps, some beer on market days. Wages were at first very low, but then food was much cheaper than it is now. The labourers were very strictly treated. If their masters struck them, they had to submit; if they wandered about without working, they were punished, and they might be taken to serve the lord and the chief officers for even a lower wage than the ordinary one. Neither they, nor in fact any one else, could leave the island without a licence from the lord. On the other hand, their masters were compelled by law to pay them their wages and to give them food of good quality. Their porridge, for instance, had to be so thick that the pot-stick would stand upright in the centre of the pot, just before dishing the porridge; and the cakes given to them were required to be one-third of an inch thick. Moreover, no Manxman could be arrested without a warrant, except for a very serious crime. But hired labourers were comparatively few in number, because most of the farms were so small that their tenants were able to cultivate them without seeking outside help.

THEIR FARMING. — They grew wheat, rye, barley, oats, hemp and flax, but there were no turnips or potatoes, and probably less than half the land was cultivated. After the harvest was over, all the fences were thrown down so that cattle might graze everywhere. These cattle, which were very small and poor, were kept in the fields all the year round, and the sheep were mainly of the sort called *loghtyn*, with brown wool.

THEIR FISHING. — Harvesting was mainly done by women, since, about the middle of July, the greater number of the men went off to the herring fishery, which seems then to have been considered of more importance than farming. They were not allowed to fish in the daytime or between Saturday morning and Sunday night, and before they set forth to the fishing they attended a service held on the quay, at which the Vicar of the parish prayed with them for the success of their labours.

THEIR TRADE. — There was but little trade at this time, and it was hedged about with what would appear to us to be very curious regulations. For instance, if a stranger came to the island with goods to dispose of, he was not allowed to sell them till "four discreet men of the country," appointed by the governor, had arranged the prices at which he was to sell. The chief exports were cattle, sheep, corn, hides, wool, flax, hemp, leather, honey, wax; with herrings, cod and ling, both fresh and salted. Except the salt fish, these commodities were mainly sent to England, Scotland and Ireland, while the salt fish went to France, Spain, and Portugal. From the last three countries, wine and salt were received in return, and, from the first three, timber, coal, iron, brass, nails, pitch, tar, soap, starch, and resin, and a small quantity of manufactured goods.

THEIR MANUFACTURES. — The people produced all their food, and possibly nearly all their clothing; their cattle and sheep provided them with meat, milk, and wool, while from their corn and flax they obtained bread, beer, and linen. Beer was usually brewed at home. The women spun both wool and flax, and the yarn was sent to weavers, some of whom were found in every parish. Their shoes, or *carranes*, were made of cow-hide, salted and dried, and laced with thongs of the same material at the top of the foot.

DEFINITION.

Warrant. — A written order giving power to arrest or execute an offender.

CHAPTER VII (*continued*)

Part 5. — *The Great Stanley (1627 — 1651).*

"Oh! I love well the *Stanlagh* name,
Though Roundies may abhor him,
Through the island, or over the sea,
Or across the Channel with Stanley;
Come weal, come woe, we'll gather and go,
And live and die with Stanley."

H IS SERVICES TO THE KING. — These lines, taken down from the lips of an old Manx woman fifty years ago, show how long the memory of James, the seventh Earl of Derby (*Yn Stanlagh Mooar*, "The Great Stanley,"as he is called in Manx), has been preserved among the people. He, indeed, and his brave wife, the famous Charlotte de la Tremoille, a French woman, are probably the most striking figures in our history. They lived in the island during the time of the Civil War in England. He was a devoted adherent of King Charles I, for whom he did many important services, not only by raising men to fight for him, but by providing him with arms and ammunition, and giving him large sums of money. The story of his wife's gallant defence of Latham House is probably familiar to you, and, as you will see, the earl himself was fated to lay down his life for the royal cause.

NATURE OF HIS RULE IN MAN. — In 1643 the king ordered him to go to Man, where the people, who were no doubt influenced by what was taking place in England, threatened to revolt. But his arrival, with English soldiers, soon put a stop to any trouble of this kind. He at once set about making himself popular, and he succeeded. In his own words:—"When first I came among the people, I seemed affable and kind to all, so I offended none. For taking off your hat, a good word, a smile or the like, will cost you nothing, but may gain you much." Truly, these were wise words. He well knew, however, how to hide the iron hand in the velvet glove. Never had the Manx people less liberty than under his rule. They enjoyed, indeed, the blessing of peace, but they were heavily taxed and sorely oppressed by the burden of supporting the troops which were quartered upon them, and they had also the more permanent grievance of being deprived of their ancient tenure, or holding, of the land. For all these things, the earl cleverly contrived that they should think his officers to blame, and not himself. But for the benefits that he conferred upon the people, he took care to receive full credit. What, then, were these benefits? Not only did the earl's residence with his family, and his numerous retinue of cavaliers, who had fled to him for refuge, bring about a much larger circulation of money than usual, but he actively bestirred himself to help the people.

HE ENCOURAGES TRADE. — Thus, perceiving that the island would never flourish till it had more trade with other countries, he tried to improve its manufactures by bringing in Englishmen to teach various handicrafts, and to help its farmers by improving the breed of Manx horses. He wore a suit made of native wool, with the object, no doubt, of inducing others to wear clothes of the same material, and he had an idea, although he did not live to carry it out, of encouraging education by establishing a college. But, after all, the welfare of the Manx people was of small importance to him as compared with the success of the royal cause. To this end he not only kept the Manx foot-militia constantly under arms, at great cost both to the country and himself, but he largely increased the horse-militia; and he established a small navy, which had some successful fights against the Parliament's vessels.

DEFIES THE PARLIAMENT. — Six months after the death of King Charles I, and three years after almost the whole of England had submitted to the Parliament, Earl James received a summons from General Ireton to surrender the island. To this request he returned the following reply:—"I received your letter with indignation, and with scorn I return you this an-swer,—that I cannot but wonder whence you should gather any hopes from me that I should, like you, prove treacherous to my sovereign; since you cannot be insensible of my for-mer actings in his late Majesty's service, from which principles of loyalty I am in no whit departed. I scorn your proffers. I disdain your favor. I abhor your treason; and am so far from delivering up this island to your advantage, that I will keep it, to the utmost of my power, to your destruction. Take this for your final answer; and forbear any further solicitations. For, if you trouble me with any more messages on this occasion, I will burn the paper and hang the bearer. This is the immutable resolution, and shall be the undoubted practice of him who accounts it his chiefest glory to be

"His Majesty's most loyal and obedient servant,
"Derby."

Parliament, which had more important matters to attend to, made no serious effort to take Man for more than two years later.

HIS DEATH. — In August, 1651, the earl left the island with some of his troops, among whom were 300 Manxmen, to join King Charles II, who was marching from Scotland into England. They were defeated in a fight at Wigan, but the earl went on with the remnant of his troops to Worcester, where he

JAMES, 7TH EARL OF DERBY
B. 1607; D. 1651

met the king and shared in the decisive defeat of the Royalists. He was captured, and confined in Chester Castle, and, after being tried by court-martial, was executed at Bolton.

DATE.

Civil War in England began, 1642.

DEFINITIONS.

To quarter Troops. — To have them supplied with lodgings and food without paying.

Court-martial. — A court consisting of military or naval officers for the trial of military or naval offences.

NOTE.

Sir Walter Scott's novel, "Peveril of the Peak," the scene of which is partly laid in the Isle of Man during this period, should be read.

CHAPTER VII (*continued*)

Part 6. — *Edward and William Christian.*

IN THE DAYS OF THE SEVENTH EARL WE FIND, for the first time since Bishop Donkan, two Manxmen who took a leading part in the government of the island. These were Edward and William Christian.

Edward Christian was the second son of John Christian, Vicar of Maughold. When quite young he went to sea, and, having become the owner as well as captain of a vessel, made a fortune in the East Indian trade. We then find him at the English Court in attendance upon the Duke of Buckingham, through whose influence he obtained the command of a frigate in the Royal Navy. After nine years of this service he returned to Man, where he met Lord Strange (afterwards the seventh Earl of Derby), who was so favourably impressed by him, that he made him governor. He performed his duties faithfully for a time, till he got into trouble for some dealings with pirates and smugglers, and was deprived of his governorship. But he regained his lord's confidence some years later, and was placed in command of the militia. Unhappily, he abused the trust placed in him by encouraging the militia to revolt; however, before their plans were ripe, the earl arrived in the island, and

Christian was thrown into prison. At his trial he was charged
with having asserted that the House of Keys should be elected
by the people, and that the deemsters should be chosen in
like manner. As a matter of fact, both these were old practices
which had been abolished by the Stanleys, so that Christian
had merely been acting as a patriot in urging their adoption.
He was condemned, on these and other charges of treason,
to perpetual imprisonment in Peel Castle. Released when the
Parliament took the island, he was again imprisoned in Peel
Castle for plotting against Chaloner, a governor of the island
under Lord Fairfax, and he died there.

William Christian, famous in Manx song under the
name of *Illiam Dhone*, "Brown William," was the third
son of Ewan Christian of Milntown, one of the deemsters. He held the office of receiver, and the earl had such
a high opinion of his trustworthiness, that he left him in
command of the militia when he went to England. Soon
after this a rumour reached the island that the Parliament
had sent a force to capture it, and that the Countess of
Derby, who was then ruling in the name of her husband,
had arranged terms with the leader of this force. Christian consequently called a meeting of the people at his
house of Ronaldsway, where eight hundred of them took
an oath to oppose the countess till she had redressed their
grievances, and it is probable that, at the same time, their
leaders came to an agreement to anticipate the countess
by themselves surrendering the island. The militia then
proceeded to capture all the forts (except Rushen and
Peel, which they failed to take), so that their leaders were
able, on the arrival of the Parliamentary troops under
Colonel Duckenfield, to surrender the island to him; and
they did so, on condition that the Manx should enjoy
their laws and liberties as formerly. A few days later the
countess gave up Castle Rushen.

The island was then, for a brief period, under the rule of the Parliament, which sent for William Christian and his brother, Deemster John Christian, described as "two of the ablest and honestest gentlemen in the island," to give the Council of State an account of the Manx laws.

Thomas, Lord Fairfax, to whom the island had been presented by the Parliament, then took possession of it as its lord. Christian acted as governor under him for a year or two, and he continued to be receiver till Chaloner, who succeeded him as governor, deprived him of that office for reasons which have never been satisfactorily explained; he then left the island. When he returned to it, after the Restoration, he was brought to trial for his rebellion against the countess ten years before. Care had been taken to turn all Christian's friends out of the court which tried him, so that it need not surprise us that he was declared to be guilty. He was sentenced to be shot, and this sentence was carried out at Hango Hill, near Castletown. Christian had been, no doubt, guilty of treason against his lord; nevertheless, there is much to be said in his favour. It is true that he had sworn allegiance to the countess; but he recognized the folly of further resistance, and he probably had good reason to believe that her surrender to the Parliament would carry with it no sort of security for the rights and liberties of her subjects, which he, by seizing the power at a critical moment, succeeded in obtaining. Manxmen, indeed, have always condoned his faults in consideration of his services. They believe him to have been a true patriot, and they consider the sentence against him a crime, as expressed in the words of the ballad:—

"Thy murder, Brown William, fills Mona with woe!"

His dying speech has been paraphrased in the following lines:—

"Mourn not for me, my people, that I die,
For I stand innocent of any crime
Against the Countess and my loyalty.

Unjustly tried, I meet my death to-day
In patience; freely offering myself
In sacrifice for those I love so well.
So be ye patient, too, but hold my name,
When I am gone, in kindly memory;
And think of me as one that did not fear
To give his life to gain your liberty.
Mourn not for me, for I shall be at rest:
Of late my days have passed in misery,
Knowing no place where I might lay my head;
But now secure in God's forgiving grace,
All persecution will be passed away.
So I at last may find the peace I crave,
For though He kill me—yet I trust in Him.
Let there be no more risings in the Isle;
But act as loyal lieges, and obey
Your rulers in all just commands, and be
Loyal to one another in your homes.
What I have said and proved in my defence
To show my guiltlessness, they may suppress;
 But ye who know me know I do not lie,
And I assert that I am innocent.
Farewell, my people! May God's blessing light
Upon you and your homes! May He forgive
Those who have injured me and wrought my doom,
As I forgive them!"

W. E. WINDUS

REIGN.

Thomas, Lord Fairfax, 1652 — 1660.

DATES.

Edward Christian, made governor, 1628; in command of the militia, 1643; died, 1661.

William Christian, born, 1608; died, 1663; receiver, 1648 — 1659.

Parliament took possession of the island, November, 1651.

DEFINITION.

Council of State. — Forty-one members selected from the House of Commons who had full executive power.

CHAPTER VII (*continued*)

Part 7. — *The Last Stanleys (1660 — 1736).*

"Oft at the Ross with Yawkins and with Dowell,
And Manxmen gabbling from the Manor hole,
What noggins have I drunk of smuggled rum,
Just from the little Isle of 'Three Legs' come."
See "Guy Mannering," SIR W. SCOTT

MANX AND ENGLISH RESTORATION COMPARED. — Like the English Charles II, the Lord of Man, Charles, the eighth Earl of Derby, was restored to his kingdom in 1660. But the state of affairs the latter Charles had to deal with was very different to that which confronted the former. In England, the whole system of government had been altered by the Commonwealth; in Man, under the rule of Lord Fairfax, everything had gone on almost exactly as before. Thus it is not surprising to find that the Restoration in Man was marked by few changes, and that there was no outburst of disorder and irreligion as in England. Indeed the Church drew the bonds of its discipline tighter than ever, and increased its power over the people.

ISAAC BARROW. — The chief mover in this, as in other matters relating to the island, was Isaac Barrow, who held the offices of both bishop and governor, and thus united practically all authority in his own person. Fortunately he was a good as well as an able man, and he used his authority for the benefit of the island. His first care was to increase the incomes of the clergy, which were wretchedly small. For this purpose, he raised a sum of money in England, with which he bought back from the lord the share of the tithes of which the Manx monasteries had been deprived at the Reformation,[1] and he also, by his influence with King Charles II, obtained a grant of £100 a year towards the maintenance of the clergy, which was called the "Royal Bounty." His next care was for education. He established a school in every parish, and gave two farms near Castletown, the rents of which were to be applied to the support of a school, called the Academic School, which many years afterwards became King William's College. The only blot upon his career was his persecution of a few poor Quakers.

Earl Charles was succeeded by his son, Earl William, who was then a boy. When he grew up, he began to take an interest in the island, especially in its manufactures and trade.

SMUGGLING. — Trade certainly did increase in his time, but chiefly in the dishonest form of smuggling, which was carried on in the following manner. Large quantities of foreign goods were shipped to Manx ports, and the Manx duties, which were very small, were paid on them.

They were then secretly conveyed to Great Britain, and landed there without paying duty. In this way very large profits were made. Such a state of affairs led Parliament, after the Union with Scotland, to consider whether it would not be better to make the Manx duties as high as the British. Alarmed by this, the Keys sent some of their number to London to lay their views before the House of Commons, and they promised that, if Great Britain would import certain Manx products duty free, they would undertake that all persons shipping foreign goods from the Isle of Man to Great Britain and Ireland should pay the duties on them. An Act of Tynwald was

---

1 This share was rather more than one-fourth the whole.

passed to confirm this arrangement; but since Parliament did not perform its part of the bargain, the Act was repealed, and smuggling went on as before. In consequence of the serious loss which this unlawful trade caused to the English revenue, an Imperial Act was passed in 1726 to enable the English Government to purchase the Isle of Man; it was not, however, put in force till 1765.

Even after the English Government had gained control over the island, the Manx smugglers proved so skilful and cunning that their trade, though less extensive than formerly, still continued to be a profitable one, and, indeed, did not finally cease till well on into the nineteenth century.

Earl William was succeeded by his brother, James, the tenth earl, the last lord of the House of Stanley who ruled over Man. I will tell you about his connexion with the Manx *Magna Carta*, with the House of Keys, and with Bishop Wilson, in the next two *Parts*.

REIGNS.

Charles (8th Earl), 1660 — 1672; *William II* (9th Earl), 1672 — 1702; *James II* (10th Earl), 1702 — 1736.

DATES.

Isaac Barrow, governor and bishop, 1664 — 1671.

Union of England and Scotland, 1707.

Act of Tynwald (*Customs Act*) passed, 1711; repealed, 1714.

King William's College founded, 1833.

CHAPTER VII (*continued*)

Part 8. — *The Manx Magna Carta and Bill of Rights.*

"For Freedom's battle once begun,
Though baffled oft is ever won."

BYRON

THE WHOLE OF THE LAND IN MAN belonged to the Stanleys. A small part of it was granted by them to the barons, on condition of their doing fealty; and all the rest of it was occupied by tenants who paid rent.

THE POSITION OF THE TENANTS. — The tenants could only keep their farms for one year without making a fresh agreement; but if they paid their rents, they were not likely to be turned out, especially as the lord had often a difficulty in getting as many tenants as he wanted. They therefore gradually came to think that their farms were their own, and a practice sprang up of selling them to others without the lord's leave. On such occasions the seller of the land handed over a piece of straw to the buyer, in the presence of a judge, and of a jury, called the setting, or letting, quest. The judge then entered in a book a record of the fact that the straw had been handed over. The buyer held his land by the possession of the straw, and this tenure was called "the tenure of the straw." When the seventh Earl of Derby came to the island, he tried to put an end to this tenure; he told the tenants that under it they might be put out of their farms at any time, but that if they took leases, they were sure of keeping them during their lives and that of their children. Nevertheless, most of the people still clung to their old tenure. Finding, then, that he could not persuade them in this way, he bribed some of his officers and of the chief among the people to take leases, in the hope that the other tenants would follow the example of their leaders. This scheme had some effect, but still was not completely successful. After the Restoration, the eighth earl, who was constantly quarrelling with the "Keys" about this and other matters, told them plainly that he claimed the right to deprive any one of his land, when his lease came to an end. This threat, combined with the attractions of fishing, and of smuggling, which began about that time, and the fact that farming was then very unprofitable, induced many of the tenants to leave their farms. This was a serious matter for the lord because he got much less rent. William, the ninth earl, tried to come to terms with the tenants but did not succeed, and nothing was done till 1704, when a bargain, which was made between James, the tenth earl, and Bishop Wilson, with three members of the Keys—Ewan Christian of Milntown, Ewan Christian of Lewaigue, and John Stevenson of Balladoole—was agreed to by the Tynwald Court.

THE ACT OF SETTLEMENT. — The Act which was passed to confirm this agreement is called the "Act of Settlement." It secured the tenants in possession of their farms for ever, on condition of the payment of a small yearly rent which is still known as "lord's rent"; this rent was then fixed at an amount which might never be altered, while a small additional charge was to be made whenever a farm was either sold or descended to children. So secure is their holding that the tenants are now called land-owners.

From the great importance of this Act to the Manx people it has been called their *Magna Carta*. As time went on, and the value of their farms increased, the rent payable to the lord became so small in proportion as to be almost nominal.

The new land-owners were thus enabled, in their turn, to let their farms to tenants.

THE COMMONS. — Another land trouble, which arose a little later, was about the commons, or mountain lands. These lands, though belonging to the lord, had been used by the people for grazing, cutting turf, and other purposes. During the eighteenth century, however, the lords gradually began to sell portions of the commons which, when fences were made round them, were called "intacks," or "intakes," as the word means. The question was finally settled by the equal division of the commons between the Crown and the land-owners; and the rent from the land-owners' part is devoted to the payment of their lord's rent once every three years.

POLITICAL POSITION. — But there were causes of complaint other than those connected with the land. After the passing of the Act of Settlement, though the people ceased to be serfs, they continued to be deprived of any share in the government. They might be fined, punished, and imprisoned, without being tried by jury, and their money might be extorted from them by the governor and officers. The self-election of the Keys had been put an end to at the Restoration, after which they were chosen by the governor, and were turned out by him, if they did not do as he ordered them. The Keys complained, again and again, about this and other matters, but though Lord Derby made many promises, he did nothing. An appeal to the English Crown produced no effect, and it was not till after the accession of the first of the Atholl rulers that their grievances and those of the people were considered.

BILL OF RIGHTS. — It was then that the Acts were passed which have been called the *Manx Bill of Rights*, after the great English Bill of that name passed in the reign of William and Mary. By these Acts the right of the Keys to share in fixing the customs duties was confirmed. No criminal could be punished without the verdict of a jury, and the more severe of the spiritual laws were done away with. In a word, despotic government was replaced by oligarchical government.[1] The Keys, who resumed their mode of self-election, were never again turned out by the governor, and they began to take an important part in the government of the country.

DATES.

Act of Settlement passed, 1704; *Manx "Bill of Rights,"* 1736; *Commons Question settled*, 1864.

DEFINITIONS.

To do fealty. — To take an oath to be faithful to a superior lord of whom land is held.

Spiritual laws. — Laws enforced by the Church.

---

1 See Introduction.

CHAPTER VII (*continued*)

Part 9. — Bishop Wilson.

"To think on Bishop Wilson with veneration is only to agree with the whole Christian world," says Dr. Johnson. Nor is there any name so dear to Manxmen as that of Thomas Wilson, because, during the fifty-seven years he was bishop, his heart and hand were set to do their utmost in everything that related to the welfare of the island and its people.

He came to the Isle of Man at a time when the people were in great distress, owing to the troubles about the land, and when their hitherto simple and uneventful lives were beginning to be affected by the exciting and demoralizing trade of smuggling. They were, therefore, disposed to rebel against the discipline of the Church; and yet the bishop was able, for nearly forty years, to prevent most of them from rebelling. What a proof this affords of his influence over them!

HIS "DISCIPLINE."— Good and kind as he was, he never shrank from enforcing this discipline, even in ways, such as are referred to in Part 2 of this chapter, which appear to us, in these days, to be cruel and unjust, if he thought that by so doing he could turn people from their sins.

I have now to tell you how quarrels rose between him and the governor, who, as well as his officers, greatly disliked the discipline.

The oath of office taken by our bishops contains words which pledge them to maintain and defend the ancient laws and customs of the isle, and so Bishop Wilson, when he thought that the governor and officers were doing anything contrary to these laws and customs, did not hesitate to rebuke them. They consequently not only opposed his administration of the discipline, but fined him for interfering with them, and since he refused to pay the fine, they imprisoned him in Castle Rushen. For more than two months he was kept there, in a dark and damp cell, till he was released by order of King George I, and the sentence against him was reversed by the Privy Council.

The governors continued to oppose his discipline till the coming of James, Duke of Atholl, who took the wiser course of inducing the Tynwald Court to do away with the most severe of the Church's laws.

But Bishop Wilson benefited the Manx Church in many ways which, unlike the discipline, were generally acceptable.

HE PROMOTES EDUCATION. — Foremost among them was the promotion of education. Before his time the clergy were, as a rule, the only schoolmasters, and since they could spare but little time from their other duties for teaching, the education of the children suffered. The good bishop appointed masters and mistresses, who had to give their whole time to teaching; he established grammar schools in the towns; and he also founded a library in every parish.

Another way in which he did good was by providing religious books in the Manx language. You know that, in those days, very few of the people could speak or read anything but Manx, so that English books were of no use to them.

BISHOP THOMAS WILSON B. 1663; D. 1755

HE BUILDS CHURCHES. — When he first came to the island most of the Manx churches were in ruins, but before his death he had rebuilt or restored them; we give a picture of one of the most interesting of these churches.

SOME OF HIS OTHER GOOD DEEDS. — This excellent man did not confine his work to the Manx Church. You have already seen how he thought himself bound to work for the Manx State also.

A notable instance of this is the part he took in obtaining the *Act of Settlement*, and, on many other occasions, he helped the Keys in their struggles for liberty. He also took a deep interest in the industries of the people. Himself the son of a farmer, he had a competent knowledge of farming, which was then in a very backward state in the island. So well did he manage his own estate at Bishop's Court that many of the farmers came to take a pattern from it, more especially when they found that, during the terrible famine between 1739 and 1741, he was able to produce good crops, though theirs had failed. This was a time of great suffering, which he did much to diminish, either by giving corn to the poor for nothing, or by selling it to them at half cost.

His interest in the fishing is shown by the encouragement which he gave to the good old custom of praying with the fishermen before they set out to their work, and by his provision of a special service for the use of the clergy at such times. It is to him, too, that we owe the beautiful petition in the Litany, "That it may please Thee to restore and continue to us the blessings of the seas."

It is impossible in this brief account to mention all that Bishop Wilson did for the Isle of Man, which he would not leave, though he might have had a much more important bishopric in England.

HIS CHARITY. — I must, however, say a word or two about the greatest of all his virtues, that of charity. He began by giving a tenth, then a fifth, afterwards a third, and, finally, half of his income to the poor. The following story, among others, is told to show how kind-hearted he was: He had ordered a cloak from his tailor, which he wished made with only one button to fasten it. "But, my lord," said the tailor, "what would become of the poor button-makers and their families, if everyone thought as you do—why they would be starved outright." "Do you say so, John," replied the bishop; "well, then, button it all over."

He died at Bishop's Court, and was buried in Kirk Michael churchyard, where the following words may be read on his tombstone:—

"Sleeping in Jesus, here lieth the body of Thomas Wilson, D.D., Lord Bishop of this Isle, who died March 7th, 1755. Aged 93, and in the 58th year of his consecration.

"This monument was erected by his son, Thomas Wilson, D.D., a native of this parish, who, in obedience to the commands of his father, declines giving him the character he so justly deserved. Let this Island speak the rest!"

DATES.

Thomas Wilson, bishop, 1698 — 1755; *imprisoned in Castle Rushen*, 1722.

BALLAUGH OLD CHURCH

CHAPTER VII (*continued*)

Part 10. — *John Stevenson and William Walker.*

JOHN STEVENSON. — The name of John Stevenson, Speaker of the House of Keys, should ever be remembered by Manxmen with respect, because he was the leader of the Keys in their patriotic struggle against the despotism of the tenth Earl of Derby. We have seen that he was one of those who made the arrangement which resulted in the Act of Settlement. But his next efforts for the good of the people were not successful. In vain did he appeal to Lord Derby against the arbitrary conduct of his servants, the governor and officers, which I have described in *Part* 8. Lord Derby's answer was to have him tried as a criminal and imprisoned in Castle Rushen; and equally vain, as we have seen, was the appeal to King George I, which was suggested by him, to compel Lord Derby to redress the grievances of the people and of the Keys. After Lord Derby's death, however, the cause for which Stevenson had been struggling triumphed, and we find his name at the head of the Keys who signed the *Bill of Rights*.

William Walker, Rector of Ballaugh and vicar-general, rose from a humble position by his diligence and good conduct. When twelve or thirteen years of age, he was a servant in the household of the John Stevenson I have just been telling you about. One day, in harvest time, he was driving one of the sledges, or carts without wheels, then in use, and, at the same time, reading a book. The horse, taking advantage of this, slipped the halter off his neck and ran away, passing before the windows of the house. Mr. Stevenson, standing at one of the windows, saw what had happened, and ran out to stop the horse. When he got up to the cart, he saw that the little reader still had his book in his hand. This fact seemed to the master to mark the character of the boy; and therefore, instead of scolding him for his neglect, he said to him: "Since thou art so fond of reading, thou shalt have enough of it." Accordingly, the next day, he sent him to the Academic School at Castletown, where he made such rapid progress that he passed all his examinations and was ordained as a clergyman when only twenty-one years old. He became Bishop Wilson's most devoted friend, and entered warmly into all his plans for the benefit of the Church. They were imprisoned in Castle Rushen together for nine weeks, during which time Walker and the other vicar-general, Curghey, translated part of the New Testament into Manx. He afterwards went to London in connexion with the lawsuit which arose out of this imprisonment. When there he met the Archbishop of Canterbury, who was so struck by his goodness and ability that he conferred the degree of LL.D. upon him. It is pleasant to learn that the honours he received did not in any way spoil the simplicity of his character. This was shown by the fact that when he saw his mother in the crowd that came to welcome him on Ramsey beach, on his return from London, he at once fell upon his knees to receive her blessing.

Bishop Wilson, who preached his funeral sermon, spoke of him as a most faithful, tender pastor of the flock committed to his care, as a dutiful son, a just magistrate, and unbounded in his charities and his hospitality.

DATES.

John Stevenson, born, 1659; died, 1737.

William Walker, born, 1679; died, 1729.

DEFINITION.

L.L.D. means Doctor of Laws.

CHAPTER VIII

THE HOUSE OF ATHOLL

Part I.—The Revestment.

"All the babes unborn will rue the day,
That the Isle of Man was sold away;
For there's ne'er an old wife that loves a dram,
But what will lament for the Isle of Man."

THE SALE OF THE ISLAND. — On the death of the tenth Earl of Derby, the Sovereignty of Man passed to James Murray, the second Duke of Atholl, who was descended from the seventh Earl of Derby's third daughter.

The brief rule of the Atholl family is connected in the minds of Manx people with the sale of the island, and the consequent suppression of smuggling, which are referred to in the foregoing lines. But the name of the first Atholl Lord of Man is also connected with Acts of Tynwald, which did much to secure the liberty and better government of the Manx people. He was succeeded by his daughter, Charlotte, and her husband, John, who became Duke and Duchess of Atholl and Lord and Lady of Man.

For some time past, the Imperial Government had been determined to put an end to the smuggling because of the great harm it had done to English trade. They had hitherto failed in their attempts to do so, owing to their not having control over the island. They therefore sought to obtain this control by buying the sovereign rights of the duke and duchess. The duke, however, was very unwilling to part with them, and he did not yield till he had received a hint that steps would be taken to compel him. The arrangement which was come to between the Government and the duke was confirmed by an Act called the *Revesting Act*, which restored to the King of England the sovereignty of Man, which had been granted by King Henry IV to Sir John Stanley, 360 years before.

Thus the Dukes of Atholl ceased to be the sovereign rulers of the island, though they continued to be its manorial lords, and they retained the right of appointing the bishop and most of the clergy.

On the 11th of July, 1765, the flag with the Manx arms was hauled down from the flagstaff of Castle Rushen, and the standard of Great Britain was hoisted in its place; while His Majesty King George III was proclaimed King of Man.

So ends the history of our island as a distinct, though dependent, kingdom.

RESULTS OF THIS SALE. — Unsatisfactory as the bargain thus made was to the Atholl family, it was still more unsatisfactory to the Manx people, who had been in no way consulted about it. Let us see how this was. To begin with, the Tynwald Court lost its share in the control of the revenue; and it was enacted that, after paying the expenses of the government, and setting aside a certain sum for the purpose of encouraging, improving and regulating the trade, manufactures and fisheries of the island, the whole balance of the revenue should be at the disposal of the Imperial Parliament. There was, however, a provision that any money that was left, when the charges mentioned were paid, was to be placed to a separate account, an arrangement which very naturally led the Manx people to suppose that it was to be kept for their use. But you will see that the English Government viewed the question differently. The Imperial Parliament also took over the management of the harbours. Thus was the authority of the Tynwald Court almost destroyed. One immediate result of these changes was greatly to alarm the smugglers and the merchants who did business with them. Large quantities of goods, which they had intended to smuggle, were hidden in different parts of the country, and bands of armed coastguards went about searching for them. Riots and tumults resulted, and the country was reduced to such a state of distress that many of the land-owners, fearing that the prosperity of the island had departed for ever, sold their farms for next to nothing.

This state of things continued for some years, without any great improvement. The lords, whose reign had now come to an end, were certainly not model rulers. Their policy may often have been tyrannical, or unwise, or influenced by motives of self-interest. But at any rate most of them had, to a greater or less extent, taken a personal share in the government of the island, and had interested themselves in the well-being of its inhabitants. When their place at the head of the Manx State was taken by the King of England, the whole direction of affairs was handed over to distant officials who regarded the island as a nest of smugglers, from which it was their duty to get as much revenue as possible, but for which they were not bound to do anything in return. Consequently, trade and agriculture suffered, and the harbours and public buildings fell into decay. So bad was the state of affairs, that the English Government tried to improve it by practically restoring Atholl rule in 1793.

REIGNS.

James III (2nd Duke of Atholl), 1736 — 1764; *John III* (3rd Duke) *and Charlotte*, 1764 — 1765.

DEFINITION.

Enacted. — Made into a law; commanded by an act of a legislative body.

NOTE.

The sovereignty of the island was purchased for £46,000, and £24,000 was paid to the duke for the customs duties, which really belonged to the Manx people. The duke and duchess also received an annuity of £1,740 a year.

CHAPTER VIII (*continued*)

Part 2. — *The Manx Bible.*

"The Sacred Book
Assumes the accent of our native tongue."

WORDSWORTH

IT IS DIFFICULT TO BELIEVE THAT, till the Gospel of S. Matthew was published, the Manx people were without any part of the Bible in their native tongue. The Gospels of S. Mark, S. Luke, and S. John, and the Acts of the Apostles had also been translated in Bishop Wilson's time, but not published.

BISHOP HILDESLEY. — When his successor, Bishop Mark Hildesley, was appointed, he saw how important it was that this want should be supplied. He therefore promptly divided the task of translating the Bible among the clergy, and while this great work was going on, he also got some of them to translate the Prayer-book and other religious books, which the people eagerly and thankfully received. Funds for the expenses of publication were obtained from the *Society for Promoting Christian Knowledge* and from some charitable friends of the bishop in England. The arduous work of correcting and copying the various translations of the Bible was carried out by the Rev. Philip Moore and his pupil, John, afterwards Dr. Kelly.

On one occasion, when the latter was taking part of the manuscript to Whitehaven, to be printed, he was shipwrecked in a storm. His one thought was for his precious charge, which he held up above the water for five hours, till he was rescued.

The Manx translation of the Bible is a very good one, and we owe a debt of gratitude to the clergy who made it.

THE METHODISTS. — Just at the time that the Bible was placed in the hands of the Manx people, Wesleyan preachers began to come over to the island, and John Wesley himself arrived in 1777. Wesley was much pleased with the people, whom he described as being "loving and simple-hearted." His efforts and those of his disciples, assisted by the possession of the Bible, brought about a religious revival which was greatly needed. The influence of the Church over the people had begun to fail during the old age of Bishop Wilson, and this process had continued, notwithstanding the earnest efforts of Bishop Hildesley. At first, the unworthy successors of this good bishop persecuted the Methodists, as the followers of John Wesley were called. But this persecution soon ceased, and both Church people and Methodists worked together in a friendly way for many years.

It was during this period that most of the religious songs, called *carvals* or carols, some of which you have perhaps heard sung, were written.

SUNDAY SCHOOLS. — Another sign of renewed religious activity was the introduction of the system of Sunday Schools. The pious Hugh Stowell started such a school in his parish of Lonan. From Lonan the system quickly spread to other parishes, and was also eagerly adopted by the Methodists who had, however, about this time, begun to separate from the Church.

DATES.

Gospel of S. Matthew printed, 1748; *Prayer-book* (1st edition), 1765; *Bible* (1st edition), 1775.

Mark Hildesley, bishop, 1755 — 1772.

Sunday Schools first started, 1808.

CHAPTER VIII (*continued*)

Part 3. — *The Fourth Duke.*

THOUGH THE THIRD DUKE and his wife complained that the English Government had not paid them enough for their sovereignty, and that the Manx people had encroached on their rights, they made no effort to obtain any redress. Their son, John, on the contrary, when he succeeded to the dukedom, at once showed that he was determined not to sacrifice the smallest part of what he considered to belong to him.

FOURTH DUKE APPOINTED GOVERNOR. — The history of his struggles with the Manx people on the one hand, and the English Government on the other, before he became governor, would not interest you. It is, therefore, sufficient to state that the English Government, which felt, perhaps, that it had not managed the island well, appointed him to that office in 1793, hoping that, in this way, they would both stop his complaints and reconcile the Manx to English rule. They were, however, entirely mistaken about the first point, and partly, about the second. The duke, who had thus been placed almost in the position of the ancient lords, since he practically had the appointment to all public offices in the island, and was able to prevent the passing of any laws which he did not like, used his power to urge his claim against the English Government for more money with greater vigour than ever, and at last he succeeded in obtaining £3,000 a year. It is possible that the Atholl family would have continued to be the owners of the island, if the fourth duke could have agreed with its people. But this was very far from being the case.

HE QUARRELS WITH THE KEYS AND THE PEOPLE. — He was constantly quarrelling with the House of Keys. On one occasion, he told them that "they were no more Representatives of the people of Man, than of the people of Peru." There was a certain amount of truth in this gibe, because, owing to the self-elective system of the Keys, the people had no control over them, and it is therefore not surprising to find that the Keys disregarded the people's interests when they came into collision with their own. For instance, the Keys, who were, for the most part, landowners, wanted to keep up the price of corn, and therefore, even when the poor were starving, they tried to stop foreign corn being brought into the island. With his Council also the duke was often at variance. The people, however, were for a time well disposed towards him, because he pleased them by using his influence with the Government to stop the press-gangs from taking Manx fishermen to serve in the navy, and by his opposition to the Keys, who were then much disliked, on the question of the importation of corn. But after a time, various circumstances arose which made even the people turn against him. They objected to his appointing Scotsmen, instead of Manxmen, to paid offices in the island; and they resented his action in supporting his nephew, Bishop Murray, in levying a tithe on turnips and potatoes. This proceeding led to such a determined opposition that it had to be given up. Thus nearly every Manxman had turned against the duke, and the English Government saw how necessary it was that his connexion with the island should cease.

SELLS HIS REMAINING RIGHTS. — They therefore offered to purchase his remaining rights here, and, after lengthy negotiations, he accepted the sum of £417,000 for them.[1] This was far too much; but the island has prospered so greatly since 1829, when the duke left it, that the bargain has turned out a very good one for the English Government, which has not only got back all the money it paid him, but has received good interest as well.

DATES.

John (4th Duke of Atholl), *manorial lord,* 1774 — 1829; *governor,* 1793 — 1829.

---

1 *i.e.,* annuity, rents, commons, tithes, ecclesiastical patronage, &c.

CHAPTER VIII (*continued*)

Part 4. — *Manx Soldiers and Sailors.*

AFTER THE REVESTMENT the ancient militia ceased to be called out for drill, though some of the militiamen were made use of as watchmen to give warning of the approach of an enemy; and the place of the lord's garrison soldiers was taken by an English regiment. But when England was at war, not only with her American Colonies, but with France and Spain as well, she was so hard pressed by her foes that she withdrew this regiment and allowed a regiment of Manx Fencibles to be formed in its place. This Fencible regiment, which is said to have covered more ground than any other regiment in the British Army, because the men composing it had such broad shoulders, served in the Isle of Man, in England, and in Ireland during the Rebellion. There were also several companies of Manx Volunteers; and we find, both during the war first mentioned and during the gigantic struggle with France, which lasted for twenty-two years, almost without cessation, a very large number of Manxmen in the Royal Navy, and a smaller, but by no means insignificant, number in the Army. Indeed, it is probable that the Isle of Man had more men in the Navy, in proportion to its population, than any other part of the Empire. I can only tell you about very few of these gallant Manxmen.

You must all have heard of *Captain John Quilliam*, the son of a farmer at the south of the island. He first came into notice at the battle of Camperdown, when Admiral Duncan made him a lieutenant. At the battle of Copenhagen he was in a frigate of such a light draught of water that she was able to get close under the batteries. Here she was exposed to such

CAPTAIN QUILLIAM, R.N. B. 1771; D. 1829

a tremendous fire that all the officers senior to Quilliam were killed, so that he was left in command. Soon afterwards, Lord Nelson came on board and asked Quilliam how he was getting on; and it is said that Quilliam—too busy to attend even to his admiral—replied by the single word "middlin'," and did not for a moment pause in his arduous task. Nelson was so pleased, not only by his pluck and coolness, but by the independence of his character, that he took an early opportunity of appointing him first lieutenant on his own ship, the *Victory*. It was this vessel which he helped to steer into action at the glorious battle of Trafalgar.

Captain William Kelly received special mention for his bravery at the capture of Cape Town, and *Lieutenant Philip Cosnahan* greatly distinguished himself in the celebrated action between the *Shannon* and the American frigate *Chesapeake*.

Nor was the gallantry of Manxmen at sea confined to those who served in the Royal Navy; for, in those days, the merchant (or trading) vessels were armed, and many brave deeds are recorded of Manx merchant captains. The exploits of two of them may be mentioned here.

Captain Thomas Moore, of the *Fame*, actually defeated no less than five French privateers. As soon as he saw them, he sailed towards them, and, reserving his fire till he was within pistol range, he fired shot after shot into the largest until she struck. Without stopping to send any of his men on board of her, he then engaged the second ship, and took her also after a brief resistance. An officer and seven men were placed in this prize, and were ordered to watch the first ship till the *Fame* returned from chasing the three remaining vessels which were crowding sail to get away. Moore overhauled two of them, and forced them both to strike.

Captain Hugh Crowe fought several actions. The most famous of them was when he fought in the *May*, of twenty-eight guns, against two English sloops of war, the *Dart*, of thirty guns, and the *Wolverine*, of eighteen guns. Mistaking them for French privateers, he engaged them from ten in the evening till daylight. Considering the greatly superior force of the men-of-war, this was a truly remarkable feat.

The most distinguished Manxman in the Army at this time was *Colonel Mark Wilks*. His earliest service was in India, where he fought under Lords Cornwallis and Wellesley, and where he afterwards held the very important position of Resident at the Court of the native prince of the great country called Mysore. He then received the appointment of Governor of St. Helena, and he was there when Napoleon I. was sent to that island after his defeat at Waterloo.

DATES.

Wars. — *With the American Colonies*, 1775 — 1783; *with France*, 1779 — 1783; 1793 — 1802; 1803 — 1815; *Irish Rebellion*, 1798.

Battles. — *Camperdown*, 1797; *Copenhagen*, 1801; *Trafalgar*, 1805; *Waterloo*, 1815.

DEFINITIONS.

Fencibles. — Soldiers of the regular army enlisted to serve in the United Kingdom, the Channel Islands, and the Isle of Man.

Resident. — Adviser and controller.

CHAPTER VIII (*continued*)

Part 5. — *The People.*

A. — THEIR WAGES, HOUSES, CLOTHING, &C.

THE CHIEF MATTERS OF INTEREST between the Restoration and the accession of the Atholls are the struggles about the land and the revenue, and the rise of smuggling, so that, as I have already told you about these, I will put what little there is left to say about the people at that time into this *Part*.

WAGES. — You have seen how badly off the farmers were during the period just before the Act of Settlement. The poor labourers were in an even worse position, since their wages had been kept by law at the same level as they were many years before, though the cost of food had greatly increased. But when the smuggling began, it was soon found that it was impossible to keep wages down in this way, or to prevent the labourers leaving the island to seek work elsewhere. The farmers, therefore, fearing that they would lose them altogether, had to give way and raise their wages.

HOUSES. — Some idea of what the houses, not only of the labourers, but of the people generally, were like, may be gathered from the fact that, at the end of the seventeenth century, there were very few chimneys, even in the towns; and the almost complete absence, half a century later, of knives, forks, and spoons shows the primitive way in which the people lived. At the end of the eighteenth century many of the cottages in the country were scarcely better than they had been three hundred years before. It was not till towards the very end of this period that such cottages began to be replaced by brick or stone houses, with roofs of slate.

DRESS. — It will, perhaps, interest you to know how our ancestors of eighty years ago were dressed. The men wore a coat, like a modern "dress-coat," and knee-breeches or trousers. These garments were made of wool from the native sheep, which was left the natural brown-colour, or dyed blue, and their stockings were also dyed blue.

On their feet they wore *carranes* or sandals, made of raw hide, and on their heads they had tall hats, most of which were made at Ballasalla. The women wore petticoats of linsey-woolsey, usually dyed either red or blue. Over this they had a loose jacket, with a broad collar, called a "bedgown," generally made of linen and dyed some bright colour, which was drawn in at the waist by a white linen apron. On their heads they wore a mob cap in winter, and a sun-bonnet in summer, and when they went out they wrapped themselves in a plaid or shawl. On their feet they had *carranes* like the men. All these garments were, as a rule, made at home.

HIGHWAYS. — Till after the Revestment there were no highways properly so called, since, as carriages and carts did not exist, the roads had only to be wide enough to accommodate horses laden with *creels* or panniers. Some few of these roads, or rather lanes, are still to be seen, and are probably familiar to you. One of the best known of them is the lane down the steep hill into the old part of Laxey by the sea.

CLEANLINESS. — At this time very little attention was paid to cleanliness and to drainage. Cattle and human beings sometimes occupied the same house, and even when this was not the case the cow-house and stable were often on a higher level than the dwelling-house, and consequently drained into it. No wonder, then, that disease was terribly common, the most deadly kind being small-pox, which sometimes carried off nearly one tenth of the inhabitants in a single year. The population, nevertheless, rapidly increased, especially in the towns.

POPULATION OF THE ISLAND.

In 1726, 14,426; in 1757, 19,144; in 1792, 27,913; in 1821, 40,081.

DEFINITION.

Linsey-woolsey. — Cloth made of linen and wool mixed.

CHAPTER VIII *(continued)*

Part 5 *(continued).* — *The People.*

B. — THEIR TRADE AND INDUSTRIES.

TRADE. — Trade, that is to say trade which was not smuggling, decreased for thirty years after the Revestment, but it then began to increase, though it was cramped and hindered by an unjust system, in accordance with which goods were allowed to be imported by a few merchants only. The result of this system was that the merchants agreed together upon the prices they would charge; and these prices were, of course, very high, so that, while the traders made fortunes, the unfortunate people paid far too much for their goods. Another check to trade was the insufficient amount of money in the island. It is hard for us at the present day to understand how it was possible to get on without money. You can imagine how great the inconvenience must have been when every bargain had to be arranged by barter; but there seems to be no doubt that, except during the period when the Cavaliers were in the island, this was the way in which Manx trade was usually conducted.

MANX COINAGES. — Such a state of things was partially remedied in 1668, by the issue of pence and half-pence, by

John Murrey, a Douglas merchant. Thirty-one years later the Manx Government issued its first coinage (also of pence and half-pence) with the Stanley crest — the eagle and child — on it. There were no Manx silver or gold coins, because the people were, as a rule, too poor to need them. But when trade increased the want of money began to be felt by all classes, and it was supplied by tradesmen issuing cards for small sums under twenty shillings, which were passed about like bank-notes. When trade became bad again, many of the tradesmen were unable to pay the amounts of their cards, which were then abolished by law.

FARMING. — Farming remained in a very backward state till the end of the eighteenth century, when clover and turnips were first cultivated. At this time a number of English and Scottish farmers, who saw that land was comparatively cheap and rents low in the Isle of Man, bought and rented land here. Their superior methods of farming were imitated by the Manx farmers, and a great improvement resulted. The implements used by the Manx farmers still, however, continued to be very primitive. Though threshing machines had just come into use, farm carts were almost unknown, the usual method of carriage being by creels on horses' backs, or by sledges, which were carts without wheels. Their ploughs, which were of a very rude make, and required two men to manage them, were drawn by four oxen yoked abreast; and their harrows had teeth made of wood hardened over the fire, which had to be sharpened every morning before being used. During the long war with France, when there was a great demand for corn, which rose enormously in price, farmers were very prosperous. But after the war, prices fell rapidly, and there was a time of very great distress. Many farmers, especially the smaller ones, were ruined, and they, to obtain employment, emigrated to America.

FISHING. — The fishing industry was largely developed and actively followed during this period, being encouraged by bounties. During a terrible storm, a number of the fishing boats were lost in Douglas Bay. One result of this was an increase in the size of the new boats built.

MANUFACTURES. — Manufactures continued, for the most part, to be carried on at home; linen and woollen cloths, nets, coarse hats, gloves, and snuff were the chief articles produced. But towards the end of the eighteenth century, encouraged by the bounties offered to those who spun the greatest quantity of linen yarn, and wove and exported the greatest number of yards of linen cloth, linen factories were established. Cotton, too, was spun at Ballasalla, and was exported to England to be woven into cloth there. This manufacture was, however, soon abandoned, but woollen factories, flour and paper mills, and tanneries were successfully carried on.

DATES.

First Manx Government coinage, 1709.

Good trade, 1793 — 1815.

Bad trade, 1815 — 1829.

Loss of the fishing boats, 21st September, 1787.

DEFINITIONS.

Barter. — The exchange of one thing for another.

Bounties. — Payments offered by a Government to those engaged in some particular branch of commerce or manufacture, for the purpose of encouraging trade. It is now understood that bounties do not really do good to trade as a whole.

CHAPTER IX

RECENT HISTORY (1829 — 1901).

Part I. — *Political Reform.*

REFORM AND PROGRESS. — The course of our recent history may be clearly indicated by two words: *Reform* and *Progress*.

When the Duke of Atholl left the island the House of Keys was still a self-elected body, and the Tynwald Court had no control over the revenue; there was no regular system of helping the poor, drunkenness and disease were practically unchecked by law, the education given was of a very poor kind, and trade was injured, not only by unwise taxation, but by the want of good harbours.

I have now to show you how improvement in all these matters was brought about.

In this *Part* I will deal with political reform, or reform of the Government, as we may call it, and describe how the House of Keys came to be elected by the people, and how the Tynwald Court obtained control of the revenue.

THE KEYS. — We have seen how formerly, when a vacancy occurred in the House of Keys, the remaining members used to meet together, and themselves elect someone to fill the vacancy, without taking any trouble to find out what the people wished. At first, no doubt, this arrangement served to promote the liberty of the people, because the Keys were near-ly all tenants on the same footing as the greater part of the country people, so that their interests were the same; and the population of the towns was very small.

But when the land question was settled, the tenants be-came virtually landlords, and the Keys were almost entirely selected from this class, so that the new class of tenant which gradually grew up, and the inhabitants of the towns, who had now largely increased in number, were practically un-represented; and consequently their interests were very apt to be neglected when they came into collision with those of the landlords.

Against this state of things the people first protested at the end of the eighteenth century; at that time English commis-sioners were in the island, inquiring into the complaints made by the Duke of Atholl, and to them a protest was made that, owing to the self-election of the Keys, the people had no voice in the government of the island. Nothing, however, came of this protest, and no further effort to obtain redress was made for nearly fifty years. Several urgent applications were then made to the English Government, but with no better result, and the reform by which the right of election was at last re-stored to the people was a consequence of another reform, of which I am now going to speak.

THE CONTROL OF THE REVENUE. — The attempts of the Keys, which had the hearty support of the people, to obtain some control of the revenue for the Tynwald Court seemed, at first, as hopeless as did the efforts for a better mode of election. The Tynwald Court had been deprived of this control at the Revestment, but some hope was then held out that it would be allowed to have the spending of any balance of money which might be left after paying the expenses of the government of

the island. Forty years later the Manx people were deprived
even of this hope, though the balance thus remaining then
amounted to a considerable sum, and, at the same time, their
harbours and public buildings had been falling into decay for
want of repair.

For a time they submitted; then for thirty years before
1866 they again and again endeavoured to obtain justice,
but till that date with little success. In 1863 an able and

LORD LOCH B. 1827; D. 1900

energetic man, Mr. Henry (afterwards Lord) Loch had been
made governor. He at once saw how necessary it was, if the
island was to prosper, that its harbours should be improved,
and he also saw that this could only be done satisfactorily
by its Legislature having more money at its disposal. With a
view to getting this money, he asked the Tynwald Court to
appoint a committee of its members to help him in arranging
terms with the English Government. The Tynwald Court did
so, and, after lengthy negotiations, he and the committee
succeeded in obtaining an undertaking that, in future, when
the expenses of the government of the island had been paid,

the Tynwald Court should have the balance of the revenue to spend as it thought proper, subject to the right of the English Government and of the governor to say "no."

This undertaking was given on the conditions that the House of Keys should be elected by the people, and that the English Government should receive £10,000 a year from the insular revenue, as the contribution by the Manx people towards supporting the Army and Navy.

Nothing was said about the repayment of the money due to the island, because the governor and the committee feared that they might risk losing what had been gained by asking too much.

Thus was Constitutional Government obtained by the Manx people.[1]

DATES.

Constitutional Government obtained, 1866.

---

1 In reading this *Part* reference should be made to the Introduction.

CHAPTER IX (continued)

Part 2. — Social Reform.

L ET US NOW CONSIDER THE REFORMS in the condition of the people and their consequent progress.

THE LABOURERS. — Towards the end of the last period the condition of the labourers, which had been a very miserable one, began to improve. There was indeed a failure of the potato crop in 1847, but the distress which resulted from it was trifling in comparison with that in Ireland at the same time.

It was partly owing to this, and partly to the discoveries of gold in California and Australia, that numbers of Manxmen, both labourers and small farmers, emigrated between 1847 and 1853. Since then wages have greatly increased.[1] Prices have also increased generally, though not so much in proportion as wages, and, thanks to lessened taxation, such articles as bread, groceries and clothes have become much cheaper. The houses of the labouring class have been greatly improved, but the poorer people in the towns are too much crowded together. Generally speaking, the labourers are no doubt better off than they were seventy years ago, though there are more very

---

1 In 1829 they were 1*s* a day; in 1866, 2*s.* 6*d*; in 1901, 3*s.*

poor people now than formerly. The chief reason of this seems to be that many of those who attend to the wants of the visitors in the summer have nothing to do in the winter.

POOR RELIEF. — Owing, however, to the improved system of helping the poor, or "poor-relief," as it is called, no one can actually starve. Formerly the only way in which the poor were helped was by voluntary contributions; that is to say, each person used to give what he liked, chiefly to the collections in the churches. It was found, however, that more money was needed than could be raised in this way, and therefore, of late years, the amount required for this purpose has, in Douglas, and in some other parts of the island, been obtained by rates, which people have to pay, whether they like to do so or not; and a house, called "The Home for the Poor," has been built for those of the poor who are too old and feeble to do sufficient work to support themselves.

This reminds me of the other house, called the "Lunatic Asylum," which was built for the unfortunate people whose minds are diseased. You will find it hard to believe that, before the Lunatic Asylum was built, many of these poor creatures had been tied up in outhouses and stables, and that they were treated more cruelly than if they had committed crimes. Now, under kind and skilful treatment, some of them recover, and all are made as happy and comfortable as possible.

HEALTH. — It was not till quite recently that the health of the people became a matter which the Manx Legislature thought worthy of consideration. Much, however, has now been done by drainage and by building better houses to make people more healthy, with the result that the number of deaths in proportion to the population has been greatly reduced. Another thing which has caused the people of our island of late years to be more healthy and to live longer is that they have become more temperate. There is no reason to suppose that the Manx people were much given to drunkenness before smuggling supplied them with cheap spirits. But it was hard to get rid of the habit of drinking when once it had been acquired; and even after smuggling had been put down, the duties on spirits were so low that their price was very little higher than before. Seventy years ago, then, drunkenness was terribly common. Its reduction since then has been due to four main causes. The first is the good work done by the Temperance Societies; the second is the increase of the duties on spirits; the third is the legislation regulating the trade in strong drink, especially an Act which closed the public-houses on Sunday; and the fourth is the establishment of an efficient police force.

EDUCATION. — Another of the great reforms which have taken place in the last half of the nineteenth century is the improvement in education, which had formerly been greatly neglected. In 1872 the State first took charge of education, and compelled every child to go to school. By a wise plan made at that time Manx children have to pass the same examinations as English children. The result of this is that education in the Isle of Man, which was made free in 1892, is as good as it is in England.

DATES.

Taverns (Sunday Closing) Act passed, 1857.

Lunatic Asylum built, 1868.

New System of Poor Relief began, 1887.

POPULATION OF THE ISLAND.

In 1861, 52,469; in 1901, 54,758.

CHAPTER IX (continued)

Part 3. — Industrial Reform.

HARBOURS. — In early days there were no harbours protected by piers and breakwaters, so that the fishermen and traders, who used Manx ports, had to run their vessels ashore and then pull them up out of the reach of the waves. When vessels grew larger, this became inconvenient, and they therefore sought the bays which afforded the best shelter. This is the reason why Derby-haven, so named from the Earls of Derby, which is too shallow for modern vessels, was, for centuries, the favourite port. We first hear of an artificial work to protect vessels in 1660. It was at Douglas and was called the "Bulworke," being, no doubt, a kind of breakwater. The only charges vessels had to pay till just before the accession of the Atholls were for anchoring, but harbour dues were then imposed, which shows that artificial harbours had been made about that time. We have seen that at the Revestment the Tynwald Court was deprived of the control of the harbours; the result was that they were neglected, and consequently became useless. Except the Red Pier, in Douglas, which was finished at the beginning of the nineteenth century, no really important harbour work was carried out till after 1866, when this control was restored. Then followed the building of the fine piers and breakwaters, which enable people to land in the island safely, whether the tide is low or high.

These improvements resulted in the bringing of more visitors, year by year, to our shores, till now they exceed the large number of 400,000 annually. Their coming has not only brought prosperity to all classes in the island, but it has led to an enormous increase in the size of our towns.

THE TOWNS. — I have not said anything about the towns hitherto, because, till quite recently, they were no bigger than villages. Castletown, as being the place where the lord and the governor formerly lived, where the chief courts were held and where the Legislature sat, was the most important of them. But when smuggling began, Douglas soon outstripped the other towns in size. All the towns were formerly very filthy, cows and pigs being allowed to wander about the streets, which, till Duke Street and Strand Street, in Douglas, were begun, were unpaved. Till after the departure of the Duke of Atholl the streets were not lighted at all, and then for forty years they were lit by a few oil lamps only. The towns were formerly governed by the captains of the garrisons, then by high-bailiffs, and, of late years, by councillors or commissioners, elected by the people. It is this growth of the towns, which now contain more than half the population of the island, that has made the health reforms, spoken of in the last *Part*, so necessary, because people are much more crowded together in the towns than in the country, and are therefore more likely to catch diseases.

CAUSES OF PROSPERITY. — Not only have our towns and their inhabitants benefited by the coming of the visitors, but the country and its inhabitants have benefited as well. So great is the quantity of milk, butter and meat required by them that it has paid the farmers to make the land more productive by cultivating and draining it well, and to have as good cattle, horses and sheep as possible. Having thus obtained better crops, the farmers have been able to make a larger profit in the shape of increased rents, and to pay higher wages. Thus landlords, tenants and labourers, have all improved their positions. Prosperity has also been increased by the provision of better means of getting to and from the island, and of moving about when once in it. Instead of sailing vessels, which, as they depend upon the wind, are uncertain,— sometimes, indeed, no vessel could leave the island or come to it for weeks—we have swift steamers coming and going every day; and we have not only good wide roads, instead of narrow lanes, but railways and tramways.

INDUSTRIES WHICH HAVE NOT PROSPERED. — There are, however, some industries which have not prospered lately. The very quickness and easiness, and also, I may add, cheapness of our communication with other countries, have led to the decline of our manufacturing industries, because people can buy their goods in places where they can be made at lower prices than are possible here. The chief articles we make now are woollen cloths and blankets, hemp ropes, flax sailcloth and cotton herring-nets.

The herring fishing, which was always very uncertain, has given very poor results of late years, and mining, which was a prosperous industry between 1850 and 1880, has not been so profitable since that period.

DATES.

Harbour dues first imposed, 1734.

High-bailiffs first appointed, 1777.

Duke Street and Strand Street built, 1810.

Gas introduced, 1860.

Victoria Pier completed, 1873.

POPULATION OF THE TOWNS.

In 1726: *Douglas*, 810; *Ramsey*, 460; *Peel*, 475; *Castletown*, 785. In 1901: *Douglas*, 19,149; *Ramsey*, 4,672; *Peel*, 3,306; *Castletown*, 1,963.

CHAPTER IX (continued)

Part 4. — Heroes of the Lifeboat.

THERE IS NO SERVICE in which Manxmen have distinguished themselves more, of recent years, than in that of saving the lives of those who have been shipwrecked round the rocky and dangerous coast of our island. A lifeboat had been presented to Douglas by the fourth Duke of Atholl, but it was dashed to pieces in a severe storm, and it was not till Sir William Hillary, one of the founders of the "National Institution for the Preservation of Life from Shipwreck," established a District Lifeboat Association in the island, that much could be done to save life in this way. A lifeboat was then placed in each of the four towns. It is to this brave and generous man, who himself frequently went out in the lifeboat, that we also chiefly owe the "Tower of Refuge," on S. Mary's Rock, or Conister, in Douglas Bay. This rock is covered at high water, so that, if it were not for the tower, those who are wrecked on it would be drowned, unless they could be promptly rescued.

When the poet Wordsworth visited Douglas he wrote the following lines about

"S. MARY'S ROCK."

"The feudal keep, the bastions of Cohorn,
Even when they rose to check or to repel

THE TOWER OF REFUGE

Tides of aggressive war, oft served as well
Greedy ambition, armed to treat with scorn
Just limits; but yon tower, whose smiles adorn
This perilous bay, stands clear of all offence;
Blest work it is of love and innocence,
A tower of refuge built for the else forlorn.
Spare it, ye waves, and lift the mariner,
Struggling for life, into its saving arms.
Spare too, the human helpers! Do they stir
'Mid your fierce shock like men afraid to die?
No; their dread service nerves the heart it warms,
And they are led by noble Hillary."

Since Hillary's day, the Manx lifeboats have increased both in number and size, and as it is impossible to mention all the gallant deeds done by their crews, I shall confine myself to quoting the following fine poem by the Rev. T. E. Brown about

"THE PEEL LIFEBOAT."

"Of Charley Cain, the cox,
And the thunder of the rocks,
And the ship *St. George*—
How he balked the sea-wolf's gorge
Of its prey—
Southward bound from Norraway;
    And the fury and the din,
        And the horror and the roar,
    Rolling in, rolling in,
        Rolling in upon the dead lee-shore!

See the Harbour-master stands,
Cries—'Have you all your hands?'
Then, as an angel springs
With God's breath upon his wings,
She went;
And the black storm robe was rent
    With the shout and with the din,
        And the horror and the roar,
    Rolling in, rolling in,
        Rolling in upon the dead lee-shore!

And the castle walls were crowned,
And no woman lay in swound,
But they stood upon the height
Straight and stiff to see the fight,

For they knew
What the pluck of men can do
 With the fury and the din,
  And the horror and the roar,
 Rolling in, rolling in,
  Rolling in upon the dead lee-shore!

'Lay aboard her, Charley lad!
Lay aboard her!—Are you mad?
With the bumping and the scamper
 Of all this loose deck hamper,
And the yards
Dancing round us here like cards,'
 With the fury and the din,
  And the horror and the roar,
 Rolling in, rolling in,
  Rolling in upon the dead lee-shore!

So Charley scans the rout,
Charley knows what he's about,
Keeps his distance, heaves the line—
'Pay it out there true and fine,
Not too much, men!
Take in the slack, you Dutchmen!'
 With the fury and the din,
  And the horror and the roar,
 Rolling in, rolling in,
  Rolling in upon the dead lee-shore!

Now the hawser's fast and steady,
And the traveller rigged and ready.
Says Charley—'What's the lot?'
'Twenty-four.' Then like a shot—
'Twenty-three,'
Says Charley, ''s all I see'—
 With the fury and the din,
  And the horror and the roar,
 Rolling in, rolling in,
  Rolling in upon the dead lee-shore!

'Not a soul shall leave the wreck,'
Says Charley, 'till on deck
You bring the man that's hurt.'
So they brought him in his shirt—
O, it's fain
I am for you, Charles Cain—
 With the fury and the din,

And the horror and the roar,
　Rolling in, rolling in,
　　Rolling in upon the dead lee-shore!

And the captain and his wife,
And a baby! Odds my life!
Such a beauty! such a prize!
And the tears in Charley's eyes.
Arms of steel,
For the honour of old Peel
　Haul away amid the din,
　　And the horror and the roar,
　Rolling in, rolling in,
　　Rolling in upon the dead lee-shore!

Sing ho! the seething foam!
Sing ho! the road for home!
And the hulk they've left behind,
Like a giant stunned and blind
With the loom
And the boding of his doom—
　With the fury and the din,
　　And the horror and the roar,
　Rolling in, rolling in,
　　Rolling in upon the dead lee-shore!

See the rainbow bright and broad!
Now, all men, thank ye God,
For the marvel and the token,
And the Word that He hath spoken!
With Thee,
O Lord of all that be,
　We have peace amid the din,
　　And the horror and the roar,
　Rolling in, rolling in,

　　Rolling in upon the dead lee-shore!"

DATES.

District Lifeboat Association formed, 1826.

The Tower of Refuge built, 1832.

CHAPTER X

SOME MANX WORTHIES

"Lives of great men all remind us,
We can make our lives sublime;
And departing leave behind us
Footprints on the sands of time."

LONGFELLOW

PERHAPS WE HAVE HAD NO GREAT MEN in the Isle of Man. Great men are very uncommon everywhere. But we have certainly had some able men, as well as many good and brave men, and a few who have combined all these qualities. I have already mentioned several of our "Worthies," and I will now tell you about some others who lived nearer to our own time.

The earliest is *John Christian Curwen*, a statesman.

He was a member both of the House of Commons and of the House of Keys, and not only a member but a leader. A determined defender of the purity and independence of Parliament, he opposed the great William Pitt when he thought that he was trying to override that independence. Many taxes, especially those which fell heavily on farmers, were removed by his influence, and he distinguished himself by his brilliant speeches against the claims of the fourth Duke of Atholl. He was a very skilful farmer, and he conferred a great benefit on the island by founding our first Agricultural Society.

The life of the *Rev. Hugh Stowell* is worthy of admiration for its holiness and simplicity.

He spent it in doing good. Deeply sincere and heavenly minded, he devoted himself with the utmost zeal to his duties. Founder of Sunday Schools and of Temperance Societies, and writer of religious memoirs both in Manx and English, he will perhaps be best remembered by his "Life of Bishop Wilson."

We now come to one who was in both the military and civil service of England—*Sir Mark Cubbon*, K.C.B.

He received an Indian cadet's appointment and went out to Madras, where he served with distinction, reaching the rank of general. He was then appointed Commissioner of Mysore, which meant that he was practically the ruler of that great province. That his rule there was acceptable to the natives, as well as to the Government of India, is shown by the fact that, during the terrible mutiny in the years 1857 and 1858, Mysore kept perfectly quiet and contented. This was recognized by a letter from the Governor-General of India, in which he said that the value of Sir Mark Cubbon's services, and the honour and esteem which his high character and ability had won from all, whether European or native, would never be forgotten by the supreme Government.

Of striking appearance, dignified yet unassuming in manner, with a calm judgment and a firm will, combined with enduring patience and great sympathy, he was beloved and respected by all who knew him.

Many of our countrymen have gone forth to find their homes in other countries, and some of them have been very successful in the larger fields thus opened out to them.

Perhaps the most remarkable among their number is the *Honourable William Kermode*, who was one of the founders of the Colony of Tasmania and a member of the upper branch of its Legislature.

Professor Edward Forbes, F.R.S., the distinguished naturalist, showed his taste for natural history even before he was ten years old, having by that age formed a little museum in which he stored minerals, fossils, shells, dried sea-weeds, flowers, butterflies, &c, all duly named and arranged. But his parents thought so much of the skill he displayed in drawing that they sent him to be trained for the profession of an artist. Natural history, however, proved to be his true vocation, and his labours in that science have caused him to be considered one of the first of British naturalists.

The *Rev. Thomas Edward Brown*, our Manx poet, may have been known to some of you.

Educated at King William's College and at Oxford, he gained the highest distinctions at both. Most of his life was spent as a schoolmaster at Clifton College, near Bristol, but Manxmen know him best as the author of the charming poems in which he describes their manners and customs.

I trust that you will read them when you are older. He himself tells us the chief aim of his poetry:—

> "Whate'er is left to us
> Of ancient heritage—
> Of manners, speech, of humours, polity,
> The limited horizon of our stage—
> Old love, hope, fear—
> All this I fain would fix upon the page;
> That so the coming age,
> Lost in the empire's mass,
> Yet haply longing for their fathers, here
> May see, as in a glass,
> What they held dear."

THE REV. T.E. BROWN B. 1830; D. 1897

DATES.

John C. Curwen, born, 1756; died, 1828.

The Rev. Hugh Stowell, born, 1768; died, 1835.

Sir M. Cubbon, born, 1775; died, 1861.

The Hon. W. Kermode, born, 1775; died, 1852.

Prof. E. Forbes, born, 1815; died, 1854.

CONCLUSION

Our Heritage.[1]

"Breathes there the man, with soul so dead,
Who never to himself hath said,
This is my own, my native land!
Whose heart hath ne'er within him burned
As home his footsteps he hath turned
From wandering on a foreign strand?"

SIR WALTER SCOTT

I HAVE FULFILLED MY PROMISE TO TELL YOU SOMETHING about the history of our native country, and I will now bring this book to an end by briefly describing the *Constitution* which our forefathers have gained for us by their self-denying struggles.

At the head of the Government of our little State is the English Sovereign, whose subjects we are and through our connexion with whom our island forms part of the British Empire. Next comes the Imperial Parliament, which has a general control over us, but does not, except on rare occasions, pass laws which affect us.

Then we have our own governing body, the Tynwald Court, which, with the governor, has both legislative and executive powers.

---

1 This chapter should be read in connexion with the Introduction.

This Court is divided into two branches: (I) The governor and the Council, appointed by the English Sovereign;[1] (2) the twenty-four Keys, elected by the people. Each of these branches has equal powers, and one cannot pass laws, raise taxes, or spend the revenue, without the consent of the other. Nor can both these branches united (*i.e.*, the Tynwald Court) do any of these things without the consent of the English Sovereign. But this consent is nearly always given, and we may feel sure that, as long as we do nothing wrong, we are free to manage our own affairs in our own way.

Thanks to our forefathers:—

"It is the land that freemen till
That sober-minded Freedom chose,
The land, where girt with friends or foes,
A man may speak the things he will."[2]

We are free to think, speak, write and print what we please, free to follow the religion we prefer, free to elect whom we wish to represent our views; in a word, we are free to do anything we like, if only it is not contrary to the laws which have been made for the good of all, and does not harm our neighbours.

Such is the glorious heritage our forefathers have gained for us.

Having thus told you what your rights are, I will now tell you what your chief duties are towards the State and its Government. They are:—

(I) To maintain, and, if possible, to improve its Constitution.

(2) To obey its laws.

(3) To take care of public property. Remember that what belongs to the State belongs to you all.

(4) To vote in elections. Every citizen is responsible through his vote for the kind of government he lives under.

---

1 Except for the vicar-general, who is appointed by the bishop.

2 Tennyson.

If you do not vote, and bad laws are passed, you are partly to blame for them.

(5) To pay taxes. Bear in mind that the money which you have to pay in taxes goes to form a fund that will be spent for the good of all the people; and that without such a fund it would not be possible to carry on the government of the country at all.

(6) To help to defend the State, when it is necessary. Every able-bodied citizen is required by law to bear arms if called upon.

(7) If you have sufficient ability and leisure, it will be your duty to take office, whether it be as a member of a School Board, of a Parish or a Town Council, or of the House of Keys. Of course it is neither necessary nor possible that every citizen should serve his country in this particular way; but the State needs good and able men to do its work, so that all of you who are capable and can spare the time from your own business should take office for the public good. A State, whose best men shrink from serving it, is sure to suffer. "The worth of a State, in the long run," says John Stuart Mill, "is the worth of the individuals composing it."

Finally, as my last words, let me impress upon you that, though

"We cannot all be heroes,
And thrill a hemisphere
With some great daring venture,
Some deed that mocks at fear;
[Yet] we can fill a lifetime
With kindly acts and true,"

Because

"There's always noble service
For noble souls to do."[3]

3 C.A. Mason.

APPENDIX A

GEOGRAPHY

THE ISLE OF MAN LIES IN THE IRISH SEA, almost midway between the coasts of England, Scotland and Ireland. It is about thirty-three miles long, and twelve miles broad in the widest part.

Except in the north, it is a hilly country, with a range of mountains extending from Ramsey to the Calf of Man. The first of these is North Barrule (1,842 feet); then comes Clagh Ouyr (1,808 feet); Snaefell, the highest (2,034 feet); Beinn-y-phot (1,772 feet); Carraghan (1,520 feet); Slieau Ruy (1,570 feet), and Greeba (1,382 feet). The range is then broken by the valley between Douglas and Peel, but is continued on the south side of it by South Barrule (1,585 feet) and Cronk-ny-Irree-Lhaa (1,449 feet). Further south are the hills called the Carnanes, Bradda and the Mull, and, to the east and west of Snaefell, there are some mountains branching off from the main range, the highest of which is Slieau Freoghane (1,602 feet).

From most of our mountains, especially Snaefell, there is a grand view of the mountains of Cumberland in England, of Wigtonshire in Scotland, of County Down in Ireland, and of the Snowdon range in Wales.

Thus Wordsworth says:—

"Off with yon cloud, old Snaefell, that this eye
Over three realms may take its widest range."

The chief headlands are, on the east coast, the Point of Ayre, Maughold Head, Clay Head, Douglas Head, Santon Head, Langness, and Spanish Head; on the west coast, Bradda Head, the Niarbyl, Contrary Head, and Jurby Head.

From Maughold Head right round by the south to Contrary Head, the coast is high and rocky, but from each of these headlands—

"The coast runs level to the Point of Ayre,
A waste of sand, sea-holly and wild thyme,
Wild thyme and bent."[1]

The chief bays are, on the east coast, Ramsey, Laxey, Douglas, Derby-Haven, Castletown, and Port S. Mary; on the west coast, Port Erin and Peel.

There are three small islands off the coast. Much the largest of these is the Calf of Man at the extreme south-west. The others are S. Michael's Island off Derby-Haven, and S. Patrick's Island off Peel. Both these last two islands are now joined to the mainland by walls.

There are also a number of isolated rocks, the best known of which are Conister, or S. Mary's Rock, in Douglas Bay, and the Chickens, to the south-west of the Calf of Man.

The five largest streams are the Sulby, falling into the sea at Ramsey, the Glass and the Dhoo, which unite their waters near Douglas, the Neb, at the mouth of which Peel is situated, and the Silverburn, which joins the sea at Castletown.

The island is divided into six Sheadings and seventeen ancient parishes.

Beginning from the north, there is Ayre Sheading, containing the parishes of Bride, Andreas, and Lezayre; Michael Sheading, containing the parishes of Jurby, Ballaugh and

---

1 T.E. Brown.

Michael; Garff Sheading, containing the parishes of Maughold and Lonan; Middle Sheading, containing the parishes of Conchan, Braddan and Santon; Glenfaba Sheading, containing the parishes of German (including Peel), Marown and Patrick; and Rushen Sheading, containing the parishes of Malew (including Castletown), Arbory and Rushen.

The parishes, on an average, are divided into ten *treens*, and each treen is generally divided into four *quarterlands*.

There are also four parishes recently formed in Douglas, viz.: S. George's, S. Matthew's, S. Barnabas' and S. Thomas'; one at Foxdale, and two in Ramsey, viz.: S. Paul's and S. Olave's.

There are four towns: Douglas, Ramsey, Peel, and Castletown.

The largest villages are Port S. Mary, Port Erin and Laxey.

The climate of the island is very mild, and there is less difference between the summer and winter temperature than almost any place in the world. It is very sunny, though rather damp and rainy, and there are frequent strong winds, chiefly from the west.

DEFINITIONS.

Treen. — The meaning of this word is not known, but it is applied to a piece of land varying from 240 to 320 acres in size.

Quarterland. — The quarter of a land or treen.

APPENDIX B

CELTIC PLACE-NAMES AND SURNAMES

IF YOU WILL LOOK AT THE MAP OF THE ISLE OF MAN you will see that by far the greater number of names on it contain the following words, which are all Celtic: *Slieau* for mountain, *cronk* or *knock* for hill, *glione* for glen, *awin* for river, and *balla* for farm. *Douglas*, from the rivers *doo*, black, and *glas*, grey or bright, is Celtic, so is *Peel*, meaning "fort," and *Castletown* is a translation of the Celtic *Balla-Cashtal*; and our commonest surnames, such as *Brew, Bridson, Cain, Caley, Callister, Callow, Cannell, Cashen, Clucas, Coole, Curphey, Kaighan, Kelly, Kewley, Mylchreest, Mylrea, Quayle*, and *Quiggin*, are the forms which early Celtic names have gradually taken in the Isle of Man.

APPENDIX C

NORSE PLACE-NAMES AND SURNAMES

OUR MAP ALSO CONTAINS A NUMBER OF NAMES of Norse origin. The ships of the Vikings ran ashore at the *Ayre* (Gravelly Bank), or lay in shelter in *Ronaldsway* (Ronald's Bay), in Ramsey (Raven's Isle), at *Laxey* (Salmon River), or in the many creeks, such as *Soderick* (South Creek); or, perchance, were wrecked on some of the rocks called by them *sker* or *stack*. Norse settlers, too, indicate their presence by the numerous words ending in *by* (their word for farm), such as *Kirby* (Church Farm), and not only have they named our largest land division the *Sheading*, but, among the mountains, *Snaefell* (Snow Hill), *Sartfell* (Black Hill), and *Wardfell* (Watch Hill), the old name of South Barrule.

Even some of their earliest names are still found here, such as *Solvi* in Sulby, *Kol* in Colby, *Narfi* in Narradale, *Kraki* in Cregneish, and so on; but, for the most part, their names in the lips of Manx people, who, as you know, are mainly Celtic, have gradually taken forms quite different to what they were originally. Thus, *Asmundr, Asketill, Ottarr, Thorketill, Thorliotr, Olafr*, and *Rognvaldr* grew into *Casement, Castell, Cottier, Corkhill, Corlett, Cowley*, and *Crennell*, surnames which are common amongst us at the present day.

THE

FOLK-LORE OF THE ISLE OF MAN

THE FOLK-LORE OF THE ISLE OF MAN, BEING AN
ACCOUNT OF ITS MYTHS, LEGENDS, SUPERSTI-
TIONS, CUSTOMS, & PROVERBS

Collected from many sources; with a GENERAL INTRO-
DUCTION; and with EXPLANATORY NOTES to each
Chapter;
BY A. W. MOORE
AUTHOR OF "*MANX NAMES*," &c.

"I would not for any quantity of gold, part with the wonderful tales which I have retained from my earliest childhood, or
have met with in my progress through life" — *Martin Luther*

INTRODUCTION

THE ISLE OF MAN HAS BEEN UNFORTUNATE in not having had competent collectors of its Legendary Lore. But few have taken the slightest interest in it, and those who have did not understand the language in which they could have learned it at first hand. The earliest of these collectors, and the one to whom we owe most of the tales which are given in the following pages, was George Waldron, an Englishman, who was in the Isle of Man, where he seems to have been acting as Commissioner from the British Government, to watch and report on the import and export trade of the country, between 1720 and 1730. He seems to have had but little knowledge of the Manx people and their ways, and the marvellous tales which he tells are given in his own language, and, probably, with many additions suggested by his fancy. After an interval of a century came Train, who had also the disadvantage of being a stranger, and who was, therefore, obliged to gather the greater number of the few additional tales he gives at second hand. The next collector of Manx Folk-Lore who began his work about 1860, was William Harrison, a Lancashire man who lived for some time on the Island, being a member of the House of Keys, and devoted considerable attention to

Manx antiquities. He has done good service in the cause of
Folk-Lore by collecting the ballads, proverbs, &c., which are
printed in volumes XVI and XXI of the Manx Society's publications, and in editing Waldron's History. And, lastly, Jenkinson inserted some scraps of Folk-Lore in his "Guide to the
Isle of Man," published in 1874. Campbell, the editor of the
"Popular Tales of the West Highlands," who visited the Island
in 1860, was a singularly competent observer, and might have
done much for Manx Folk-Lore, even at such a late period,
and in spite of his also being a stranger, if he had thought it
worth his while. His visit was, however, only a very brief one,
and, being discouraged at his Gaelic not being understood,
and at the difficulty of extracting any information from the
Manx peasantry, did not persevere. He describes his difficulties in getting into the confidence of the Manx peasants as
follows:—"I found them willing to talk, eager to question,
kindly, homely folk, with whom it was easy to begin an acquaintance. I heard everywhere that it used to be common to
hear old men telling stories about the fire in Manx; but any
attempt to extract a story, or search out a queer old custom, or
a half-forgotten belief seemed to act as a pinch of snuff does
on a snail. The Manxman would not trust the foreigner with
secrets; his eyes twinkled suspiciously, and his hand seemed
unconsciously to grasp his mouth, as if to keep all fast." It is remarkable that no native Manxmen have, till recently, troubled
themselves about collecting what, we suppose, they considered
idle, if not mischievous, tales.[1] If they had done so, and had
recorded them in the original Manx, they would have conferred a boon upon those who are interested in such research-
es. Now it is, unfortunately, too late. The Manx language is
moribund, and Manx superstitions, except in the more remote
districts, are in a similar condition. Since even so recent a date

---

1 The Isle of Man Natural History and Antiquarian Society has
appointed a Committee for this purpose.

as 1860, the change in the condition of the natives is simply marvellous. The constant and rapid intercourse with England, Scotland, and Ireland, the large emigration of the Manx, and immigration of strangers, the shoals of visitors who come over in the summer, and the consequent increase of wealth and prosperity, have produced their natural results. There are, however, remote parts of the Island, away from the towns and the main highways, where beliefs in Fairies, Goblins, Demons, and Ghosts still remain; where the "Evil Eye" is still a power; where there is still a vague distrust of solitary old crones; and where the "Charmer" has a larger practice than the ordinary medical practitioner. But these things are not spoken of either to the stranger or to the educated Manxman, especially if a clergyman, and, even among themselves, they are mentioned with some sense of shame, and with a wish to keep them as secret as possible, so that the most diligent and craftily-put enquiries have extracted but little that has not been hitherto known.[2] On the whole, the present state of the Isle of Man is so antagonistic to such superstitions that, to place the reader in a position which will enable him to understand the sort of people and the state of society in which they originated, it is necessary to draw a veil over the present, and to uncover the past as far as possible. This we are able to do only to a very limited extent, as the old historians, or rather annalists, were not at all concerned with the people whose history they were supposed to write, but merely with the movements of their rulers, dynastic and episcopal changes, battles and ecclesiastical squabbles. We append such meagre accounts as exist. The first writer who mentions the people in anyway was Merick, who was Governor and Bishop in 1577, and who confines himself

---

2 The results of these enquiries, which have chiefly been made by Professor Rhys and the writer, are given in the following pages, together with the Folk-Lore taken from previously published accounts.

to the astounding statement that the women, when they went
abroad, girded themselves with the winding sheet that they
proposed to be buried in, "to show themselves mindful of their
mortality." Speed, writing in 1627, copies this, and adds on
his own account the fiction that "such of them (the inhabitants) as are at any time condemned to dye are sowed within a
sack, and flung from a rocke into the sea." Blundell, writing 30
years later, corrects the error about the winding sheets, which,
he shows, were merely blankets or plaids, and mentions their
houses, &c., as follows:—"These men's habitations are mere
hovels, compacted of stones and clay for the walls, thatched
with broom, most commonly containing one room only. Very
few have two rooms, have no upper rooms—such as in their
town they call lofts—nor any ceiling but the thatch itself, with
the rafters, yet in this smoking hut . . doth the man, his wife,
and children cohabit and in many places with ye geese and
ducks under ye bed, the cocks and hens over his head, the cow
and calf at the bed's foot . . . their constant diet is only salt
butter, herrings, and oat cakes, here made almost as thin as a
paper leaf . . . their drink is either simple water, or water mixt
with milk, or at best buttermilk." Beer, he says, is only drunk
when they meet at market.[1] Chaloner, who was Governor of
the Island at this time, says that the Manx are "very civil . . . la-
borious, contented with simple diet and lodgings; their drink,
water; their meat, fish; their bedding, hay or straw, generally;
much addicted to the musick of the violyne . . . bearing a
great esteem and reverence for the publique service of God."[2]
Bishop Gibson's account, in the edition of Camden's *Britannia* published in 1695, adds nothing new. Waldron (1720-30)
says that the houses of the peasantry "are no more than cabins
built of sods, and covered with the same, except a few belonging to the better sort of farmers, which are thatched with

1 Manx Society, vol. XXV., p. 57.
2 Manx Society. vol. X., p. 11.

straw . . . the greater part of them (the peasants) of both sexes go barefoot, except on Sunday or when they are at work in the field, and have then only small pieces of cow's or horse's hide at the bottom of their feet, tyed on with packthread, which they call carranes. Their food is commonly herrings and potatoes, or bread made of potatoes."[3]

Thomas Quayle, a Manxman, who wrote in 1812 about the agriculture of the Island, also mentions the cottages of the peasantry as follows: "The walls are about seven feet high, constructed of sods of earth; at each side the door appears a square hole containing a leaded window. Chimney there is none, but a perforation of the roof, a little elevated at one end, emits a great part of the smoke from the fire underneath. The timber forming the roof is slender, coarse, and crooked. It is thatched with straw, crossed chequerwise, at intervals of twelve or eighteen inches, by ropes of the same material, secured either by being tied to the wall by means of coarse slates fixed and projecting, or by stones hanging from the ends of the ropes. From that end of the roof whence the smoke issues to the other end, the roof gently declines in height. If the means of the inhabitant enable him to keep a cow, a continuation of the roof covers another hovel of similar materials, accommodating this valuable inmate. . . The floor (of both portions of the hovel) is hardened clay; the embers burn on a stone placed on a hearth, without range or chimney; the turf-smoke, wandering at random, darkens every article of furniture, till it finds exit at the aperture in the roof or elsewhere. A partition separates the cottage into two room; over the chamber end is sometimes a loft, to which the ascent is by a ladder from the keeping room. The aspect of the inhabitants is in unison with their abode. The mother and children are bare-legged and bare-footed; their dark-coloured woollen garments squalid and unseemly. Yet, perhaps, this wretchedness is but in externals. This homely

abode is warm and evidently not unhealthy . . . In the northern district, where quarries of stone are less accessible and lime
more distant, the cottages continue to be built in the primitive
manner. In the southern, where building materials are comparatively more plentiful, stone and lime are used in the new
cottages more frequently. The ancient mode of thatching and
roping is still general." [1]

He is followed, in 1816, by Bullock, who declares that
"what any English peasant would consider a state of actual
starvation is scarcely regarded by Manxman as including any
particular deprivation; from their birth they are habituated to
live very hardly. Herrings, potatoes, oatmeal, and these in very
moderate quantities, are the general fare equally of the small
native farmer and the labourer. The latter resides contentedly
in a cottage of mud, under a roof of straw, so low that a man
of middling stature can hardly stand erect in any part of it. If
to the common necessaries above stated the good people add a
stock of turf for the fire and a cow, fed in the lanes and hedges,
they enjoy the utmost abundance of which they have any idea.
A chaff bed for the whole family, a stool, and a wooden table
constitute the furniture of their mansion." [2] Finally, Campbell,
in 1860, tells us that, "Of the poorer classes living in the mountain farms, and on the points and distant corners of the Island,
these are still many who can hardly speak anything but Manx.
Their hair is dark; the sound of the voices, even their houses,
are Celtic. I know one turf dwelling which might be a house
in North Uist. There was the fire on the floor, the children
seated around it, the black haired Celtic mother on a low stool
in front, the hens quarrelling about a nest under the table, in
which several wanted to lay eggs at once." From other sources
we gather the following further facts about the Manx people

1 Quayle; General view of the Agriculture of the Isle of Man, pp.
22-3.

2 History of the Isle of Man, pp. 350-1.

of by-gone times:—A fireplace or chimney in their houses was quite a modern luxury. The *chiollagh*, or hearth, was made of a few stones laid on the floor, and the smoke found its way out either through the door or a hole in the roof. Frequently, from the scarcity of wood in the Island, they were too poor to afford a door, and used a bundle of gorse in its place. For burning they used turf, or even dried seaweed, from which latter they also got kelp for washing. Of their costume we have been able to collect the following particulars:—Train tells us, but without giving his authority, that the ancient Manx wore their hair long, and bound behind with a leather thong. The dress of the peasantry was made of *kialter*, a woollen cloth, neither milled nor tucked. It consisted of trousers, more recently of knee breeches, when blue stockings were worn, and a short coat and waistcoat. The colour of these garments was usually *keeir*, or dark brown, from the undyed fleece of the *loghtan*, or native sheep; but sometimes it was *keeir-as-lheeah*, "brown and gray," or *keeir-as-gorrym*, "brown and blue," the colours being mixed in the wool. *Gorrym*, "blue", was also a favourite colour. On their feet they wore *oashyr-voynee*, a stocking without a foot, but having a string to fasten it under the sole; or *oashyr-slobbagh*, a stocking having no sole to the foot, but a lappet covering the top of the foot, with a loop to the fore toe, and a heel strap. Over these they had the *carrane* or *kerrane*, a cover for the sole and sides of the foot, made of raw hide, salted and dried, and laced with thongs of the same at the top of the foot. Train says that, in 1836, these were still worn by the peasantry in the uplands, but that they were being rapidly displaced by a shoe with a large buckle; and with the buckles the knee breeches came in vogue. Sometimes elderly people made inner soles to their *carranes* of pitched sheep skin, but this was generally regarded as effeminate. On their heads they had a *bayrn*, or cap, like the Scotch bonnet, but, at the beginning of the present century, this was discarded in favour of the tall beaver hat. The women wore a petticoat, or *oanrey*, of *eglhinolley*, or linsey-woolsey, which was usually dyed dark-red with *scriss-ny-greg*, a moss which grows upon the rocks by the sea, but it was also blue, *keeir*, or *keeir* and white chequered. It was full and loose, and fell to within six inches of the ground. Over this there was a loose jacket with a broad collar, called the "bedgown", usually made of linen, and dyed some bright colour, drawn in at the waist by a linen apron. On the head a mob cap, called *quoif cooil corran*, or cap shaped like the back of a sickle; dark blue or *keeir* stockings and *carranes*, or, at a later date, buckled shoes, completed the attire. A sun-bonnet was substituted for the mob cap in the summer, but frequently no cap at all was worn in the house, and when they went out they wrapped themselves in the plaid or shawl, which Bishop Merick called their winding sheet. It seems probable that in early days, before the time of English rule, the men wore the Scotch kilt, which at that time was worn by both Scotch and Irish. It must be remembered that all these garments we have mentioned were made either at home, or in the immediate vicinity of it. The women spun both wool and linen, which was woven by the weaver, or *fidder*, who was to be found all over the country. When the cattle were killed at Martinmas, and salted for winter consumption, their hides were kept and tanned at home; and the light beer, or *jough*, which was the usual drink, was generally home-brewed. The woollen and linen cloths were made into garments by tailors, who travelled from farm house to farm house, and who were usually famous gossips and story tellers. Stories, or *skeeal*, were told also by the old people during the long winter nights, which stories they had heard from their forefathers, and which they in their turn handed on to their children. As an illustration of this method of oral tradition, it is recorded that the poem of "Fin and Ossian" was written down a century ago from the recitation of an old woman, who, when she was asked how and where she had learned it, replied "from her mother and grandmother and many more." She told them also that she remembered the name of *Farg-hail*, the man with the terrible eyes; and *Lhane-jiarg*, the man with the bloody red hand. Can the existence of superstitions among a people so excluded from the outer world be wondered at? It is difficult in these days to estimate how complete this seclusion was, but a fair idea of what it was, even at the beginning of the present century, may be arrived at from considering the fact that the Battle of Waterloo was not heard of in the Isle of Man till the beginning of September, six weeks after it had taken place. Apart from their isolation, too, the people, who are of mixed Celtic and Scandinavian race, were naturally superstitious, so much so that Waldron stated "he verily believed that, idolisers as they were of their clergy, they would be even refractory to them were they to preach against the existence of fairies;" and at the beginning of the present century, we have the evidence of Sir Walter Scott, who was well informed about the Folk-Lore of the Island by his brother, who lived there, to the effect that "Tales of Goblins, Ghosts, and Spectres; legends of Saints and Demons, of Fairies and familiar Spirits, in no corner of the British dominions are told and received with more absolute credulity than in the Isle of Man."

We have divided our consideration of the Folk-Lore of the Isle of Man into the following chapters:—

(1) Legendary Myths.
(2) Hagiological, and Mytho-Historical Legends.
(3) Fairies and Familiar Spirits.
(4) Hobgoblins, Monsters, Giants, Mermaids, and Apparitions.
(5) Magic, Witchcraft, Charms, &c.
(6) Customs and Superstitions connected with the Seasons.
(7) Superstitions connected with the Sun, Animals, Trees, Plants, Sacred Edifices, &c.
(8) Customs and Superstitions, connected with Birth, Marriage, Death, &c.

(9) Customs formerly enforced by Law.

(10) Proverbs and Sayings.

Folk-Lore may be defined as being "the comparison and identification of the survivals of archaical beliefs, customs, and traditions, in modern ages"; and though many will doubtless think that the attempt to perpetuate these figments of an ignorant and superstitious past is a mistaken one; yet, on the other hand, there has been a disposition of late years to recognise that they contain elements of instruction as well as of amusement, for they are "often the only possible means of penetrating to the historic past of nations," and they are "certainly the only means of tracing out many of the landmarks in the mental development of man."

PREFACE

THE WONDERS OF THE ISLE OF MAN, according to Nennius, are "a strand without a sea . . . . a ford which is far from the sea, and which fills when the tide flows, and decreases when the tide ebbs"; and "a stone which moves at night in Glen Cinden, and though it should be cast into the sea, yet at morning's dawn it would be found in the same valley." I cannot display such wonders as these in this little Compilation, yet I think there will be found in it many quaint and curious "things not generally known"; and I trust that it may not only interest Manx Folk and Visitor Folk, but that it may be accepted as a contribution—though an insignificant one—to the science of Folk-Lore.

Thanks are due to the many kind friends* who have contributed scraps of Folk-Lore, and to Professor Rhys and Mr. Alfred Nutt, for assistance in Chapter I.

A. W. MOORE.

Cronkbourne, June, 1891.

*In some cases the name of the contributor has been attached; but in others, as similar information has been given by so many different personas, this has not been practicable. Stories told to the writer, which have not been committed to writing by the teller, are marked *Oral.*

TABLE OF CONTENTS

INTRODUCTION 131

MYTHS CONNECTED WITH THE LEGENDARY HISTORY OF THE ISLE OF MAN: 146

Manannan Mac Lir—Lug—The Story of the Isle of Falga—Culann—Finn—Oshin—The Stories of Sigurd Fafni's Bane, and of the Punishment of Loki.

HAGIOLOGICAL AND MYTHO-HISTORICAL LEGENDS: 170

Introductory—*Stories*: The Conversion of the Manx; the Conversion of St. Maughold; St. Maughold's Fish; St. Maughold and Gilcolum; A Legend of Myrescogh Lake; The Stone Cross of Ballafletcher; Goddard Crovan's Stone; Olave Goddardson and the Sword Macabuin; Alswith the Swift; Ivar and Matilda.

FAIRIES AND FAMILIAR SPIRITS: 187

Introductory—*Stories*: Origin of the Arms of the Island; The Discovery of the Island; The Fairy Horn; The Fairy Saddle; The Fairy Horse Dealer; Fairy Music; The Fairy Lake; The Unfortunate Fiddler; Objection of Fairies to Noise; The Fairy Cup of Kirk Malew; Fairy Elf; The Kidnappers; A Fairy detected in Changing an Infant; Abduction of a Boy by Fairies; The Christening; The

School Boys; Fairy Punishment; The Whipping of the Little Girl; Mischief done by Fairies; Fairy Dogs; The Cup of the Lhiannan-Shee; The Fairy Sweetheart; The Dooiney-oie.

HOBGOBLINS, MONSTERS, GIANTS, MERMAIDS,
APPARITIONS, &C.: 212

Introductory—*Stories*: The Phynnodderee; The Glashtin or Glashan; The Water Bull, or Tarroo-Ushtey; The Buggane; The Black Dog, or Moddey Doo; The Spellbound Giant; The Old Man; The Three-headed Giant; Jack the Giant Killer; The Captured Mermaid; The Mermaid's Courtship; The Mermaid's Revenge; Dwellings under the Sea; The Apparition of Castle Rushen; Ben Veg Carraghan; A Legend of the Sound; The Chasms; The Spirit "Hoa Hoa."

MAGIC, WITCHCRAFT, &C.: 243

Introductory—Cases of Witchcraft from Insular Records—*Stories*: The Magician's Palace; Origin of King William's Sands; The Devil's Den; The Submerged Island; Tehi-Tegi, the Enchantress; Caillagh-ny-Ghueshag; The Glencrutchery Well; The Effigy; The Witch of Slieu-Whallian; The Burnt Besom; Butter Bewitched; The Manx Witch; Popular Antidotes to Witchcraft; The Evil Eye, Dust as an Antidote; Charmers and their Charms.

CUSTOMS AND SUPERSTITIONS CONNECTED WITH
THE SEASONS: 279

Introductory—New Year's Day; Twelfth-day; St. Paul's Feast-day; Bridget's Feast-day; Candlemas Day; Shrove Tuesday; Periwinkle Fair; Weather Sayings for March and April; Patrick's Feast-day; Good Friday; Easter Sunday; St. Mark's and Maughold's Feast-day; May-day Eve; May-day; Spitlin's Summer Feast-day; Perambulation of Parish Boundaries; Midsummer-eve; Midsummer-day; Luanys's Day; Harvest Festival; Maughold's Feast-day; Hallowe'en;

The Twelfth of November; Spitlin's Winter Feast-day; Catherine's Feast-day; Thomas's Feast-day; Christmas-eve; Christmas-day; The White Boys; Stephen's Feast-day ("Hunt the Wren"); John's Christmas Feast-da; Feast-day of the Children; New Year's Eve.

SUPERSTITIONS CONNECTED WITH THE SUN, ANIMALS, TREES, PLANTS, SACRED EDIFICES, &C.: 330
Nature Worship; The Sun; The Moon and the Stars; Animal Worship; Totemism; Sacrifices; Blood; Nail and Hair Cuttings; Criminals hung by Hair Ropes; Tree Worship; Adoration of Re-productive Power of Nature; May-day, Midsummer, and Harvest Celebrations; The Hare, Herring, Cow, Cock, *Bollan*; Animals' Weather Wisdom—Stories: The *Ushagreaisht*; The *Lhondoo*; The Blackbird and the Thrush; How the Herring became King of the Sea; The Seven Sleepers; The Thorn, Elder, Shamrock, &c.; Virtues of Iron and Salt; The Sin of Sacrilege and its Punishment; Piety of the Manx, &c.

CUSTOMS AND SUPERSTITIONS CONNECTED WITH BIRTH, MAR-RIAGE, AND DEATH:...350
Birth. — Precautions taken to Preserve Women after Childbirth and Children before Baptism from Evil Influences and Fairies; Powers of a Posthumous Child, &c.; Virtues of Salt, and of a Caul.

Marriage. — Waldron's Description of a Manx Wedding; Blowing of Horns; The *Dooinney-Moyllee*; Train's and Harrison's Descriptions of a Manx Wedding.

Death. — Omens which preceded it; Preparations for Burial; Bishop Merick's Mistake about the Windingsheet; Waldron's Description of Death and Funerals; Road Crosses; a Funeral Entertainment; Further Death Signs; Modern Custom after a Funeral; Second Sight; A Supernatural Warning; Mock Funerals.

CUSTOMS FORMERLY ENFORCED BY LAW: 361
Introductory—Watch and Ward; Customs connected with Land Tenure; Jury for Servants; Custom about Servants Giving Notice; Yarding; The Deemster's Oath; Legal Purgation; The Stocks; The Pillory; The Wooden Horse; Bishop Wilson on Peculiar Laws and Customs; Other Curious Laws; Manx Ecclesiastical Law; Excommunication; Penance; The Nuns' Chairs; The Bridle; The Punishment of being Dragged after a Boat; Bowing to the Altar; Observation of Sunday; The Three Reliques; Games, &c.

PROVERBS AND SAYINGS: 382
Introductory— (I) Proverbs relating to General Truths; (2) Proverbs inculcating Caution, Contentment, Thrift, Independence, Industry, and Charity; (3) Proverbial Weather-Lore; (4) Miscellaneous Sayings and Proverbs.

CHAPTER I

MYTHS CONNECTED WITH THE LEGENDARY HISTORY
OF THE ISLE OF MAN

THE RELIABLE HISTORY OF A COUNTRY may be said to date from the period when its written records begin. Before that time, there is an epoch during which the place of history is usually supplied by tales of imaginary personages, whose doings are calculated to gratify the national pride. An unfailing characteristic of such an epoch is the personification of the race in an eponym, who is its supposed ancestor and founder. Thus, in the Isle of Man, we have the famous magician and navigator Manannan Mac Lir in this capacity, and there are various other mythical personages connected with the Island, all of whom appear in ancient Irish tales, though nothing can be discovered with regard to them from purely native sources of early date. In fact, the Isle of Man was so intimately associated with Ireland till the coming of the Northmen, that it is not likely that it would have any early myths distinct from those in Ireland. It is, therefore, to the early Irish legends that we have to refer for any mention of the Isle of Man, and they tell us that it was considered to be a sort of Fairy-land to which the Irish gods and heroes occasionally resorted. In the legends of the heroic period in Ireland, we find the deities and heroes called Lug, Cúchulainn, Cúroi, and Cúlann connected with Man as well as Manannan; while, in the later or Ossianic Cycle of legends, we have Finn and his son Oisin, who, in the only really early native legend, are made to associate with the Scandinavian Oree. But of all these deities, the most important in Man is Manannan, about whom many tales have accumulated. To understand his place in the Legendary History of Ireland we must bear in mind that, according to the *Leabhar Gabhala*, or Book of Invasions (a compilation of the late 10th or early 11th century), there were five conquests of Ireland, the first by Parthol or Bartholemew, and his followers; the second by Nemed and his followers; the third by the Firbolg; the fourth by the Tuatha Dé Danann; the fifth by the Milesians. It is with the fourth body of invaders, the Tuatha Dé Danann, who conquered the Firbolg, that Manannan is connected. In the legendary and romantic literature of Ireland the Tuatha Dé Danann are celebrated as magicians. By the Milesians and their descendants they were regarded as belonging to the spirit world, and, in the imagination of the people, they became Fairies, who were supposed to lie in splendid palaces in the interior of green hills. There can be little doubt that the Tuatha Dé Danann represent the Olympus of the ancient Irish, that hierarchy of divine beings which the Celts possessed as well as other Aryan people. In this hierarchy Manannan occupied the position of god of the sea. But as early as the 9th and 10th centuries of our era he had suffered the change known as euhemerisation, from an immortal he had become a mortal. It is thus we meet him in one of the oldest monuments of Irish literature, the so-called glossary of Cormac, King-bishop of Cashel, killed in 903:—"Manannan Mac Lir, a celebrated merchant who was in the Isle of Man. He was the best pilot that was in the west of Europe. He used to know, by studying the heavens, the period which would be the fine weather and the bad weather, and when each of these two times would change. *Inde Scoti et Brittones eum deum vocaverunt maris, et inde filium maris esse dixerunt*, i.e., *Maclir*, 'son of sea.' *Et de nomine Manannan* the Isle of Man *dictus est*."[1] This theory of the Isle of Man being named after Manannan, when so called, has been shown to be highly improbable by Professor Rhys, who thinks that "Manannan gave his original name corresponding to *Manu* and its congeners to the Island, making it *Manavia Insula*. . . . for which we have in Welsh and Irish respectively *Manaw* and *Manann*. Then from these names of the Island the god derives his in its attested forms of Manawydan and Manannan, which would seem to mark an epoch when he had become famous in connection with the Isle of Man."[2]

To Cormac's account, O'Donovan has added the following note:—"He was the son of Allot, one of the Tuatha Dé Danann chieftains. He was otherwise called Orbsen, whence Loch Orbsen, now Lough Corrib. He is still vividly remembered in the mountainous district of Derry and Donegal, and is said to have an enchanted castle in Lough Foyle. According to the traditions in the Isle of Man and the Eastern counties of Leinster, this first man of Man rolled on three legs like a wheel through the mist."

We can follow the process of euhemerisation in later texts. Thus, according to the Book of Fermoy, a MS. of the 14th to the 15th century, "he was a pagan, a lawgiver among the Tuatha Dé Danann, and a necromancer possessed of power to envelope himself and others in a mist, so that they could not be seen by their enemies." The Book of Lecan (14th century) mentions a Manannan whom it calls 'son of Athgus, King of Manain (Man) and the islands of the Galls" (the Western Isles), who "came with a great fleet to pillage and devastate the Ul-

1 Cormac's Glossary. (O'Donovan's edition). p. 114.

2 Rhys, Hibbert Lectures, 1886, pp. 663-4.

tonians, to avenge the children of Uisnech." These children of Uisnech, when compelled to fly "from Erinn," had sailed eastwards and conquered "what was from the Isle of Man northwards of Albain," and after having killed Gnathal, King of the country, were induced to return to Ireland under a pledge of safety from Conchobar, King of Ulster. The sons of Gnathal, who also sought the protection of Conchobar, "killed the sons of Uisnech," in consequence of which Gaiar, the grandson of Uisnech, banished Conchobar to the islands of Orc and Cat (the Orkneys and Caithness), and Gaiar having reigned over Ulster for a year, went into Scotland with Manannan, and died there. The 15th century version of a story called "The exile of the children of Uisnech" tells us that Gaiar was assisted against Conchobar by Manannan, who was the fourth of his name and dynasty who had ruled in Man.

O'Flaherty speaks of him in his *Ogygia* as follows: "The merchant Orbsen was remarkable for carrying on a commercial intercourse between Ireland and Britain. He was commonly called Mananan Mac Lir, that, is, Mananan, on account of his intercourse with the Isle of Man; and Mac Lir, *i.e.*, *sprung from* the sea, because he was an expert diver; besides, he understood the dangerous parts of harbours; and, from his prescience of the change of weather, always avoided tempests."[3]

The same author, in his *West Connaught*, states that Orbsen's proper name was Manannan, and that Lough Orbsen was called from him, because when his grave was being dug the lake broke forth; and he says that, at the adjacent *Magh Uillin*, "Uillin, grandchild of Nuadh (silver-hand), King of Ireland twelve hundred years before Christ's birth, overthrew in battle, and had the killing of Orbsen Mac Alloid, commonly called Mananan (the Mankish man), Mac Lir (son of the sea) for his skill in seafaring."[4]

3 Ogygia, p. 26, Dublin, 1793.

4 *West Connaught*, Irish Arch. Soc., Dublin. 1849. p. 54.

A. W. MOORE

Keating, in his *General History of Ireland*, written early in the 17th century, gives Manannan's genealogy as follows: "Mananan, the son of Alladh, the son of Elathan, son of Dalboeth, an immediate descendant of Nemedius, the progenitor of the Tuatha de Danans in Ireland; that weird and mystic colony who never, through the lapse of ages, have relinquished their dominion over the superstitions of the peasantry of Ireland; but who are still believed to rule the spirit or fairy land of Erin; to reign paramount in the *lis*, the cave, the mine; to occupy genii palaces in the deepest recesses of the mountains, and under the deep water of our lakes."

But supplementing this pseudo-historical account of Manannan, we find numerous romantic references to him at all stages of Irish literature. Thus, the "Sick-bed of Cúchulainn," a tale which goes back, substantially, to the fifth century of our era, although we only possess it in transcripts of the 11th century, relates that Manannan became jealous of Cúchulainn, with whom his wife Fand had fallen in love. He shook a cloak of invisibility of forgetfulness between the two and carried off Fand with himself to fairy-land, whereupon Cúchulainn returned to his own wife.

Professor Rhys remarks of him that "In Irish literature he appears mostly as King of the Fairies in the Land of Promise, a mysterious country in the lochs or the sea. His character seems to have been a most contradictory one—many tricky actions are ascribed to him, while he was very strict about other people's morality. At his court no one's food would get cooked if, while it was on the fire, any one told an untrue story, and he is said to have banished three men from fairy-land to the Irish court of Tara for lying or acting unjustly. . . . In the Welsh Mabinogi, bearing the name of Manannan's counterpart, Manawydan, the latter is not much associated with the sea, excepting, perhaps, his sojourn . . . in the lonely Isle of Gresholm. It makes him, however, take to agriculture, especially the growing of wheat. . . . He is also called one of the three Golden Cordwainers of Britain, owing to his having engaged successively in the making of saddles, shields, and shoes. . . . The sinister aspect of Manannan is scarcely reflected by Manawydan, who is represented as gentle, scrupulously just, and always a peacemaker; neither is he described as a magician; but he is made to baffle utterly one of the greatest wizards known to Welsh literature." It would appear also that he was connected with the other world, and he figures as one of the three landless monarchs of Britain. He had, however, a huge prison in the shape of a bee-hive, the walls of which consisted of human bones. King Arthur was once incarcerated there for three months.[1]

The Gaelic Manannan is represented in Brythonic (Welsh) literature by Manawydan, but it is uncertain if there really was a Brythonic sea-god corresponding to the Gaelic one, or if the Welsh tales are not simply literary adaptations of Irish ones. Professor Rhys favours the former view.

The connection of Manannan with the Isle of Man probably arose in this way. It was the practice of the earliest Irish to represent their divinities as living in Islands to which, under exceptional circumstances, mortals might sail. It is uncertain if this conception of the Island home of divinities is really older or not than that which figures them as dwelling in the hollow hills. All one can say is that we find it earlier in the Irish texts. It has been well studied by Professor Zimmer in his admirable essay on the Brendan voyage,[2] in which he shows that a number of texts which have come down to us are still completely pagan in conception, and reflect a belief which must still have been officially dominant in parts of Ireland as late as the sixth century. Unofficially these beliefs linger in the traditions

1 Rhys, Hibbert Lectures, 1886. pp. 665-7.

2 Zeitschrift für deut, Alt., 1889. Mr. Alfred Nutt's Summary Folk-Lore.

respecting Hy Breasil. But, as a rule, the Gaelic peasant figures "Faery" as inside a hill, or under the water, and probably this belief is the older of the two.

Manannan MacLir is an actor in so many of the ancient Irish heroic tales that it is impossible, with a due regard to space, to give more than outline of a few of them as we have done. The magic powers of his sword are frequently mentioned, *e.g.*, in the curious tale of Diarmait and Grainne. Those interested in such matters will find in Vol. III of the Ossianic Society's Publications a marvellous romance of the adventures of Cormac MacArt in the fairy palace of Manannan in Man; but enough will have been given to exhibit Manannan in his various attributes as King, warrior, trader, navigator, and magician; and to show that his connection with the Isle of Man was supposed to have begun after he and his Tuatha dé Dananns were defeated by the Milesians, when he was chosen by the warriors as their leader, and that he and they were supposed to have taken refuge in the Western Isles and Man, whose inhabitants acknowledged him as their ruler.

From purely local sources we glean the following information about Manannan; but it must be remembered that in its present form it is all of comparatively recent origin, as the "Supposed True Chronicle of Man," and "The Traditionary Ballad," both probably date from the sixteenth century, though doubtless founded on older traditions. The former tells us that "he was the first man that had Mann, or ever was ruler of Mann, and the land was named after him," and that "he reigned many years, and was a Paynim, and kept, by necromancy, the Land of Man under mists, and if he dreaded any enemies, he would make of one man to seem an hundred by his art magick, and he never had any form of the comons; but each one to bring a certain quantity of green rushes on Midsummer Eve—some to a place called Warfield (now South

Barrule), and some to a place called Man,[1] and yet is so called. And long after St. Patrick disturbed him, the said Manannan, and put Christian folks into the said land."[2] The ballad gives practically the same account. More recent tradition has endowed him with the stature of a giant, who by his strength and ferocity became the terror of the whole Island. It is said that he used to transport himself with great ease across the gorge between Peel Castle and Contrary Head. On one occasion, either for amusement or in a fit of rage, he lifted a large block of granite from the Castle rock, and though it was several tons in weight, he hurled it with the greatest ease against the slope of the opposite hill, about three miles distant, where it is seen to this day, having, as an evidence of the truth of the story, the print of his hand on it. His grave is said to be the green mound, thirty yards long, outside the walls of Peel Castle.

The connection of Lug (an Irish divinity, corresponding partly to Hermes, partly to Apollo) with Manannan and Man, is said to have been a close one, as will be seen from the following account of him; and, as will be shown later, his cult had spread to Man as well as to other Celtic lands (see "August I" chap. vi). Lug is thus described: "Like to the setting sun was the splendour of his countenance and his forehead; and they were not able to look in his face from the greatness of its splendour. And he was *Lugh Lamh-fada*,[3] and (his army was) the Fairy Cavalcade from the land of Promise, and his own foster brothers, the sons of Manannan."[4] He is said to have been brought up at the Court of Manannan, here called the Land of Promise, which in many of the ancient tales is identified with Man. Lug was famous for his mighty blows, and his spear

1 This can scarcely mean the Island.

2 Manx Soc., vol. XII., p. 6.

3 Long Hands.

4 The Fate of the Sons of Turren, published by O'Curry, in the Atlantis. Vol. IV, p. 160-3.

became one of the treasures of the Tuatha Dé Danann. When he fought against the sons of Turenn and imposed upon them the impossible eric-fine of procuring certain fabulous weapons, he rode Enbarr of the flowing mane, Manannan's steed, who was "as swift as the clear, cold wind of spring," and travelled with equal ease on land and sea. He wore Manannan's coat of mail, through, or above and below which no one could be wounded; also his breastplate, which no weapon could pierce. His helmet had two glittering precious stones set in front, and one behind, and Manannan's sword, called "The Answerer," hung at his side. From the wound of this sword no one ever recovered, and those who were opposed to it in the battlefield were so terrified by looking at it, that their strength left them. He was accompanied by his foster brothers, and by the Fairy Host, as already mentioned. The sons of Turenn were told that they could not obtain the eric-fine without the help either of Lug or Manannan, and they were advised to ask Lug for the loan of Manannan's steed, and if he refused, for his canoe, the "Wave Sweeper."

Lug, the great warrior of the Tuatha Dé Danann, has his counterpart among the Ultonians in Cúchulainn, who is said to have been the son of Lug, or Lug re-born. It is only in the story of "The Isle of Falga," given below, that he is mentioned in connection with the Isle of Man, though there were former-ly songs sung about him, and there is a tradition to the effect that he was called "King of the Mists," like Manannan. His adversary, Cúroi Mac Daire, was a great magician. The following tale gives an account of their rivalry for the fair daughter of the king of Man.

THE STORY OF THE ISLE OF FALGA

The Isle of Falga is variously supposed to have been the Isle of Man, or *Insi Gall*, *i.e.*, the Western Isles. Cúchulainn and the heroes of Ulster once on a time resolved to go on a plundering expedition to the Isle of the Men of Falga, a fairy land ruled by Mider as its King. Cúroi, who was a great magician, insinuated himself among the raiders in disguise, and by means of his arts he succeeded in leading the Ultonians into Mider's stronghold, after they had repeatedly failed in their attempts. He did this on the condition that he was to have of the plunder the jewel that pleased him best. They brought away from Mider's castle Mider's daughter, Bláthnat, as she was a damsel of exceeding beauty; also Mider's three cows and his cauldron, which were objects of special value and virtues. When they came to the division of the spoils, the mean-looking man in grey, who had led the victorious assault, said that the jewel he chose was Bláthnat, whom he took to himself. Cúchulainn complained that he had deceived them, as he had only specified a jewel, which he insisted on interpreting in no metaphorical sense; but, by means of his magic, the man in grey managed to carry the girl away unobserved. Cúchulainn pursued, and the dispute came to be settled by a duel on the spot, in which Cúchulainn was so thoroughly vanquished that Cúroi left him on the field bound hand and foot, after having cut off his long hair, which forced Cúchulainn to hide himself for a whole year in the wilds of Ulster, while Cúroi carried away to his stronghold of Caher Conree both Bláthnat and her father's cows and cauldron. Later it would appear that Cúchulainn got the better of Cúroi, and took Bláthnat away from him, for Bláthnat proved a faithless wife to Cúroi and plotted with Cúchulainn to kill him. At the time fixed upon by her, namely, November eve, Cúchulainn and his followers stationed themselves at the bottom of the hill, watching the stream that came down past Cúroi's fort; nor had they to wait long before they observed its waters turning white: it was the signal given by Bláthnat, for she had agreed to empty the milk of Mider's three cows from Mider's cauldron into the stream, which has ever since been called the Finnghlais, or White Brook. The sequel was that Cúchulainn entered Cúroi's fort unopposed, and slew its owner, who happened to be asleep with his head on Bláthnat's lap. Cúchulainn took away Bláthnat, with the famous cows and cauldron; but he was not long to have possession of his new wife, for Cúroi's poet and harper, called Ferceirtne, resolved to avenge his master; so he paid a visit to Cúchulainn and Bláthnat in Ulster, where he was gladly received by them; but one day, when the Ultonian nobles happened to be at a spot bordering on a high cliff, Ferceirtne suddenly clasped his arms round Bláthnat, and flinging himself over the cliff they died together.[1] This old story has been embodied in a poem, called "Blanid,"[2] by Robert D. Joyce, of which the following, lines describing the combat between Cúroi and Cúchulainn are perhaps the best:—

> "I come to win back thy misgotten prize,
>   Mine own beloved, the bloom-bright Maid of Man!"
> "Thou com'st to dye this grass with ruddy dyes
>   Of thy best blood," cried Curoi, "and to ban
> All knighthood with thy word forsworn! Her eyes
>   Shall see the fight, so let him take who can!
> Lo! there she stands, with her fear-whitened face;
> Look thy last on her now, and take thy place!"
> Meanwhile, as one who on a wreck doth stand,
>   That the wide wallowing waves toss to and fro,
> And sees the saving boat put from the land,
>   Now high, now in the sea-trough sunken low,
> Trembling 'tween fear and hope, each lily hand
>   Pressed on her heart, as if to hide her woe,
> And pale as one who had forsaken life,
> Young Blanid stood to watch the coming strife.

> *   *   *   *

> Then sprang they to their feet, and warily
>   Looked in each other's eyes with look of hate,
> And crossed their jarring swords, and with bent knee
>   Fought a long time, their burning ire to sate,
> Till like a storm-uprooted stately tree
>   Cuhullin fell, and Curoi stood elate,
> Eyeing him as the hunter eyes the boar,
> That fighting falls, but yet may rise once more.

---

1 This tale is taken from Rhys, Hibbert Lectures, pp. 473-6, who quotes, as his authorities, Book of Leinster, Keating, and O'Curry.

2 Published by Roberts Brothers, Boston U.S.A.

Another mythic Irish figure connected with the Isle of Man is Culann, the smith, who in this capacity may be compared with Hephœstus, or Vulcan. Culann was, however, also a Divine and Prophet. He was the possessor of a terrible hound, which was slain by the youthful Setanta, who was in consequence called Cú-Chulainn, *i.e.*, Culann's hound. Culann is said to have lived for a time in the Isle of Man, where he manufactured sword, spear, and shield of such transcendent excellence for Conchobar, that he was invited by him to dwell in his realm. The story about this may perhaps be found of sufficient interest to be related at length:—Conchobar, who had not yet become King of Ulster, but was an ambitious young man seeking to gain a kingdom, consulted the famous oracle at Clogher as to how he might best attain his end. The oracle advised him to proceed to the Isle of Man and get Culann to make these weapons for him. Conchobar did so, and prevailed on Culann to begin his task; but, while awaiting its completion, he sauntered one morning along the shore, and in the course of his walk met with a mermaid fast asleep on the beach. He promptly bound the syren, but she, on waking and perceiving what had happened, besought him to liberate her; and to induce him to yield to her petition, she informed him that she was Teeval, the Princess of the Ocean; and promised that if he caused Culann to form her representation on the shield surrounded with this inscription, 'Teeval, Princess of the Ocean,' it would possess such extraordinary powers that whenever he was about engaging his enemy in battle, and looked upon her figure on the shield, read the legend, and invoked her name, his enemies would diminish in strength, while he and his people would acquire a proportionate increase in theirs. Conchobar had the shield made according to the advice of Teeval, and, on his return to Ireland, such extraordinary success attended his arms, that he won the kingdom of Ulster. Culann accepted Conchobar's offer, referred to above, and settled on the plain of Murthemne, which was fabled to have been formerly situated beneath the sea. It was here that he was visited by Conchobar, accompanied by his Court and Cúchulainn.

Of the later legends, which form a cycle entirely distinct from that of the heroic age, Finn, the son of Cumall (Finn MacCumaill), is the chief hero. He is said to have been the chief of a band of mercenaries, or robbers, called Fianns, and to have flourished in the second part of the third century. If this were so, he lived on the very threshold of the historical period in Ireland. Ossin, his son, was a famous warrior and a great poet, in both of which roles he only reproduced the character of his father, who was not merely celebrated as a warrior and huntsman, but especially as a poet and diviner, as already stated. Finn is connected with the Scandinavian Orree in a Manx heroic poem, and if, as has recently been conjectured,[1] Finn is identical with Kettle Finn, a Norseman who yielded great influence in Ireland and Man about the middle of the ninth century, the connection is a very natural one. The poem referred to above is undoubtedly the oldest known poetical composition in the Manx language. We append it, together with some interesting notes by Deemster Peter John Heywood, who died in 1790. It is not known by whom the spirited English translation was made. With the exception of lines 9 and 10, which rendered literally are—

> "Full threescore whelps, and not one less,
> With three old dames to look after them."

it is fairly close to the original.

FIN AS OSHIN

Hie Fin as Oshin magh dy helg,
[2]Fal, lal, lo, as fal, lal, la,

---

1 See Mr. Alfred Nutt's abstract of Professor Zimmer's theory of the Ossianiac Saga in "The Academy," of Feb. 14, 1891.

2 Chorus after every line.

Lesh sheshaght trean as moddee elg,
Cha row un dooinney sloo ny keead,
Coshee cha bieau cha row ny lheid,
Lesh feedyn coo eisht hie ad magh,
Trooid slieau as coan dy yannoo cragh,
Quoi daag ad ec y thie agh Orree beg[3]
Cadley dy kiune fo scadoo'n creg!
Slane three feed quallian aeg gyn unnane sloo,

    *   *   *   *

Lesh three feed cailleeyn dy yeeaghyn moo,
—Dooyrt inneen Fin ayns craid as corree,
"Kys yiow mayd nish cooilleen er Orree?"
Dooyrt inneen Oshin: "kiangle mayd eh,
Lesh folt y ching chionn gys y clea,
As chur mayd aile gys y cass cha bieau."
Clysht tappee eisht hug Orree ass,
Tra dennee'n smuir roie ass e chiass,
Loo[4] *Mollaght Mynney* ad dy stroie,
Va er n'yannoo craid er mac y ree,
Dy farbagh breearrey ry ghrian as eayst,
Dy losht ad hene as thieyn neesht.
—Hie Orree beg magh dys ny sleityn,
As speih mooar connee er e geayltyn,
Hoght bart mooar trome hug eh lesh cart,
Hoght kionnanyn currit ayns dagh bart.

---

3 Orree beg—Young Orree—not from his size, but his age;—where there are two of the same family, Father and Son, of the same name, the younger is styled beg—*i.e.,* the lesser. This Orree beg is supposed to have been a Scandinavian prince, prisoner on parole, with Fingal and like some modern gallants, to make love to both young ladies at the same time,—and thus they shew their resentment. He declines the hunting party, for an opportunity of intrigueing (sic) with one or other of the ladies. Meantime he falls asleep in a grotto in the heat of the day; but when he awoke and found the indignity done to him, he resolves, in revenge, to burn Fingal's palace—takes his huge bill, an instrument like a hoe, with which they hack and grub up gorze and heath, or ling, &c., for firing—hies him to the forest, and made up eight large burthens, such as eight modern men could not heave from the ground, and with these he fired the house as above described.

4 *Mollaght Mynney*, is the bitterest curse in our language, that leaves neither root nor branch, like the Skeabthoan, the besom of destruction.

Hoght deiney lheid's 'sy theihll nish t'ayn,
Cha droggagh bart jeh shoh ny v'ayn
Ayns dagh uinnag hug eh bart as ayns dagh dorrys,
Agh mean y thie mooar hene yn bart mooar sollys.
—Va Fin as Oshin nish shelg dy chionn,
Lesh ooilley nyn treanee ayns ollish as loan,
Yaagh wooar ren sheeyney ass y glion, neear,
Troggal ayns bodjallyn agglagh myr rere;
Roie Fin as roie Oshin derrey d'aase Oshin skee,
Agh she Fin mooar hene chum sodjey nish roie;
Eisht dyllee Fin huggey lesh coraa trome,
"Cha vel faagit ain nish agh tholtanyn lhome,
 Quoi ren yn assee shoh nagh re Orree beg?"
 V'an chosney voue chelleerid gys oig fo yn creg,
Raad plooghit lesh yaagh hayrn ad magh er y cass.

———————

FIN AND OSHIN

Fin and Oshin went out to hunt,
[1]Fal, lal, loo, as fal, lal, la.
With a noble train of men and dogs,
Not less in number than one hundred men,
So swift of foot and keen, none were their like;
With scores of Bandogs fierce they sallied forth,
O'er Hill and Dale, much Havock for to make.
 —Whom left they then at home, but youthful Orree!
Who slept secure beneath the shadowy rock;
 Full three score Greyhounds, with their whelps they left,
(With three score lovely maidens, young and fair,)*
As many old dames to attend the young.
Says Fin's fair Daughter, in Disdain and Scorn,
How on young Orree shall we be avenged?
—Says Oshin's Daughter
Fast to the Harrows we will tie his Hair,
And to his nimble feet, we'll set a train of Fire.
Then up starts Orree, with a nimble Spring;
 Feeling his Feet a broiling with the heat.
 With Curses direful, vowing to destroy,
Those who presum'd t' affront a King, his Son!
Swearing most bitterly by Sun and Moon.
To burn themselves and all their habitations;
—Then to the Mountain hies he fast away,
His heavy Gorse-hack poised upon his shoulder,
Eight pond'rous Burthens thence he carried off,
And eight large Faggots cram'd in ilka Burthen.
Not eight such Men as in the world are now

———————

1 Chorus after every line.

Could from the Ground one of these Burthen's raise.
Into each Window, he a Burthen thrust.
Into each Door, a Burthen of the same,
But, the grand blazing Burthen, on the Floor,
Of the great Hall he laid, and set on Fire.
—Meanwhile, our Heroes, Fin and Oshin hight,
They and their hardy men pursued the chase,
Eager, in sweat and dust, all cover'd o'er.
—Vast clouds full floating from the west
Were seen like Billows dreadful, as I ween.
—Then Fin he ran, and Oshin also ran,
Till faint, and out of breath, he sat him down;
But Fin, the hardy chief, still held it out,
Then lift he up his lamentable Voice,
Calling to Oshin, who was far behind,
"We've nothing left but rueful, ruin'd walls!
—"This mischief who has done?" Who but young Orree,
Who fled, and in a rocky Cavern hid himself,
—Then choak'd with Smoke, they drag him by the heels,
[2](And tore him Limb from Limb (they say) with Horses wild.)

CÆTERA DESUNT. — But the Catastrophe is said to be that they tore him Limb from Limb with wild horses. The tearing criminals asunder with Horses fastened to each limb is the punishment in the old Statutes of the Isle of Mann to be inflicted on those who should presume to draw a weapon, or strike, or violate the peace within the verge of the Court of Tynwald, or any Court held by the King of Mann, or his Governor.

We have a tradition, that Mann for about a century was governed by a Norwegian race of kings called Orrys. According to the *Supposed True Chronicle*: "Then there came a Son of the King of Denmark; he conquered the Land, and was the first that was called King Orrye, &c, After him remained Twelve of the Stock, that were called King Orryees inso much that the last (named Reginald) had no Son but one Daughter, named Mary, to whom the right descended, which Mary was Queen of Mann & Countess of Straherne, who, taking with her all her Charters, fled to the King of England, Edward the 1st in the 20th year of his reign, being in St. John's Tower in

---

2 Not in the Manx.

Scotland, otherwise called Perthe in Anno Dom., in 1292, for Alexander King of Scots arrived at Ranoldsway, near Castletown, and took possession of the Land of Mann." (*See* the Manx Statute Book, p. 1st.) *See* also the Ancient Chronicle of the Kings of Man in Camden's Brittannia Edition, 1637, which says "1270, the 7th day of October, a Navy set out by Alexander King of Scots arrived at Rogalwath; and the next morning before Sun rising a Battaile was fought between the People of Man, and the Scots in which were slaine of the Manx men 537, whereupon a certain Versifier play'd upon the number—

> 'L. decies Xter, et pente duo cecidere,
> Mannica gens de te, damna futura cave.

> 'L. ten times told, X thrice, with five beside and twaine,
> Ware future harmes; Tread (sic) of thy Folke Mann were slaine.'"[1]

A verse from an old song and a proverbial saying contain the only other references to Finn in Manx tradition:—

In the following verse, Finn Mac Coole is associated with. Fairies and Demons:—

> Finn Mac Coole, as ooilley e heshaght,
> Ferrish ny glionney, as y Buggane,
> Dy jymsagh ad cooidjagh mysh dty lhiabbee,
> As eisht roie lesh oo ayns suggane.

> "Finn Mac Coole, and all his company,
> The Fairy of the Glen and the Buggane,
> If they would gather together about thy bed,
> And run off with thee in a straw-rope"

The following quaint saying also relates to him:—

> Ny three geayghyn s'feayrey dennee Fion Mac Cooil,
> Geay henneu, as geay huill, as geay fo ny shiauill.

"The three coldest winds that came to Fion Mac Cooil, wind from haw, wind from a hole, and wind from under the sails."

---

1 ["Ten L. thrice X. with five and two did fall, ye Manx beware of future evil's call," is the translation given by Munch in his edition of the Chronicle, Manx Society, vol. XXII., p. 3.—ED.]

There are only two Scandinavian tales remaining on record in Man. They are *Sigurd Fafni's Bane* and *The Punishment of Loki*. These tales have been preserved neither by tradition, nor by written record, but by having been carved on stone. Both are found on a stone in Kirk Andreas Church-yard, and the first only on a stone in Malew Church-yard.[2] We take the following abstract of the two tales, which are mythologico-historical lays in the Elder Edda, from an account of the Andreas stone given by Mr. G. F. Black in the *Proceedings of the Society of Antiquaries of Scotland*.

THE STORY OF SIGURD FAFNI'S BANE

"There was a king named Sigmund Völsungsson, who married Hiordis, a daughter of King Eylimi, for his second wife. Some time after his marriage Sigmund was attacked in his kingdom by King Lingvi Hundingsson and his brothers, and was mortally wounded through being opposed by a one-eyed man, with a broad-brimmed hat and blue cloak (Odin), who held his spear against the sword of Sigmund, which was shivered into fragments. At night, Hiordis came to the battle-stead and asked Sigmund whether he could be healed, but he did not wish to be healed, for his good fortune had forsaken him since Odin had broken his sword, of which he requested Hiordis to collect the fragments, and give them to the son she would bear, who should become the greatest of the Völsung race. Hiordis was carried off by Alf, son of King Hialprek of Denmark, who had just landed at the battle-stead with a band of Vikings, and who married her after she gave birth to

---

2 Mr. P.M.C. Kermode has the credit of being the discoverer of the former, and Canon G.F. Browne of the latter. Canon Browne, indeed, was the first to indicate the existence of this tale on any sculptured stone in the United Kingdom, he having identified it on a cross in Leeds Parish Church-yard and having pointed out its historical and arcaheological significance.

Sigmund's child. This child was named Sigurd[1] and grew up in Hialprek's court, under the care of the dwarf Regin, who taught him all the branches of knowledge known at that time. He also urged him to demand his father's treasure of Hialprek, but Sigurd only asked a horse of the king, who allowed him to choose one; and Odin, in the guise of an old man with a long beard, aided him to find out Grana, that was of Sleipnir's[2] race. Regin then counselled Sigurd to go in quest of Fafni's gold, of which he gave him the following account:—

"Hreidmar had three sons, Fafni the Dragon, Ottur, and Regin the dwarf-smith. Ottur could transform himself into an otter, under which form he was in the habit of catching fish in Andvari's waterfall, so called from a dwarf of that name. One day as Ottur was sitting with his eyes shut eating a salmon, Odin, Hœnir, and Loki passed by; and Loki cast a stone at Ottur and killed him. The Æsir (gods) then skinned him, and came well satisfied with their prize to Hreidmar's dwelling. Hreidmar caused them to be seized, and compelled them to redeem themselves with as much gold as would both fill and cover the otter's skin. To obtain the gold Loki borrowed Rán's[3] net, cast it into the waterfall, and caught in it the dwarf And-vari, who was accustomed to fish there under the form of a pike. The dwarf was compelled to give all his gold-hoard as the price of his liberty; but on Loki taking from him his last ring, with which he hoped to redeem his fortune, he foretold that

1 The Sigurd here mentioned is the same person as the Siegfried of the Old High German *Nibelungenlied*. The northern version, however, is the older, more mythical, and more simple of the two. A bold attempt has lately been made by Dr. G. Vigfusson to iden-tify Sigurd with the noble Cheruscan youth Arminius.—*Sigfried Arminius*, pp. 1-21.

2 *Sleipnir*, "the slipper," was the eight-footed steed of Odin. *Grana* (commonly *Grani*) means the "grey steed."

3 *Rán* was the goddess of the sea. and caught in her net all those who were drowned.

it should prove the bane of all its possessors. With this gold the Æsir covered the otter's skin; but on Hreidmar perceiving a hair of the beard still uncovered, Odin threw on it the ring of Andvari. Fafni afterwards slew his father Hreidmar, took possession of the gold, became one of the worst of serpents, and now watched over his treasures at Gnitaheid."

Sigurd then asked Regin to forge him a sword, and Regin forged one that could cleave an anvil, and cut through floating wool. Armed with this weapon Sigurd fared forth, first to his maternal uncle Grip, who spaed his fortune. He then sailed with a large fleet collected for him by King Hialprek to avenge his father's death. During a storm they were hailed by an old man (Odin) from a cliff, whom they took on board. He told them his name was Hnikar, together with many other things. The storm abating, he stepped ashore and vanished. Hunding's son, with a large army, encountered Sigurd, but were all slain, and Sigurd returned with great honour. Sigurd now expressed a wish to slay the dragon Fafni, whose lair had been pointed out to him by Regin. After a hard fight Sigurd pierces the dragon through the body, but nevertheless it holds a long conversation with its slayer, in which it answers Sigurd's questions relative to the Norns and Æsir but strives in vain to dissuade him from taking the gold.

After the death of Fafni, Regin cut out his heart, and told Sigurd to roast it for him while he took a sleep. Sigurd took the heart and roasted it on a spit, and when he thought it roasted enough, and as the blood frothed from it, he touched it with his finger to see if it were quite done. He burned his finger, and put it in his mouth, and when Fafni's heart's blood touched his tongue, he understood the language of birds. He heard a bird telling its companions that Sigurd should himself eat the dragon's heart. A second bird said that Regin would deceive him; a third said that he ought to kill Regin; another one counsels that he should take the dragon's treasure. All these things Sigurd performs, and rides off with the treasure on Grana's back."

In the upper left-hand corner of what, for convenience, we may call the front of the stone, is carved the figure of Sigurd roasting the heart of Fafni. Only the upper part of Sigurd's body is now visible on the stone, the remainder being broken off. In his left hand Sigurd is represented holding a spit containing the heart of Fafni, which is divided into three gobbets, while at the same time he inserts the finger of his right hand into his mouth. The flames are represented by three small isosceles triangles, one for each gobbet. Immediately above Sigurd's shoulders is shown the head and neck of one of the talking birds which warned him of Regin's intended treachery, and counselled him to forestall the deceiver by cutting off his head. The head of the bird is shown with the neck stretched forward, and the beak open as if addressing Sigurd.

The head and neck of Sigurd's horse Grana is also shown above that of the bird. The whole subject is thus referred to in *Fafnismál*:—

> The first bird[1] says:
>> "There sits Sigurd sprinkled with blood
>> Fafni's heart at the fire he roasts.
>> Wise methinks were the ring-dispenser,
>> If he the glistening life-pulp ate."
>
> Second bird:
>> "There lies Regin communing with himself;
>> He will beguile the youth who in him trusts:
>> In rage he brings evil words together,
>> The framer of evil will avenge his brother."
>
> Third bird:
>> "By the head shorter, let him the hoary sage[2]

---

1 The original word is *igoa*, which has been variously interpreted eagle, hawk, nuthatch, woodpecker, or magpie; *Egoir* is the poetical word for eagle.

2 The original word is *pulr*, the technical meaning of which is obscure. In the Cleasby-Vigfusson *Icelandic Dictionary* it is rendered

Send hence to Hell; all the gold then can he
Possess alone, the mass that under Fafni lay."

Fourth bird:
"He would, methinks, be prudent,
If he could have your friendly counsel, my sisters!
If he would bethink himself and Hugin gladden.
There I expect the wolf where his ears I see."

Fifth bird:
"Not so prudent is that tree of battle,
As I that warlike leader had supposed.
If he one brother lets depart,
Now he the other has of life bereft."

Sixth bird:
"He is most simple, if he longer spares
That people's pest. There lies Regin,
Who has betrayed him. He cannot guard against it."

Seventh bird:
"By the head shorter let him
Make the ice-cold Jötun,
And of his rings deprive him; then of that treasure thou,
Which Fafni owned, sole lord wilt be."

Sigurd replies:
"Fate shall not so resentless be,
That Regin shall my death-word bear;
For the brothers both shall speedily
Go hence to Hell."

In the lowest left-hand corner is shown the upper half of a human figure, holding a sword at arm's length. It no doubt represents Sigurd, but whether before or after slaying the dragon, it is impossible to say.

An historical connection with this tale of Sigurd Fafni's Bane has been suggested by Professor Browne, which, though not strictly in place in a book of this kind, is so interesting and suggestive that it may be briefly narrated—Among the coins found when digging the foundations of the tower at Andreas Church was one, either of Aulaf Sihtric's son, surnamed the Red, who was King of Northumbria 941-945, and

"a sayer of saws, a wise man, a sage (a bard?)."

King of Dublin till the battle of Tara in 980, or of Aulaf God-
frey's son, Sihtric's brother's son, who was King of Northumbria till 941. Now, the Sigurd of Sigurd Fafni's Bane was the
great-great-grandfather of these two Aulafs, and it is, therefore, a reasonable surmise that the crosses both at Andreas and
Malew are memorials to the memory of one of them. This is
particularly interesting to historians as showing the connection of these Aulafs, probably that of Aulaf Sihtric's son with
Man, and of equal interest to archæologists as demonstrating
that these crosses are of much earlier date than has generally
been supposed.

THE STORY OF THE PUNISHMENT OF LOKI

After Loki had enraged the gods by his many treacheries,
he was chased by them, and took refuge in the waterfall of Fra-
rangr, where he was caught by the gods in a net under the form
of a salmon. After his capture he changed to his human form,
and as a punishment the gods caused him to be bound to a
rock with the entrails of his own son Nari. After he was bound
Skadi (a goddess, daughter of Thiassi and the wife of Njörd)
took a venomous serpent and fastened it up over Loki's head.
The venom dropped down from it on to Loki's face. Sigyn, Loki's wife, sat beside him, and held a basin under the serpent's
head to catch the venom, and when the basin was full she took
it away to empty it. Meanwhile the venom dropped on Loki,
who shrank from it so violently that the whole earth trembled.

Of all the mythical personages mentioned in this chapter, the only one remaining in the Folk-Lore of the present
day is Manannan, and even about him comparatively little
is known. He is usually called *Maninagh* "the Manxman,"
and is supposed to have been the first man in Man, which
he protected by a mist. If, however, his enemies succeeded in
approaching in spite of this, he threw chips into the water,
which became ships. His stronghold was Peel Castle, and he

was able to make one man on its battlements appear as a thousand. Thus he routed his enemies. These, together with the notion that he went about on three legs at a great pace, are all the popular ideas about Manannan which still survive.

CHAPTER II

THE FOLLOWING LEGENDS are of entirely different character and origin from the early myths. Those relating to the "Conversion of St. Maughold," "St. Maughold and Gilcolm," "The Legend of Myrescogh Lake," and "The Stone Cross of Ballafletcher" are pious stories invented by monks and priests for the edification of simple-minded laymen; while the legends entitled "Goddard Crovan's Stone," "Olave Goddardson and the Sword Macabuin," "Ivar and Matilda," and "Alswith the Swift" are tales which, fostered by the love of the marvellous, have sprung up about personages, some of whom are historical, centuries after the events related are supposed to have taken place. The account of the conversion of the Manx which follows is probably semi-historical, but will serve as an introduction to the legends.

THE CONVERSION OF THE MANX

The *Tripartite Life of St. Patrick* contains the following interesting account of the conversion of Manxmen to Christianity:—St. Patrick having by means of a miracle converted a wicked man of Ulster, called Macc Cuill, and his men, the following incident is related:—"Then they were silent, and said,

170

'Truly this man Patrick is a man of God.' They all forthwith believed, and Macc Cuill believed, and at Patrick's behest he went into the sea in a coracle of (only) one hide. . . . Now Macc Cuill went on that day to sea, with his right hand towards Maginis, till he reached Mann, and found two wonderful men in the island before him. And it is they that preached God's Word in Mann, and through their preaching the men of that island were baptized. Conindri and Romuil were their names. Now, when these men saw Macc Cuill in his coracle, they took him from the sea, and received him with a welcome; and he learnt the divine rule with them, until he took the bishopric after them. This is Macc Cuill from the sea," the illustrious bishop and prelate of Arduimen.[1] It has been conjectured with reasonable probability, for reasons that need not be given here, that Macc Cuill is identical with Maughold. In this story of the conversion of the Manx there is probably a substratum of fact mingled with fiction. The "Traditionary Ballad" gives the following account of it:—

> Then came Patrick into the midst of them;
> He was a saint, and full of virtue;
> He banished Mannanan on the wave,
> And his evil servants all dispersed.
> And of all those that were evil,
> He showed no favour nor kindness,
> That were of the seed of the conjurors,
> But what he destroyed or put to death
> He blessed the country from end to end,
> And never left a beggar in it;
> And also cleared off all those
> That refused or denied to become Christians.
> Thus it was that Christianity first came to Man,
> By St. Patrick planted in,
> And to establish Christ in us,
> And also in our children.
> He then blessed Saint German,
> And left him a bishop in it,
> To strengthen the faith more and more,
> And faithfully built chapels in it.
> For each four quarterlands he made a chapel

For people of them to meet in prayer;
He also built German Church in Peel Castle,
Which remaineth there until this day.
Before German had finished his work,
God sent for him, and he died;
As ye yourselves know that this messenger
Cannot be put off by using means.
He died and his corpse was laid
Where a great bank had been, hut soon was levelled;
A cross of stone is set at his feet
In his own church in Peel Castle.
Then came Maughold, we are told,
And came on shore at the Head,
And built a church and yard around
At the place he thought to have his dwelling.
The chapels which Saint German ordered
For the people to come to prayers in them,
Maughold put a parcel of them into one,
And thus make regular parishes.
Maughold died, and he is laid
In his own church at Manghold Head.
And the next Bishop that came after
To the best of my knowledge was Lonnan.
Connaghan then came next,
And then Marown the third;
There all three lie in Marown,
And there for ever lie unmolested.
Now we will pass by these holy men,
And commit their souls to the Son of God.
It profiteth them not to praise them more
Until they appear before the King of Kings.[1]

The St. Maughold referred to above is said to have been one of St. Patrick's earliest disciples. The "Book of Armagh"gives the marvellous story of his conversion by St. Patrick, and in the other accounts of St. Patrick's life are equally marvellous tales about his episcopate. These are all, perhaps, surpassed by the circumstantial statements in the *Chronicon Manniæ* (see below), concerning his reappearance in the twelfth century to strike dead with his staff a daring pirate who had profaned his sanctuary.

---

1 Manx Society, vol. XXI., pp. 29-33; or Train's History of the Isle of Man, p. 52.

THE CONVERSION OF THE ROBBER CHIEF MACALDUS, OTHERWISE ST. MAUGHOLD

A district adjoining the Boyne was invested by a band of robbers under the command of a chief named Macaldus. Some of these had been converted from the error of their ways by the Missionaries, and their chief was very wroth in consequence against St. Patrick. Hearing that he was to pass along a road in their neighbourhood on a certain day, he and some of his band took up a position by its side, intending to murder him; but as they caught sight of him slowly approaching, and apparently sunk in profound contemplation, they found themselves deprived of all desire to injure him. Still they would not let the opportunity pass without endeavouring to bring ridicule on him by some stratagem. So one of them lay down by the side of the woodland path as if dead, and Macaldus, as the Saint passed by, besought him to restore his dead comrade to life. "I dare not intercede for him," said the Saint, and passed on. Though very well inclined to offer him some insult, they could not muster resolution for the purpose, and when he had gone on a little way, Macaldus ordered the man to rise. But while this poor wretch had been feigning death, life had really deserted his body, and consternation and remorse now seized on his comrades. Macaldus, foremost in wickedness, was the first to feel repentance. Following St. Patrick, and throwing himself on his knees before him, he besought him to return and intercede for his comrade's restoration, acknowledging the deception they had attempted, and his own readiness to undergo the severest penance the Saint might impose.

The Apostle, retracing his steps, knelt by the dead body, and did not cease to pray till the breath of life entered it again. All the band present vowed on the spot to embrace the faith preached by Patrick, and Macaldus besought the imposition of some most rigorous penance upon himself. Patrick conducted him to the Boyne, and taking a chain from a boat he flung it round him, secured the ends by a padlock, and threw the key into the river. He then made him get into the boat, and trust his course to Providence. "Loose not your chain," said he, "till the key which now lies at the bottom of this river is found and delivered to you. Strive to maintain (with God's help) a spirit of true sorrow; pray without ceasing." He then unmoored the hide covered canoe; it drifted down the river, out by the old seaport of Colpa, and so into the sea.

In twenty hours it was lying by a little harbour in Man, and those who assembled wondered much at the robust form of the navigator, his dejected appearance, and the chain that bound his body. On making enquiry for the abode of a Christian Priest, he found that the Bishop of the Island lived near. He went to his house, told him his former life and present condition, and besought instruction. This was freely given, and the man's conversion found to be sincere. Feeling a strong vocation for the clerical office, he studied unremittingly, and at last came to the eve of the day on which he was to receive holy orders. On that evening the cook, suddenly entering the room in which the Bishop and postulant were conferring, cried out, "Behold, O my master, what I have taken from the belly of a fish just brought in." Macaldus, catching sight of the key in the cook's hand, at once recognised it as the one with which St. Patrick had secured his chain. It was at once applied to its proper use, and he had the happiness of being ordained next day, unencumbered by spiritual or material bonds. At the death of his kind patron and instructor, he was raised to the dignity of the Bishop of Man.[1]

ST. MAUGHOLD'S FISH

The following story about St. Maughold, when residing in the Isle of Man, is from the *Triadis Thaumaturgæ* of Colgan:—

1 From Kenned's *Legendary Fictions of the Irish Celts*, London 1866; original authority *The Book of Armagh*, probably written in the eighth century.

And when he had for some time abided there, a fish was one day taken in the sea, and brought into their dwelling, and when the fish was opened before them, a key was found in his belly, and Machaldus being released from his chains, gave thanks unto God, and went henceforth free; and he increased in holiness, and after the decease of these holy Bishops,[2] attained to the episcopal degree, and being eminent in his miracles and in his virtues, there did he rest. In that Island there was a city called after him, of no small extent, the remains of whose walls may yet be seen, and in the cemetery of its church is a sarcophagus of hollow stone, out of which a spring continually exudes, nay, freely floweth, which is sweet to the palate, whole some to the taste, and healeth divers infirmities, and the deadliness of poison; for whoso drinketh thereof, either receiveth instant health or instantly dieth. In that stone the bones of St. Machaldus are said to rest, yet nothing is found therein save the clear water only; and though many have oftentimes endeavoured to remove the stone, and especially the king of the Norice (of Norway?), who subdued the Island, that he might at all times have sweet water, yet they have all failed in their attempts; for the deeper they dug to raise the stone, so much the more deeply and firmly did they find it fixed in the heart of the earth.

This well is still celebrated for its sanative properties (see ch. vi., "August 12th.")

The next story about him relates to a much later period.

ST. MAUGHOLD AND GILCOLUM

"Thenne, of Maughold, the Saynte, thys storye is,
    Of wycked Gil Colum by Kewyse;
A wonderous tale, yett so trewe ytt is,
    That noe bodye ytt denyes."

While Somerlid was at Ramsey, in Man, in 1158, he was informed that his troops intended to plunder the Church

---

2 Conidrius and Romuilus, supposed to have been the two first Bishops of the Island.

of St. Maughold, where a great deal of money had been deposited, in hopes that the veneration due to St. Maughold,
added to the sanctity of the place, would secure everything
within its precincts. One GilColum, a very powerful chieftain, in particular, drew the attention of Somerlid to these
treasures; and, besides, observed that he did not see how it
was any breach of the peace against St. Maughold, if, for the
sustenance of the army, they drove off the cattle which were
feeding round the churchyard. Somerlid objected to the pro-
posal, and said that he would allow no violence to be offered
to St. Maughold. On this, GilColum earnestly petitioned
that he and his followers might be allowed to examine the
place, and engaged to take the guilt upon his own head. Somerlid, at last, though with some reluctance, consented, and
pronounced these words: "Let the affair rest between thee
and St. Maughold—let me and my troops be innocent—we
claim no share of thy sacrilegious booty." GilColum, exceedingly happy at this declaration, ran back and ordered his vas-
sals to assemble. He then desired that his three sons should
be ready at daybreak, to surprise the church of St. Maughold,
about two miles distant. Meanwhile, news was brought to
those in the church that the enemy were advancing, which
terrified them to such a degree that they all left the sanctuary, and sought shelter in caves and subterraneous dens. The
other inhabitants of the district, with loud shrieks, spent the
whole night in imploring the forgiveness of God, through the
merits of Maughold. The weaker sex, also, with dishevelled
locks, ran frantic about the walls of the church, yelling and
crying with a loud voice, "Where art thou departed, Holy
Maughold? Where are the wonders that, in the old time before us, thou wroughtest in this spot—hast thou abandoned
us for our transgressions—wilt thou forsake thy people in
such an extremity? If not in compassion towards us, yet for
thine own honour, once more send us deliverance."

Maughold mollified, as we suppose, by these and the like supplications, pitied the distress of his votaries. He snatched them from their imminent danger, and consigned their adversary to instantaneous death. GilColum had no sooner fallen asleep in his tent than St. Maughold, arrayed in a white garment, and holding a pastoral staff in his hand, appeared to the robber. He placed himself opposite to the couch, and thus addressed him:—"What hast thou against me, GilColum? Wherein have I, or any of my servants, offended thee, that thou shouldest thus covet what is deposited within my sanctuary?" GilColum answered, "And who art thou?" He replied, "I am the servant of Christ; my name, Maughold, whose church thou purposest to violate; but vain are thy endeavours!" On this, raising the staff which he held, he struck him to the heart. The impious man was confounded, and awakened his soldiers, who were sleeping in their tents. The Saint struck him again, which made the ruffian utter a shriek, so hideous, that his son, and followers, ran in the greatest consternation to see what was the matter. The wretch's tongue clove to his mouth in such a manner that it was with much difficulty he could utter the following sentence:—"Maughold," said he with a groan, "was here, and thrice he struck me with his rod. Go, therefore, to the church, bring his staff, and also priests and clerks, that they may make intercession for me, if, peradventure, St. Maughold will forgive what I devised against him." In obedience his attendants straightway implored the priests to bring the staff, and to visit their master apparently in the agonies of death, relating at the same time what had happened. The priests and clerks and people, on hearing of the miracle, were exceedingly rejoiced indeed, and despatched some clergymen with the crosier. Coming into the presence of the afflicted wretch they found him almost breathless, wherefore one of the clerks pronounced the following imprecation:—"May St. Maughold, who first laid his vengeful hand upon thee, never remove thy plagues till he has bruised thee to pieces. Thus shall others by seeing and hearing thy punishment learn to pay due respect to hallowed ground." The clergy then retired, and immediately such a swarm of monstrous, filthy flies come buzzing about the ruffian's face and mouth, that neither he himself nor his attendants could drive them away. At last, about the sixth hour of the day, he expired in great misery and dismal torture. The exit of this man struck Somerlid and his whole host with such dismay that, as soon as the tide floated their ships, they weighed anchor, and with precipitancy returned home.

A LEGEND OF MYRESCOGH LAKE

There was a certain person called Donald, a veteran Chieftain, and a particular favourite of Harald Olaveson. This man, flying the persecution raised by Harald Godredson, took sanctuary with his infant child in St. Mary's Monastery, at Rushen. Thither Harald Godredson followed, and as he could not offer violence in this privileged place, he, in flattering and deceitful language, addressed the aged man to this purpose:—"Why dost thou thus resolve to fly from me? I mean to do thee no harm." He then assured him of protection, adding that he might depart in peace to any part of the country he had a mind. The veteran, relying on the solemn promise and veracity of the King, followed him out of the Monastery. Within a short space, however, his Majesty manifested his sinister intentions, and demonstrated that he paid no regard to truth, or even his oath. He ordered the old man to be apprehended, bound, and carried to an Isle in the Lake at Myrescogh where he was consigned over to the charge of a strong guard. In this distress, Donald still had confidence towards God. As often as he could bend his knees, he prayed the Lord to deliver him from his chains, through the intercession of the blessed Virgin, from whose Monastery he had been so insidiously betrayed. The Divine interposition was not withheld. One day as he was sitting in his chamber, and guarded only by two sentinels, for the others were absent, suddenly the fetters dropped from his ankles, and left him at full liberty to escape. He reflected, notwithstanding, that he could elope more successfully during the night while the sentinels were a sleep, and from this consideration attempted to replace his feet in the fetters, but to his astonishment found it impossible. Concluding, therefore, that this was wrought by the might of Heaven, he wrapped himself in his mantle, and taking to his heels, made the best of his way. One of the sentinels, a baker by trade, observing him, immediately started up and pursued. Having run a good way, eager to overtake the fugitive, he hit his shin a severe blow against a log; and thus while posting full speed he was so arrested by the power of the Lord that he could not stand. Hence the good man, by the help of Heaven, got clear, and on the third day he reached St. Mary's Abbey at Rushen, where he put up thanksgivings to God and the most merciful Mother for the deliverance. This declaration, adds the chronicler, we have recorded from the man's own mouth. This took place in 1249.[1]

THE STONE CROSS OF BALLAFLETCHER

In a wild and barren field near Ballafletcher there was formerly a large Stone Cross, but in the many changes and revolutions which have happened in this Island has been broken down, and part of it lost; but there still remains the cross part. This has several times been attempted to be removed by persons who pretended a claim to whatever was on that ground, and wanted this piece of stone; but all their endeavours have been unsuccessful. Nor could the strongest team of horses be able to remove it, though irons were placed about it for that purpose. One day a great number of people being gathered about it, contriving new methods for the taking of it away, a very venerable old man appeared among the crowd, and, seeing a boy of

---

1 Founded on the account given in the *Chronicon Manniae*.

about six or seven years of age, he bade him to put his hand to the stone, which the child doing, it immediately turned under his touch, and under it was found a piece of paper, on which were written these words: "Fear God, obey the priesthood, and do to your neighbour as you would have him do to you." Everybody present was in the utmost surprise, especially when looking for the old man in order to ask him some questions concerning the miraculous removal of the stone, he was not to be found, though it was not a minute that they had taken their eyes off him, and there was neither house nor hut in a great distance where he could possibly have concealed himself. The paper was, however, carefully preserved, and carried to the vicar, who wrote copies of it, and dispersed them over the Island. They tell you that they are of such wonderful virtue to whoever wears them that on whatever business they go they are certain of success. They also defend from witchcraft, evil tongues, and all efforts of the devil or his agents. — *Waldron*.

GODDARD CROVAN'S STONE

Down in the valley of St. Mark's, near a little purling brook, lies the famous granite boulder, weighing between twenty and thirty tons, known by the name of Goddard Crovan's stone. It was cast into this situation one day by Goddard Crovan, son of Harold the Black, of Iceland, who lived with his termagant wife in a great castle on the top of Barrule. Unable to endure the violence of her tongue, he turned her unceremoniously out of doors. After descending the mountain some distance, imagining herself out of reach, she turned round and began again to rate him so soundly at the full pitch of her voice that, in a rage, he seized on this huge granite boulder, and hurling it with all his might killed her on the spot. This took place about the year 1060. — *Cumming*.

This stone was broken up and used in building the parsonage house at St. Mark's, and has been considered effectual as a specific for the cure of a termagant by every occupier.

OLAVE GODDARDSON AND THE SWORD MACABUIN

According to tradition, there resided in Man, in the days of Olave Goddardson, a great Norman baron, named Kitter, who was so fond of the chase that he extirpated all the bisons and elks with which the Island abounded at the time of his arrival, to the utter dismay of the people, who, dreading that he might likewise deprive them of the cattle, and even of their purrs in the mountains, had recourse to witchcraft to prevent such a disaster. When this Nimrod of the north had destroyed all the wild animals of the chase in Man, he one day extended his havoc to the red deer of the Calf, leaving at his castle, on the brow of Barrule, only the cook, whose name was Eaoch (which signifies a person who can cry aloud), to dress the provisions intended for his dinner. Eaoch happened to fall asleep at his work in the kitchen. The famous witch-wife Ada caused the fat accumulated at the lee side of the boiling pot to bubble over into the fire, which set the house in a blaze. The astonished cook immediately exerted his characteristic powers to such an extent that he alarmed the hunters in the Calf, a distance of nearly ten miles.

Kitter, hearing the cries of his cook, and seeing his castle in flames, made to the beach with all possible speed, and embarked in a small currach for Man, accompanied by nearly all his attendants. When about half way, the frail bark struck on a rock (which, from that circumstance, has since been called Kitterland), and all on board perished.

The fate of the great baron, and the destruction of his boat, caused the surviving Norwegians to believe that Eaoch the cook was in league with the witches of the Island, to extirpate the Norwegians then in Man; and on this charge he was brought to trial, and sentenced to suffer death. The unfortunate cook heard his doom pronounced with great composure; but claimed the privilege, at that time allowed to criminals in Norway, of choosing the place and manner of passing from time to eternity. This was readily granted by the king. "Then," said the cook, with a loud voice, "I wish my head to be laid across one of your majesty's legs, and there cut off by your majesty's sword, Macabuin, which was made by Loan Maclibuin, the Dark Smith of Drontheim."

It being generally known that the king's scimitar could sever even a mountain of granite, if brought into immediate contact with its edge, it was the wish of everyone present that he would not comply with the subtle artifice of such a low varlet as Eaoch the cook; but his majesty would not retract the permission so recently given, and, therefore, gave orders that the execution should take place in the manner desired.

Although the unflinching integrity of Olave was admired by his subjects, they sympathised deeply for the personal injury to which he exposed himself, rather than deviate from the path of rectitude. But Ada, the witch, was at hand: she ordered toads' skins, twigs of the rowan tree, and adders eggs, each to the number of nine times nine, to be placed between the king's leg and the cook's head, to which he assented.

All these things being properly adjusted, the great sword, Macabuin, made by Loan Maclibuin, the Dark Smith of Drontheim, was lifted with the greatest caution by one of the king's most trusty servants, and laid gently on the neck of the cook; but ere its downward course could be stayed, it severed the head from the body of Eaoch, and cut all the preventives asunder, except the last, thereby saving the king's leg from harm.

When the Dark Smith of Drontheim heard of the stratagem submitted to by Olave to thwart the efficacy of the sword Macabuin, he was so highly offended that he despatched his hammerman, Hiallus-nan-urd, who had only one leg, having lost the other when assisting in making that great sword, to the Castle of Peel to challenge King Olave or any of his people to walk with him to Drontheim. It was accounted very dishonourable in those days to refuse a challenge, particularly if connected with a point of honour. Olave, in mere compliance with this rule, accepted the challenge, and set out to walk against the one-legged traveller from the Isle of Man to the smithy of Loan Maclibhuin, in Drontheim.

They walked o'er the land and they sail'd o'er the sea.

And so equal was the match that, when within sight of the smithy, Hiallus-nan-urd, who was first, called at Loan Maclibhuin to open the door, and Olave called out to shut it. At that instant, pushing past he of the one leg, the King entered the smithy first, to the evident discomfiture of the swarthy smith and his assistant. To show that he was not in the least fatigued, Olave lifted a large forehammer, and under pretence of assisting the smith, struck the anvil with such force that he clove it not only from top to bottom, but also the block upon which it rested.

Emergaid, the daughter of Loan, seeing Olave perform such manly prowess, fell so deeply in love with him that during the time her father was replacing the block and the anvil, she found an opportunity of informing him that her father was only replacing the studdy to finish a sword he was making, and that he had decoyed him to that place for the purpose of destruction, as it had been prophesied that the sword would be tempered in Royal blood, and in revenge for the affront of the cook's death by the sword Macabuin. "Is not your father the seventh son of old *windy cap*, King of Norway?" said Olave. "He is," replied Emergaid, as her father entered the smithy. "Then," cried the King of Man, as he drew the red steel from the fire, "the prophecy must be fulfilled." Emergaid was unable to stay his uplifted hand till he quenched the sword in the blood of her father, and afterwards pierced the heart of the one-legged hammerman, who he knew was in the plot of taking his life.

This tragical event was followed by one of a more agreeable nature. Olave, conscious that had it not been for the timely intervention of Emergaid, the sword of her father would indeed have been tempered in his blood, and knowing the irreparable loss which she had sustained at his hands, made her his queen, and from her were descended all succeeding Kings of Man down to Magnus, the last of the race of Goddard Crovan, the Conqueror. — *Train*.

ALSWITH THE SWIFT

Alswith, a son of Hiallus-nan-ard, the dark smith of Drontheim, whom Olave Goddardson slew in the smithy of Loan Maclibuin, undertook to walk round all the churches in the Isle of Man in one day. Now, in these days there were a great number of churches and chapels which St. Germanus had caused to be built, and the roads were then very rough and steep over the mountains, so that it was no easy task to accomplish this. However, Alswith started off very early one fine summer's morning, and he walked and walked till he had almost accomplished his task. As the evening was drawing on he approached the Tynwald Chapel at St. John's, and from thence pursued his way along the old road leading to the Staarvey, the road up Craig Willey's hill not having been made till long after this. It was now getting very late, and he had still to visit Kirk Michael before his task would be completed; so he pushed on faster than ever, so that when going up the hill leading over "The Driney" he fell down quite exhausted with fatigue and feeling utterly miserable at not having accomplished his undertaking. Since then that hill has been called *Ughtagh breesh my chree*, "Break my heart hill."

IVAR AND MATILDA

"The course of true love never did run smooth."— SHAKESPEARE

"In the year 1249 Reginald began to reign on the 6th May, and on the 30th May of the same month was slain by the Knight Ivar and his accomplices."— *Chronicon Manniæ*.

There was a young and gallant knight, named Ivar, who was enamoured of a very beautiful maiden, named Matilda.

He loved her ardently, and she reciprocated his affection. From childhood they had been companions, and as they grew up in years, the firmer became they attached to each other. Never, indeed, were two beings more indissolubly bound by the fetters of love than Ivar and Matilda. But storms will overcast the serenest sky. At this period Reginald was King of the Isle of Man; and, according to ancient custom, it was incumbent upon Ivar to present his betrothed at the Court of the Monarch, and obtain his consent, prior to becoming linked in more indissoluble fetters with her. The nuptial day had already been fixed, the feast had been prepared, and it was noised abroad that the great and noble of the Island were to be present at the celebration of the marriage. King Reginald resided in Rushen Castle, in all the barbaric pomp which was predominant in those olden times; and thither Ivar, accompanied by Matilda, proceeded to wait upon him. Dismounting from their horses at the entrance of the keep, they were conducted to the presence of the King. Ivar doffed his jewelled cap, and made obeisance; then, leading forward Matilda, he presented her to him. Reginald was greatly enraptured with the maiden's beauty from the first moment she had met his gaze, and swore inwardly that he would possess her for himself, and spoil the knight of his affianced bride. To carry into effect his wicked purpose, he accused Ivar of pretended crimes; and, ordering in his guards, banished him from his presence; detaining, however, the maiden. Vain would it be to depict Matilda's anguish at this barbarous treatment. Reginald endeavoured to sooth her agitation, but it was to no purpose. He talked to her of his devoted love, but the maiden spurned his impious offers with contempt. Exasperated at her resistance, he had her confined in one of the most solitary apartments in the Castle. In the meantime, Ivar exerted himself to avenge the deep injury which he had received; but Reginald had such despotic sway, that all his endeavours proved abortive. At length he resolved to retire from the world, to assume the monastic habit, and to join the pious brotherhood of the Monastery of St. Mary's of Rushen. The brethren received him with joy, commiserating the bereavement which he had sustained. Ivar was now devoted to acts of piety; but still he did not forget his Matilda. Sometimes he would ascend the Hill, and gaze towards the Castle, wondering if Matilda were yet alive. One day, matin prayers having been offered up, Ivar wandered as usual through the woods, thinking of his betrothed, and bowed down with sorrow. At last he reclined on the grass to rest; when, looking around, he beheld a fissure in a rock which abutted from an eminence immediately opposite. Curiosity induced him to go near; and he discovered that it was the entrance to a subterranean passage. Venturing in, he proceeded for some distance. Onward he went, till a great door arrested his progress. After some difficulty it yielded to his endeavours, and he passed through. Suddenly a piercing shriek, which reverberated along the echoing vaults fixed him horror-struck for a moment to the place. It was repeated faintly several times. A faint glimmer of light now broke in upon his path, and he found himself in a vaulted chamber. Passing through it, another cry met his ear; and rushing impetuously forward, he heard a voice in a state of exhaustion exclaim, "Mother of God, save Matilda!" Whilst, through a chink in the barrier, he beheld his long lost love, with dishevelled hair and throbbing bosom, in the arms of the tyrant Reginald. Ivar instantly sprang through the barrier, rushed upon the wretch, and, seizing his sword, which lay carelessly on the table, plunged it into Reginald's bosom. Ivar, carrying Matilda in his arms, continued on through the subterranean passage, which brought them to the sea side where they met with a boat, which conveyed them to Ireland. There they were united in holy matrimony, and passed the remainder of their days in the raptures of a generous love, heightened by mutual admiration and gratitude.

CHAPTER III

FAIRIES AND FAMILIAR SPIRITS

THE BELIEF IN FAIRIES OR ELVES was formerly very prevalent in the Isle of Man, and cannot be said to have altogether died out even at the present day. The Manx conception of a Fairy seems to be very much the same as that in other Celtic lands, with, perhaps, a tinge of the somewhat more sombre Scandinavian superstition. They are supposed to be like human beings in form and feature, though very much smaller and more delicately constructed. At a distance they seem to be handsome, but on closer inspection they are often found to be decrepit and withered. They are usually represented as being clad in blue or green, with red peaked caps. They live in green hill sides, more especially affecting the ancient tumuli. Any one straying near these on a fine summer's evening would probably hear delightful music; but he must take care, especially if he is a musician, not to linger lest he should be entrapped. Sometimes, too, they may be seen playing like children, or dancing, the rings seen on the grass being caused by this; at other times feasting. They hunt, being for the most part very furious riders. They are partly human and partly spiritual in their nature, and are visible to men only when they choose. Some of them are benevolent, curing men of diseases and delivering them from misfortune. Others are malevolent, stealing children, even abducting grown people, and bringing misfortune. The flint arrow heads which are occasionally picked up, are the weapons with which the Fairies avenge themselves upon human beings who had wronged them. Their impact is not felt, and does not break the skin, but a blue mark is found on the body of the victim after death. The good Fairies are, fortunately, more powerful than the bad, and will enable those who are considerate in their behaviour to them to prevail over the latter. It is, therefore, very desirable to keep on good terms with them, and to propitiate them by taking care not to wound their feelings; with this view, they are called "the little people," or "the good people," the word Fairy being never mentioned, as they are supposed not to like it. Indeed, the Manx word *Ferrish* is merely a recent corruption of the English word, there being no such word in the Manx language 150 years ago. It was an old custom to keep a fire burning in the house during the night, so that the Fairies might come in and enjoy it. If any one was rash enough not to do this, or to abuse them in any way, he would be sure to suffer for it. It was also customary to leave some bread out for the Fairies, and to fill the water crocks with clean water for them before going to bed. This water was never used for any other purpose, but was thrown out in the morning. The Manx women, formerly, would not spin on Saturday evenings, as this was deemed displeasing to the *Mooinjer-Veggey* (Fairies), and at every baking and churning a small bit of dough and butter was stuck on the wall for their consumption. Besides keeping on good terms with the benevolent Fairies, there are various other methods of defeating the machinations of the malevolent ones. Among these are the incantations and herbs got from men and women who had acquired the reputation of being Fairy Doctors, or Charmers, though their nostrums were usually applied to

the cure of cattle. One of the most renowned of these practitioners, Teare of Ballawhane, told Train, in 1833, that the
malevolence of the Fairies had caused the seed potatoes to become tainted in the ground, and, in order to convince him
that this was the case, he said that all the potatoes which he
had taken under his protection had vegetated vigorously.

But there are methods for protecting human beings and
animals against Fairies, which are so well known that there is
no need to apply to a Charmer before applying them. Thus,
salt is very efficacious, and so is iron, as will be seen from stories which follow. It was necessary to take great care of children, especially before baptism, as one of the commonest actions of the malevolent Fairies is to steal children. If a child
were taken away, a decrepit and emaciated Fairy would be
found in its place, and the prettier the child, the greater the
risk of this. One way of preventing this catastrophe was to lay
an iron poker, or other iron implement, on the child when
left alone, another was to tie a red thread round the child's
neck, and when taking her child to be christened, a woman
would take a piece of bread and cheese with her, which she
gave to the first person she met for the same purpose. Another
protective measure, both for human beings and animals, is to
have the *cuirn*, or mountain ash, in the form of a cross, made
without a knife, put over the threshold of their dwellings.
Flowers growing in a hedge, especially if yellow, are also useful
in this respect, and ploughmen were wont to throw chamber
lee over their ploughs to protect them. On Midsummer Eve,
when their power is at its height, flowers and herbs are the
only barriers to their incursions, and these are regularly spread
at the doors of the houses to protect the inmates. They are also
supposed to be always abroad during the harvest moon; and
many stories are related of their excursions through the Island,
and particularly of their merry-makings in Glentrammon. The
interior of Fairy Hill, in Rushen, is supposed to be the palace

of the Fairy King, and many a tale was told of the midnight revels of the fairy court of Mona.

Waldron,[1] to whom we owe most of our stories about Fairies, after referring to the ignorance of the Manx people as being the cause of their excessive superstition, writes:—"I know not, idolizers as they are of the clergy, whether they would even be refractory to them, were they to preach against the existence of fairies, or even against their being commonly seen. . . . . They confidently assert that the first inhabitants of their Island were fairies, so do they maintain that these little people have still their residence among them. They call them the good people, and say they live in wilds and forests, and on mountains, and shun great cities because of the wickedness acted therein; all the houses are blessed where they visit, for they fly vice. A person would be thought impudently profane who should suffer his family to go to bed without having first set a tub, or pail full of clean water, for these guests to bathe themselves in, which the natives aver they constantly do, as soon as ever the eyes of the family are closed, wherever they vouchsafe to come. If anything happens to be mislaid, and found again, in some place where it was not expected, they presently tell you a fairy took it and returned it; if you chance to get a fall and hurt yourself, a fairy laid something in your way to throw you down, as a punishment for some sin you have committed."

Cumming, writing in 1849, says, "It is not often now-a-days that we can meet with persons not ashamed to own their belief in the existence of the good people, and still more seldom is it that we can extract affirmative testimony of eye-witnesses to their tiny pranks upon the green sward. It would be a mistake, however, to suppose that the minds of the Manx peasantry are uninfluenced by a superstitious feeling of reverence for the Fairy Elves, and for places which tradition has

1 See Preface.

rendered sacred to their revels. The superstition has with them its use, it causes them to keep good hours; and in some parts of the Island it would be difficult to prevail on a native to stir out after dark. Yea, it is said, that on dark, dismal and stormy nights, up in the mountain parts of parishes, the tender-hearted peasants retire earlier to rest, in order to allow to the weather-beaten Fairies the unmolested and unwatched enjoyment of the smouldering embers of their turf fire."

Campbell, in writing of the Fairies in the Highlands and the Western Isles, says "Men do believe in fairies, though they will not readily confess the fact. And, although I do not myself believe that fairies *are*, in spite of the strong evidence offered, I believe there once was a small race of people in these Islands, who are remembered as fairies. . . . They are always represented as living in green mounds. They pop up their heads when disturbed by people treading upon their houses. They steal children. They seem to live on familiar terms with the people about them, who treat them well, and to punish them when they ill-treat them." He then proceeds to compare these fairy structures with the abodes of the modern Laplanders, and to state, with a considerable show of probability, that many of the stories about Fairies have originated from tradition about these curious little people.

Further on in his book, after giving a number of Gaelic fairy tales, he continues: "The Manks fairy creed is again the same. Similar beings are supposed to exist, and are known by the name of *Ferish*, which a Mankman assured me was a genuine Manks word.[2] If so, fairy may be old Celtic, and derived from the same root as Peri, instead of being derived from it. The fairies in the Isle of Man are believed to be spirits. They are not supposed to throw arrows as they are said still to do in the Highlands. None of the old peasants seemed to take the least interest in "elf shots," the flint arrows, which generally lead to

---

2   Here we think Campbell's informant was mistaken.

a story when shown elsewhere. One old man said, "the *ferish* have no body, no bones," and scorned the arrow heads. It is stated in Train's History that there are no flintarrow heads in the Isle of Man; but as there are numerous barrons, flint weapons may yet be discovered when some one looks for them.[1] Still these Manks fairies are much the same as their neighbours on the main land. They go into mills at night and grind stolen corn; they steal milk from the cattle; they live in green mounds; in short, they are like little mortals invested with supernatural power."

It will be seen from the first two stories that follow that the Fairies are supposed to have been the earliest inhabitants of the Island. In addition to the Fairies proper, there are familiar or household Spirits, who are implacable in their resentment, but unchanging in their friendship. There are two of these in the Isle of Man, viz., the *Lhiannan-Shee*, or "spirit friend," a guardian spirit, identical with the Irish *Lianhannshee* and *the Dooiney-oie*, or "night man," who seems peculiar to the Island, though he bears a faint resemblance to the Irish *Banshee*.

ORIGIN OF THE ARMS OF THE ISLAND

"Quocunque Jeceris Stabit."— MOTTO

The natives say that many centuries before the Christian era the Island was inhabited by Fairies, and that all business was carried on in a supernatural manner. They affirm that a blue mist continually hung over the land, and prevented mariners, who passed in ships that way, from even suspecting that there was an Island so near at hand, till a few fishermen, by stress of weather, were stranded on the shore. As they were preparing to kindle a fire on the

---

1 Train was certainly wrong, as numeorus flint arrow-heads have been discovered both before and after his time. Campbell's informnat was also in error, as these flint weapons are certainly supposed by the Manks to have been used by Fairies.

beach, they were astounded by a fearful noise issuing from the dark cloud which concealed the Island from their view. When the first spark of fire fell into their tinder box, the fog began to move up the side of the mountain, closely followed by a revolving object, closely resembling three legs of men joined together at the upper part of the thighs, and spread out so as to resemble the spokes of a wheel. Hence the Arms of the Island. — *Train*.

THE DISCOVERY OF THE ISLAND

"Mona, once hid from those who search the main,
Where thousand elfin shapes abide."— COLLINS

Some hundred years before the coming of our Saviour, the Isle of Man was inhabited by a certain species called Fairies, and everything was carried on in a supernatural manner; a blue mist hanging continually over the land, prevented the ships that passed by from having any suspicion there was an island. This mist, contrary to nature, was preserved by keeping a perpetual fire, which happening once to be extinguished, the shore discovered itself to some fishermen, who were there in a boat on their vocation, and by them notice was given to the people of some country, who sent ships in order to make a further discovery. On their landing, they had a fierce encounter with the little people, and having got the better over them possessed themselves of Castle Rushen, and by degrees, as they received reinforcements, of the whole Island. These new conquerors maintained their ground some time, but were at length beaten out by a race of giants, who were not extirpated, as I said before, till the reign of Prince Arthur, by Merlin, the famous British enchanter. They pretend, also, that this Island afterward became an Asylum to all the distressed princes and great men in Europe, and that those uncommon fortifications made about Peel Castle were added for their better security. — *Waldron*.

THE FAIRY HORN

A young sailor, coming off a long voyage, though it was late at night, chose to land rather than lie another night in the vessel; being permitted to do so, he was set on shore at Douglas. It happened to be a fine, moonlight night, and very dry, being a small frost; he, therefore, forbore going into any house to refresh himself; but made the best of his way to the house of a sister he had at Kirk Malew. As he was going over a pretty high mountain, he heard the noise of horses, the halloo of a huntsman, and the finest horn in the world. He was a little surprised that anybody pursued those kind of sports in the night; but he had not time for much reflection before they all passed by him, so near that he was able to count what number there was of them, which, he said, was thirteen, and that they were all dressed in green, and gallantly mounted. He was so well pleased with the sight that he would gladly have followed, could he have kept pace with them. He crossed the footway, however, that he might see them again, which he did more than once, and lost not the sound of the horn for some miles. At length, being arrived at his sister's, he tells her the story, who presently clapped her hands for joy, that he was come home safe. "For," said she, "those you saw were fairies; and 'tis well they did not take you away with them."— *Waldron.*

Manx Fairies seem to have been especially fond of the chase. If a horse were found in his stall wet with perspiration, for which no particular reason could be given, it would be said that he must have been ridden by them. Of this superstition, the following story is an instance:—

THE FAIRY SADDLE

Once upon a time an old Vicar of Braddan was very much troubled by having his horse taken out of the field during the night, and finding him in the morning sweating all over, and as much exhausted as if he had been furiously ridden many miles. In spite of all enquiries, he could never learn who had done this. But one morning, just at day-break, as he was returning home from the bedside of one of his sick parishioners, to whom he had been administering the Sacrament, he observed, just as he was passing his field, a little man in a green jacket, and carrying a riding whip in his hand, in the act of turning his horse loose into the field. On this little individual turning round, he saw the Vicar standing by the gate, on which he immediately vanished, and the saddle, which he had placed at the side of the fence was turned into stone in the shape of a saddle. It has remained there ever since, and so the road which passes this point is called "The Saddle-road" to this day. It is almost needless to state that the old Vicar's horse was never molested again. — *Oral.*

THE FAIRY HORSE DEALER

A Manxman, who had the reputation of the utmost integrity, being desirous of disposing of a horse he had at that time no great occasion for, and riding him to market for that purpose, was accosted, in passing over the mountains, by a little man in a plain dress, who asked him if he would sell his horse. "'Tis the design I am going on," replied the person who told the story. On which the other desired to know the price. "Eight pounds," said he. "No," resumed the purchaser, "I will give no more than seven; which, if you will take, here is your money." The owner thinking he had bid pretty fair, agreed with him, and the money being told out, the one dismounted and the other got on the back of the horse, which he had no sooner done than both beast and rider sunk into the earth immediately, leaving the person who had made the bargain in the utmost terror and consternation. As soon as he had a little recovered himself, he went directly to the parson of the parish, and related what had passed, desiring he would give his opinion whether he ought to make use of the money he had received or not. To which he replied that, as he had made a fair bargain, and in no way circumvented, nor endeavoured to circumvent, the buyer, he saw no reason to believe, in case it was an evil spirit, it could have any power over him. On this assurance, he went home well satisfied, and nothing afterwards happened to give him any disquiet concerning this affair. — *Waldron.*

FAIRY MUSIC

> Such a soft floating witchery of sound,
> As twilight elfins make, when they at eve
> Voyage on gentle gales from fairyland. — COLERIDGE

An English gentleman, the particular friend of our author, to whom he told the story, was about passing over Douglas Bridge before it was broken down, but the tide being high he was obliged to take the river, having an excellent horse under him and one accustomed to swim. As he was in the middle of it he heard, or imagined he heard, the finest symphony, he would not say in the world, for nothing human ever came up to it. The horse was no less sensible of the harmony than himself, and kept in an immoveable posture all the time it lasted; which, he said could not, be less than three-quarters of an hour, according to the most exact calculation he could make when he arrived at the end of his little journey and found how long he had been coming. He, who before laughed at all the stories told of fairies, now became a convert, and believed as much as ever a Manxman of them all. — *Waldron.*

THE FAIRY LAKE

> What cursed foot wanders this way to-night,
> To cross my obsequies. — SHAKESPEARE

A little beyond the "Devil's Den," is a small lake, in the midst of which is a huge stone, on which formerly stood a cross; round this lake the fairies are said to celebrate the obsequies of any good person. I have heard many people, and those of a considerable share of understanding, protest that, in passing that way, they have been saluted with the sound of such music as could proceed from no earthly instruments. — *Waldron*.

THE UNFORTUNATE FIDDLER

Then let them all encircle him about,
And, fairy like, to pinch the unclean knight,
And ask him why that hour of fairy revel-
In their so sacred paths he dares to tread
In shape profane. — SHAKESPEARE.

A fiddler, having agreed with a person, who was a stranger, for so much money, to play to some company he should bring him to, all the twelve days of Christmas, and received earnest for it, saw his new master vanish into the earth the moment he had made the bargain. Nothing could be more terrified than was the poor fiddler; he found he had entered himself into the Devil's service, and looked upon himself as already damned; but having recourse to a clergyman, he received some hope. He ordered him, however, as he had taken earnest, to go when he should be called; but that whatever tunes should be called for, to play none but Psalms. On the day appointed, the same person appeared, with whom he went, though with what inward reluctance 'tis easy to guess; but, punctually obeying the minister's directions, the company to whom he played were so angry that they all vanished at once, leaving him at the top of a high hill, and so bruised and hurt, though he was not sensible when, or from what hand he received the blows, that he got not home without the utmost difficulty. — *Waldron*.

There are many stories of fairy music, of even later date than this. The most definite of these is to the effect that the music of the famous song called *The Bollan Bane*, or "The White Herb," a plant known to the Fairy Doctors, and of great healing virtues, was taken from a tune sung by the Fairies one evening on the mountains, which was heard by a belated, wanderer, some fifty years ago. — *Oral*.

OBJECTION OF FAIRIES TO NOISE

It is well known that all Fairies and their like have a great objection to noise, especially to the ringing of church bells. This is illustrated by the following story:—About seventy years ago, a man, very early one spring morning, heard a low murmuring, wailing noise. On going to the door to see what occasioned it, he beheld "multitudes of the good people passing over the stepping stones in the river, and wending their way up the side of the hill, until they were lost in the mist that then enveloped the top of Bearey Mountain. They were dressed chiefly in *Loaghtyn*, with little pointed red caps, and most of them were employed in bearing upon their shoulders various articles of domestic use, such as kettles, pots, pans, the spinning wheel, and such like, evidently seeking fresh and more quiet quarters, having been disturbed, as was supposed, by the noise of a fulling mill lately erected in their neighbourhood."— *W. Harrison*.

THE FAIRY CUP OF KIRK MALEW

I have heard many Manxmen protest they have been carried insensibly great distances from home, and without knowing how they came there, found themselves on the top of a mountain. One man had been led by invisible musicians for several miles together, and not being able to resist the harmony, followed, till it conducted him into a large common, where were a great number of little people sitting round a table, and eating and drinking in a very jovial manner. Among them were some faces whom he thought he had formerly seen, but forbore taking any notice, or they of him, till the little people offered him drink; one of them, whose features seemed not unknown to him, plucked him by the coat, and forbade him, whatever he did, to taste anything he saw before him; "for if you do," added he, "you will be as I am, and return no more to your family." The poor man was much affrighted, but resolved to obey the injunction. Accordingly a large silver cup filled with some sort of liquor, being put into his hand, he found an opportunity to throw what it contained on the ground. Soon after, the music ceasing, all the company disappeared, leaving the cup in his hand; and he returned home, though much wearied and fatigued. He went the next day and communicated to the minister of the parish all that had happened, and asked his advice how he should dispose of the cup; to which the parson replied, he could not do better than to devote it to the service of the Church; and this very cup, they tell me, is that which is now used for the consecrated wine in Kirk Malew. — *Waldron.*

A similar tale is told of the "Altar Cup in Aagerup," a village in Zeland:—One Christmas Eve a farmer's servant in the village borrowed his master's horse and rode down to see the "troll meeting," and while he was wondering to see how well and gaily the little dwarfs danced, up came a troll to him and invited him to dismount and take a share in their merriment. Another troll held his horse, while he went down and danced with them all night long. As it was drawing near day he mounted his horse to return home, when a maiden, who held a gold cup in her hand, invited him to drink the stirrup cup. He took it, but having some suspicion, while he made as if he was raising the cup to his mouth, threw the contents over his shoulder. He then clapped spurs into his horse's sides and rode away with the cup in his hands as fast as the horse could gallop. The trolls set off in full pursuit, and gained on him every minute. In his distress he prayed to God, and he made a vow that, if he should be delivered, he would bestow the cup on the Church. As he rode along by the wall of the churchyard he hastily flung the cup over it, that it at least might be secure; and pushing on at full speed, and just as they were on the point of catching hold of the horse, he sprang in through the farmer's gate and closed the wicket after him. Thus was he saved, and the cup was presented to the Church.

Chancellor Gervase, of Tilbury, writing in the thirteenth century, makes mention of a knight who on being presented with a large horn by the "ancient people," rode off with it, instead of returning. For this he is said to have been condemned to death. A cup with some mysterious drink is common in Celtic traditions. There was the Cup of Fionn which healed diseases, and the Saint Graal, of mediæval romance. In more recent times there was the well-known cup called "The Luck of Eden Hall," and the "Ballafletcher Drinking Glass."

THE FAIRY ELF

Yee fairies, who,
Into their beds did foist your babes,
And theirs exchanged to be.—
—ALBION'S ENGLAND, 1612.

The story of infants being exchanged in their cradles is here in such credit that mothers are in continual terror at the thought of it. I was prevailed upon to go and see a child, who, they told me, was of these changelings, and indeed must own I was not a little surprised, as well as shocked, at the sight; nothing under heaven could have a more beautiful face; but, though between five and six years old, and seemingly healthy, he was so far from being able to walk, or stand, that he could not so much as move any one joint—his limbs were vastly long for his age, but smaller than infant's of six months; his complexion was perfectly delicate, and he had the finest hair in the world; he never spoke or cried, eat scarce anything, and very seldom seen to smile, but if anyone called him a *Fairy Elf* he would frown, and fix his eyes so earnestly on those who said it, as if he would look them through. His mother, at least his supposed mother, being very poor, frequently went out a charing, and left him a whole day together; the neighbours, out of curiosity, have often looked down at the window to see how he behaved when alone, which, whenever they did, they were sure to find him laughing, and in the utmost delight. This made them judge that he was not without company more pleasing to him than any mortals could be, and what made this conjecture seem the more reasonable was that if he were left ever so dirty, the woman, at her return, saw him with a clean face, his hair combed with the utmost exactness and nicety. — *Waldron.*

THE KIDNAPPERS

From fairies, and the tempters of the night,
Guard me, beseech you. — SHAKESPEARE

An account of this nature I had from a woman, to whose offspring the fairies seemed to have a particular fancy. The fourth or fifth night after she was delivered of her first child, the family were alarmed by a most terrible cry of fire, on which everybody ran out of the house to see whence it proceeded, not excepting the nurse, who, being as much frighted as the others, made one of the number. The poor woman lay trembling in her bed alone, unable to help herself, and her back being turned to the infant, saw not that it was taken away by an invisible hand. Those who had left her having enquired about the neighbourhood, and finding there was no cause for the outcry they had heard, laughed at each other for the mistake; but as they were going to re-enter the house, the poor babe lay on the threshold, and by its cries preserved itself from being trod upon. This exceedingly amazed all that saw it, and the mother being still in bed, they could ascribe no reason for finding it there, but having been removed by fairies, who by their sudden return, had been prevented from carrying it any further.

About a year after the same woman was brought to bed of a second child, which had not been born many nights before, a great noise was heard in the house where they kept their cattle. Everybody that was stirring ran to see what was the matter, believing that the cows had got loose; the nurse was as ready as the rest, but finding all safe, and the barn-door close, immediately returned, but not so suddenly but that the new-born babe was taken out of the bed, as the former had been, and dropped on their coming in the middle of the entry. This was enough to prove the fairies had made a second attempt; and the parents sending for a minister, joined with him in thanksgiving to God who had twice delivered their children from being taken from them.

But in the time of her third lying-in everybody seemed to have forgot what had happened in the first and second, and on a noise in the cattle house ran out to know what had occasioned it. The nurse was the only person, excepting the woman in the straw, who stayed in the house, nor was she detained through care or want of curiosity but by the bonds of sleep, having drunk a little too plentifully the preceding day. The mother, who was broad awake, saw her child lifted out of the bed and carried out of the chamber, though she could not see any person touch it, on which she cried out as loud as she could, "Nurse, nurse my child my child is taken away"; but the old woman was too fast to be awakened by the noise she made, and the infant was irretrievably gone. When her husband and those who had accompanied him returned they found her wringing her hands and uttering the most piteous lamenta-tions for the loss of her child, on which, said the husband, looking into the bed, "The woman is mad, do not you see the child lies by you?" On which she turned and saw indeed some-thing like a child, but far different from her own who was a very beautiful, fat, well-featured babe, whereas, what was now in the room of it was a poor, lean, withered, deformed crea-ture. It lay quite naked, but the clothes belonging to the child that was exchanged for it lay wrapt up all together on the bed.

This creature lived with them near the space of nine years, in all which time it eat nothing except a few herbs, nor was ever seen to void any other excrement than water. It neither spoke nor could stand or go, but seemed enervate in every joint, like the changeling I mentioned before, and in all its actions showed itself to be of the same nature. — *Waldron*.

A FAIRY DETECTED IN CHANGING AN INFANT

The wife of a fisherman had to go into the harvest to help with the reaping, as there were very few hands, in consequence of so many being away at the fishing. She took her young child with her, which up to that time had not been christened, because of the absence of her husband, and placed it between two sheaves on the headland, taking the precaution to place an open pair of scissors across it, for fear the fairies should take the *boght millish* (poor, sweet thing), and leave one of their own bantlings in its place. She was engaged at the other end of the field, when, hearing great wailings, and thinking that something, had happened to the child, she hastened to the spot where she had placed it; but found that it was not there. Being half distracted with the fear of losing her infant, she ran towards the entrance of the field, from whence she saw two little people engaged in dragging the child between them. She at once rushed after them, seized the child, and carried it home. It was supposed that the scissors had slipped off, and thus left the child unprotected. — *W. Harrison*.

The following story is very similar:—A woman during harvest was in a field helping her husband to stook the corn, when she heard her child crying. She had previously placed it behind one of the stooks, and when she arrived at the spot it was missing, and another child in its place, it having been exchanged by the Fairies. Soon afterwards, hearing this child cry, she began to run to it; but her husband knowing it was not the voice of their own child, held the woman back, and would not let her go till the cry had ceased. She then went back and found her own child. The Fairies having heard their child in distress, and seeing it uncared for, had taken it away, and left the woman her own. — *Jenkinson*.

Nor, were the misdeeds of Fairies confined to children, as will be seen from the next two stories: Many years ago, the Fairies stole away the fair wife of the owner of Ballaleece. After some time, the man took to himself a second partner, and then the first paid him a visit in company with a troop of sister Fairies, riding on small horses. She arranged with her husband that they should come again at a stated time, when she would be on the second horse, and he was, therefore, to seize hold of the bridle and detain her; but it was stipulated that he should not succeed in doing so, unless he swept the barn floor so clear, that there was not left a single bit of straw. He made everything ready for the meeting, but in the meantime told the secret to his second wife, and she, through jealousy, and in order to circumvent her rival, placed a single straw secretly under a bushel on the barn floor. The result was, that when the Fairies came, the farmer seized hold of the second horse by the bridle, as prearranged, but could not detain it, and away went all the troop. — *Jenkinson.*

ABDUCTION OF A BOY BY FAIRIES

Not so many years ago a farmer's son, in the parish of Andreas, was taken away by the Fairies, and was lost for four years. One day, as his two brothers were passing by a thorn bush not far from their house, they heard a crack that startled them, so that they ran back home. Not long afterwards their mother heard a footstep near the house, upon which she remarked that if John (the lost boy) had been at home, she would have said that it was his footstep. At the expiration of the four years, the boy returned, and told them his adventures. He asked his brothers if they remembered the crack from the bush, and, on receiving a reply in the affirmative, he explained that it was one of the Fairies, with whom he had been galloping about all the time, who was shooting an arrow at them, and that he had lifted up a plate to intercept the arrow; hence the crack that they had heard. As to the footstep his mother had heard, he said that was his, and he told them that he was near them all the time, but could not get to them; in fact he saw all they were doing, and, as an instance of this, he mentioned the day on which they had taken corn to Ramsey. He could give no account of how he had been let loose by the Fairies, merely remarking that he seemed as if he had been unconscious, and then waked up in this world, and at once came to his people. — *Rhys*.

THE CHRISTENING

The wife which is of Fairie,
Of suche a childe delivered is. — GOWER

A woman told me that, being great with child, and expecting every moment the good hour, as she lay awake one night in bed, she saw seven or eight little women come into her chamber, one of whom had an infant in her arms; they were followed by a man of the same size with themselves, but in the habit of a minister. One of them went to the pail, and finding no water in it, cried out to the others, "What must they do to christen the child?" On which they replied it should be done in beer. With that the seeming parson took the child in his arms, and performed the ceremony of baptism, dipping his hand into a great tub of strong beer, which the woman had brewed the day before, to be ready for her lying-in. She told me that they baptised the infant by the name of Joan, which made her know she was pregnant of a girl, as it proved a few days after, when she was delivered. She added, also, that it was common for the fairies to make a mock christening when any person was near her time, and that according to what child (male or female) they brought, such should the woman bring into the world. — *Waldron*.

THE SCHOOL BOYS

A gentleman, my near neighbour, who affirmed with the most solemn asseverations that, being entirely averse to the belief in fairies, or that any such beings were permitted to wander for the purposes related of them, had been at last convinced by the appearance of several little figures, playing and leaping over some stones in a field, whom, a few yards distance, he imagined were school boys, and intended, when he came near enough, to reprimand, for being absent from their exercises at that time of the day, it being then, he said, between three and four of the clock. But when he approached, as near he could guess, within twenty paces, they all immediately disappeared, though he had never taken his eye off them from the first moment he beheld them; nor was there any place where they could so suddenly retreat, it being an open field, without hedge or bush, and, as is said before, broad day. — *Waldron*.

FAIRY PUNISHMENT

As an instance that fairies will not suffer any abuse without resorting to some mode of punishment, the following occurred some six years ago, and was notorious. A man of Laxey, some what intoxicated, met a party of them, and began forthwith to abuse and curse them as the devil's imps; they wreaked their vengeance on him by piercing his skin with a shower of gravel. My guide, perhaps recollecting that the fairies were within hearing, took their part, and expressed his assurance that they would not have molested him had he not provoked them by his insults. The catastrophe did not terminate here. The offender sickened that night, his favourite horse died next morning, his cows died also, and in six weeks he himself was a corpse! — *Lord Teignmouth's Sketches*, 1836.

THE WHIPPING OF THE LITTLE GIRL

A girl about ten years old, daughter of a woman who lived about two miles from Ballasalla, being sent over the fields to the town for a pennyworth of tobacco for her father, was, on the top of a mountain, surrounded by a great number of little men, who would not suffer her to pass any farther. Some of them said she should go with them, and accordingly laid hold of her; but one seeming more pitiful, desired they would let her alone; which they refusing, there ensued a quarrel, and the person who took her part, fought bravely in her defence. This so incensed the others, that to be revenged on her for being the cause, two or three of them seized her, and whipped her heartily; after which it seems, they had no further power over her, and she ran home directly, telling what had befallen her, and showing her back on which were the prints of several small hands. Several of the townspeople went with her to the mountain, and, she conducting them to the spot, the little antagonists were gone, but had left behind them proofs, that what the little girl had informed them was true; for there was a great deal of blood to be seen on the stones. — *Waldron*.

MISCHIEF DONE BY FAIRIES

The following item of news was communicated to the *Mona's Herald* newspaper, by a correspondent, in 1847:—"We are sorry to state that the same disgraceful conduct has again been manifested in breaking the windows of the house of Mr Quayle, Maughold. Several panes have again been broken, and all efforts to trace the depredators have been abortive. Every precaution has been taken—the door has been thrown open, but when the neighbours rushed after those who did it, all was as still as if nothing had been there. A number of the most active and stout-hearted young men in the parish assisted in the search; three fierce dogs were brought from neighbouring farms, but they shrunk affrighted, and refused to follow the instinct of their nature. No means were resorted to, but it remains as great a mystery as ever, and nothing will convince the people but that it is the mischievous tricks of the fairies or ghosts! They say that Mr Quayle ploughed lately a small plot of ground that was never ploughed before, and that he turned over some bones in an old grave-yard, which was the sole cause!"

FAIRY DOGS

A man, with some fresh fish, was once followed home by a lot of Fairy Dogs. When he arrived at his own door he picked up a stone and threw it among them, whereupon they disappeared, but not without his being struck or stung. He was consequently ill for six months afterwards. My informant told me that this man would have been left alone if he had put a pinch of salt in the fish, as the Fairies could not stand salt or baptism, and baptised children were safe from being changed by them. He also told me that when he was engaged in the fishing and had a fish given him to take home, they would never let him start, if it was in the evening, without putting a pinch of salt in the mouth of the fish to prevent the Fairies setting on him. — *Rhys.*

Another story about Fairy Dogs was related by an old man in 1874, who said that when a lad, he and a companion were travelling one fine moonlight night in the East Baldwin Valley, and hearing something in a *gill* (small glen) they stopped, and on looking about saw little creatures, like small dogs with red caps, running away.

THE CUP OF LHIANNAN-SHEE

The estate of Ballafletcher, on which stands the Parish Church of Braddan, now called Kirby, was long in the possession of a family named Fletcher. Colonel Wilks, the late proprietor of this estate, had in his possession an antique crystal goblet, resembling those old-fashioned wine glasses still to be met with in the store of the curious housewife. This goblet was presented to him by an old lady, a connection of the family of Fletcher, the former proprietor of the estate. It is larger than a common bell-shaped tumbler, and is ornamented with carved

sprigs and white lines. It is supposed to have been dedicated to the *Lhiannan-Shee*, or "peaceful spirit" of Ballafletcher,
by the former owners of the estate, and to have been held in
great esteem, being only used once a year, at Christmas, when
the Lord of the Manor drank a bumper from it to the *Lhiannan-Shee* of his hearth and domain. To break this fragile
memorial would have been deemed a great misfortune to the
family, and displeasing to the spirit of peace. Colonel Wilks,
honouring and respecting the fancies of the olden times,
caused it to be encased in a strong oaken box, mounted with
silver; and, in all probability, the old lady donor was glad at
having got it safe out of her hands. — *Train.*

William Harrison, in his notes to Waldron, written about
twenty years later than Train's history, gives the following account
of this cup, which he calls "The Ballafletcher Drinking Glass":
This drinking cup, now in the possession of Major Bacon, of
Seafield House, upwards of two hundred years ago adorned the
beaufet of Ballafletcher House. It was purchased at the sale of
the effects of the last of the Fletchers, in 1778, by Robert Cæsar,
who gave it to his niece for safe keeping, in consequence of an
ancient tradition 'that whosoever had the misfortune to break
the glass would surely be haunted by the *Lhiannan-Shee* of Ballafletcher. The cup is a crystal cyathus engraved with floral scrolls,
having between the designs, on two sides, upright columellæ of
five pillars. . . . The following is the legend:—In ancient times
there stood in the parish of Braddan a mansion called Kirkby.
It was so named because it was the place of entertainment for
the Bishops of Sodor, in their progresses to and from the Isle.
Of this building nothing remains except its site, near an ancient
encampment, and the picturesque churchyard of Braddan with
its numerous runes and runic crosses. More than two centuries
ago, when Kirkby merged into the Fletcher family, its ancient
name was changed, and the place took the designation of the
new owner. To the first of this family was given the cup, with

the injunction "that as long as he preserved it peace and plenty would follow; but woe to him who broke it, as he would surely be haunted by the *Lhiannan-Shee.*" The glass stood in a recess, and was never taken from its place or used except on Christmas and Easter days. It was then filled with wine and quaffed off at a breath by the head of the house only, as a libation to the spirit for her protection. The cup belonged, it is said, to Magnus, the Norwegian King of Man, who took it from the shrine of St. Olave when he violated the saint's oratory."

THE FAIRY SWEETHEART

There was a man who lived not long ago near Port Erin who had a *Lhiannan-Shee*. "He was like other people, but he had a fairy sweetheart; but he noticed her, and they do not like being noticed, the fairies, and so he lost his mind. Well, he was quite quiet like other people, but at night he slept in the barn, and they used to hear him talking to his sweetheart, and scolding her sometimes; but if anyone made a noise he would be quiet at once." Now, the truth of this story is clear enough. The man went mad, but this madness took the form of the popular belief, and that again attributed his madness to the fairy mistress. I am convinced that this was believed to be a case of genuine fairy intercourse, and it shows that the fairy creed still survives in the Isle of Man. — *Campbell.*

THE DOOINEY-OIE

The *Dooiney-oie*, or night-man of the Manx peasantry, is reverenced as the tutelar demon of certain families, as it appeared only to give monitions of future events to particular persons. His voice was sometimes very dismal, when heard at night on the mountains, something like H-o-w-l-a-a, or H-o-w-a-a. When his lamentation in winter was heard on the coast, being a sure prediction of an approaching tempest, it was so awful that even the brute creation trembled at the sound. — *Train.*

Of late years there has been a disposition to confound the characteristics of the *Dooiney-oie* with those of the *Phynnodderee* and *Glashtin*, as he is supposed to do work, such as threshing corn, for those with whom he is connected.

CHAPTER IV

HOBGOBLINS, MONSTERS, GIANTS, MERMAIDS, APPARITIONS, &C.

THE DISTINCTION BETWEEN FAIRIES proper and Hob-goblins seems to be mainly that the former are nim-ble, merry, and clever, and the latter heavy, plodding, and stupid. The characteristics of the two creatures called, in the Isle of Man, the *Phynnodderee* and the *Glashtin*, or *Glashan*, are certainly of the lower, rather than of the high-er, class. For, as will be seen from the tales given concerning them, they combine the attributes of the Scotch Brownie, and of the Scandinavian Troll, though the *Glashtin* seems to be a water-horse also. (See p. 54.) The Brownies are sturdy Fair-ies, who, if well fed and kindly treated, will do a great deal of work; and the Trolls are beings who unite preterhuman strength with demoniac malice. They are bigger and stronger than men, with fiendish tempers, and are of deformed and hideous appearance. They dwell in rocks and caverns. In their intercourse with men they are usually cruel and mischievous, and take vengeance if they have been slighted or insulted. But sometimes they can be thankful and reward such kindnesses as they may have received from men, and even do them services of their own accord. Whoever is fortunate enough to do a Troll a service is sure to be lucky for the rest of his life. They know things man does not, such as the whereabouts of hidden treasure, though, generally speaking, they are stupid and devoid of reasoning powers. They hate Christianity and the sound of church bells, so much so, that any one pursued by a Troll can get rid of him by ringing the church bells. Trolls were probably once well known by name in Man, as they still survive in place-names such as Trollaby.

The *Phynnodderee* is defined by Cregeen[1] as a "satyr," and he quotes the following text to show that his name is used in the Manx Bible in that sense:—*Hig beishtyn oaldey yn aasagh dy cheilley marish beishtyn oaldey yn ellan, as nee yn phynnodderee gyllagh da e heshey:* "The wild beasts of the desert shall also meet with the wild beasts of the island, and the satyr shall cry to his fellow" (Isaiah 34, 14). The popular idea of the *Phynnodderee* is that he is a fallen Fairy, and that in appearance he is something between a man and a beast, being covered with black shaggy hair and having fiery eyes. Many stories are related by the Manx peasants of his prodigious strength. He may be compared with the *Gruagach*, a creature about whom Campbell writes as follows:—"The *Gruagach* was supposed to be a Druid or Magician who had fallen from his high estate, and had become a strange hairy creature." The following story is told about one of these:—"The small island of Inch, near Easdale, is inhabited by a brownie, which has followed the MacDougalls of Ardincaple for ages, and takes a great interest in them. He takes care of their cattle in that island night and day, unless the dairy-maid, when there in summer with the milk cattle, neglects to leave warm milk for him at night in a knocking-stone in the cave, where she and the herd live during their stay in the island. Should this perquisite be for a night forgot, they will be sure in the morning to find one of the

1 Manx Dictionary.

cattle fallen over the rocks with which the place abounds. It is a question whether the brownie has not a friend with whom he shares the contents of the stone, which will, I daresay, hold from two to three Scotch pints."

The following account is given of the *Phynnodderee* in prose and verse by Mrs E. S. Craven Green:—"Once upon a day, an Elfin Knight fell in love with one of the daughters of Mann, as she sat in her bowery home beneath the blue tree of Glen Aldyn. Offering to abandon the Fairies for a domestic life with this sweet nymph, and absenting himself from Fairy-Court during the celebration of the 'Rehollys vooar yn ouyr,' or royal high harvest festival (kept by the Fairies with dancing in the merry Glen Rushen), he so offended the little people that the Elfin King expelled him from Fairy Hall, and cursed him with an undying existence on the Manx mountains in the form of a satyr,—thus metamorphosed he became a strange, sad, solitary wanderer, known as the Phynnodderee. We compassionate his misfortune, as it fell upon him in consequence of his true love for a Manx maiden."

> "His was the wizard hand that toil'd,
>   At midnight's witching hour;
> That gather'd the sheep from the coming storm
>   Ere the shepherd saw it lower.
> Yet asked no fee save a scatter'd sheaf
>   From the peasants' garner'd hoard,
> Or cream-howl kissed by a virgin lip
>   To be left on the household hoard."

The *Glashtin* or *Glashan* is defined by Cregeen[1] as "a goblin, a sprite." The popular idea of him is that he is a hairy goblin or sprite of somewhat similar characteristics to the *Phynnodderee*. He is said to frequent lonely spots, and is useful to man, or otherwise, as the caprice of the moment leads him. In addition to the above, we have Monsters called *Tarroo-Ushtey*, or "water-bull," and *Cabbyl-Ushtey*, or "water horse," sometimes called the *Glashtin*. These would seem to be analogous

1 Manx Dictionary.

to the Irish *Phooka*, who is said to appear sometimes as a bull and sometimes as a horse, and to the Scandinavian *Nykr*, or *Vatna-Hestr*, "river-sprite" or "water horse." The *Vatna-Hestr* is supposed to live either in salt or fresh water, and to associate with ordinary cattle. In 1859 it was reported that an animal of this kind was to be seen in a field near Ballure Glen, and hundreds of people left Ramsey in order to catch a sight of it, but they were doomed to disappointment. The people about Glen Meay believed that the glen below the waterfall was haunted by the spirit of a man who one day met the *Glashtin*, or *Cabbyl-Ushtey*, and, thinking it was an ordinary horse, got upon its back, when it ran off and disappeared in the sea, and the rider was drowned.

Campbell says that in the Western Highlands and Islands, and the Isle of Man, there is a whole series of tales which relate to water-horses, and which show that people still firmly believe in their existence. He proceeds: "In Sutherland and elsewhere many believe that they have seen these fancied animals. I have been told of English sportsmen who went in pursuit of them, so circumstantial were the accounts of those who believed they had seen them. The witnesses are so numerous, and their testimony agrees so well that there must be some old deeply rooted Celtic belief which clothes every dark object with the dreaded form of the *each uisge*. . . . The bay or grey horse grazes at the lake-side, and when he is mounted, rushes into the loch and devours his rider. His back lengthens to suit any number; men's hands stick to his skin; he is harnessed to a plough, and drags the team and the plough into the loch, and tears the horses to bits; he is killed and nothing remains but a pool of water; he falls in love with a lady, and when he appears as a man and lays his head on her knee to be dressed, the frightened lady finds him out by the sand in his hair . . . and when he sleeps she makes her escape. He appears as an old woman, and is put to bed with a bevy of damsels in a mountain shealing, and he sucks the blood of all, save one, who escapes over a burn, which, water-horse as he is, he dare not cross. . . . These tales and beliefs have led me to think that the old Celts must have had a destroying water-god, to whom the horse was sacred, or who had the form of a horse." He also says that the water-bull is known all over the islands. "There are numerous lakes where the water-bulls are supposed to exist, and their progeny are supposed to be easily known by their short ears. When the water-bull appears in a story he is generally represented as friendly to man."

We have also Spirits or Fiends, who are for the most part of evil and malicious natures, such as the *Buggane*, the famous *Moddey Dhoo*, or black dog, the *Cughtagh*, who was a spirit whose abode was in caves by the sea, and whose voice was the soughing of the wavelets, and the *Keimagh* who haunted the church-yard stiles (*Keim*) and guarded the graves. *Giants*, who performed superhuman feats, abound, as in all Celtic lands. The *Mermaid*, too, was well-known. She had no special name in Manx, being called simply *Ben-varry*, or "Woman of the sea," and had the same form, half fish, half woman, as represented in the tales of other countries. She was generally of an affectionate and gentle disposition, though terrible when angered, and she was greatly given to falling in love with young men. Of her mate, the *Merman*, *Dooiney-varrey*, "Man of the sea," or *Phollinagh*, as he is variously called, less is known. Such are the names of the various dwellers in Fairy-land, most of whose characteristics will be illustrated by the following stories:—

HOBGOBLINS

THE PHYNNODDEREEE

A gentleman having resolved to build a large house and offices on his property, a little above the base of Snafield Mountain, at a place called Tholt-e-will, caused the requisite quantity of stones to be quarried on the beach, but one immense block of white stone, which he was very desirous to have for a particular part of the intended building, could not be moved from the spot, resisted the united strength of all the men in the parish. To the utter astonishment, however, of all, not only this rock, but likewise the whole of the quarried stones, consisting of more than an hundred cart-loads, were in one night conveyed from the shore to the site of the intended onstead by the indefatigable *Phynnodderee*, and, in confirmation of this wonderful feat, the white stone is yet pointed out to the curious visitor.

The gentleman for whom this very acceptable piece of work was performed, wishing to remunerate the naked *Phynnodderee*, caused a few articles of clothing to be laid down for him in his usual haunt. The hairy one, on perceiving the habiliments, lifted them up one by one, thus expressing his feelings in Manx:

> "Bayrn da'n chione, dy doogh da'n chione,
> Cooat da'n dreeym, dy doogh da'n dreeym,
> Breechyn dan toin, dy doogh da'n toin,
> Agh my she lhiat ooilley, shoh cha nee lhiat Glen reagh Rushen."

> "Cap for the head, alas! poor head,
> Coat for the back, alas! poor back,
> Breeches for the breech, alas! poor breech,
> If these be all thine, thine cannot he the merry Glen of Rushen."

Having repeated these words, he departed with a melancholy wail, and now

> "You may hear his voice on the desert hill
>   When the mountain winds have power;
> 'Tis a wild lament for his buried love,
>   And his long-lost Fairy Bower."

Many of the old people lament the disappearance of the *Phynnodderee*, for they say, "There has not been a merry world since he lost his ground."

The *Phynnodderee* also cut down and gathered meadow grass, which would have been injured if allowed to remain exposed to the coming storm. On one occasion a farmer having expressed his displeasure with the Phynnodderee for not having cut his grass close enough to the ground, the hairy one in the following year allowed the dissatisfied farmer to cut it down himself, but went after him stubbing up the roots so fast that it was with difficulty the farmer escaped having his legs cut off by the angry sprite. For several years afterwards no person could be found to mow the meadow, until a fearless soldier from one of the garrisons at length undertook the task. He commenced in the centre of the field, and by cutting round as if on the edge of a circle, keeping one eye on the progress of the *yiarn foldyragh*, or scythe, while the other

> Was turned round with prudent care
> Lest Phynnodderee catched him unaware.

He succeeded in finishing his task unmolested. This field, situate in the parish of Marown, hard by the ruins of the old Church of Saint Trinian's, is, from the circumstance just related, still called *yn lheéanee rhunt*, or the Round Meadow. — *Train*.

He is said to have borrowed a sickle and to have cut down two fields of corn in the parish of Bride in the course of one night. Among the many stories of his having brought sheep home for his farmer friends, there is an often told one of his having, on one occasion, brought home a hare among the rest, and of his having explained that the *loghtan beg*, or "little native-sheep" (*i.e.*, the hare) had given him more trouble than all the rest, as it made him run three times round Snaefell before he caught it. — *Oral*.

In the following curious old song the doings of the *Phynnodderee* are thus commemorated:—

> The Phynodderee went to the meadow
> To lift the dew at gray cock-crow,
> The maiden-hair and the cattle-herb,
> He stamped them under both his feet.
> He was stretching out on the ground of the meadow,
> He threw the grass on the left hand,
> He caused us to wonder last year,

And this year he is far better.
He was stretching out on the ground of the meadow,
Cutting the herbs in bloom,
The hog-bane herb in the rushy curragh,
As he went out it was all shaking.
The scythe he had was cutting everything,
Skinning the meadow to the sods,
And, if a leaf were left standing,
He stamped it down with his heels.

(The same in Manx.)

Yn Phynnodderree hie dy'n lheeanee,
Dy hroggal druight y vadran glass,
Luss-y-voidyn as luss-yn-ollee
V'eh dy stampey fo e ghaa chass.
V'eh sheeney magh er laare yn lheeanee,
Cheaayn faiyr er y cheu chiare,
Hug y yindys orrin nuirree,
As t'eh ny bleeaney foddey share.
V'eh sheeney magh er laare yn lheeanee,
Ghiarey yn lussey ayns y vlaa,
Lubber-lub ayns y curragh shuinagh,
Myr v'eh goll va ooilley craa.
Yn yiarn va echey y ghiarey ooilley,
Scryssey yn lheeanee rise y foaidyn,
As, my va rybbag faagit shassoo,
V'eh cur stampey lesh e voydyn

In the same song the vengeance of the water-bull and the *Glashtin* is invoked upon some person unknown:—

What if the spotted water-bull,
And the Glashtin take thee,
And the Phynnodderee of the glen, waddling
To throw thee like a bolster against the wall?

Cred dy jinnagh yn tarroo-ushtey spottagh,
As yn Ghlashtin oo y ghoaill,
As yn Phynnodderee ny glionney, sprangagh
Clooisagh y yannoo jeed noi'n voal.

As an instance of the strength of the Phynnodderee, it was stated he met a blacksmith one night as he was going from his shop, and on accosting him, and requesting to shake hands, the blacksmith gave him hold of the iron sock of a plough which he happened to have with him, and the strange visitor instantly squeezed it just as though it were a piece of clay.

THE GLASHTIN, OR GLASHAN

With regard to this creature, Campbell relates the following, which was told him by a woman who lived near the Calf of Man, who said:—

"Well, you see, in the ould times they used to be keeping the sheep in the folds, and one night an ould man forgot to put them in, and he sent out his son, and he came back and said the sheep were all folded, but there was a year-old lamb, *oasht*, playing the mischief with them, and that was the Glashan. You see they were very strong, and when they wanted a stack threshed, though it was a whole stack, the Glashan would have it threshed for them in one night. And they were running after the women. There was one of them once caught a girl, and had a hould of her by the dress, and he sat down and he fell asleep, and then she cut away all the dress, you see, round about, this way, and left it in his fist, and ran away; and when he awoke, he threw what he had over his shoulder, this way, and he said something in Manx. Well, you see, one night the ould fellow sent all the women to bed, and he put on a cap and a woman's dress, and he sat down by the fire, and he began to spin; and the young Glashans they came in, and they began saying something in Manx that means 'Are you turning the wheel? are you trying the reel?' Well the ould Glashan he was outside, and he knew better than the young ones; he knew it was the ould fellow himself, and he was telling them, but they did not mind him, and so the ould man threw a lot of hot turf, you see it was the turf they burned then, over them, and burned them; and the old one said (something in Manx). You'll not understand that now?" "Yes I do, pretty nearly." "Ah, well, and the Glashans went away, and never came back any more." "Have you many stories like that, guid wife?" "Ah!" said she, "there were plenty of people that could tell those stories once. When I was a little girl I used to hear them telling them in Manx over the fire at night; but people is so changed with pride now that they care for nothing."

In commenting on the *Glashan* story, he says "Now, here is a story which is all over the Highlands in various shapes. Sometimes it is a Brollichan, son of the Fuath, or a young water-horse transformed into the likeness of a man, which attacks a lonely woman and gets burned or scalded, and goes away to his friends outside. . . . The Glashan, as I found out afterwards, frequented neighbouring farms till within a very late period."

MONSTERS

THE WATER BULL; OR, TARROO-USHTEY

Among the prodigies of Nature, I know none which more justly may be called so, at least, of those which I am convinced of the truth of, than that of the Water Bull, an amphibious creature which takes its name from the so great resemblance it has of that beast, that many of the people, having seen him in a field, have not distinguished him from one of the more natural species. A neighbour of mine, who kept cattle, had his fields very much infested with this animal, by which he had lost several cows; he, therefore, placed a man continually to watch, who bringing him word that a strange bull was among the cows, he doubted not but it was the Water Bull; and having called a good number of lusty men to his assistance, who were all armed with great poles, pitch forks, and other weapons proper to defend themselves, and be the death of this dangerous enemy, they went to the place where they were told he was, and ran altogether at him; but he was too nimble for their pursuit; and after tiring them over mountains and rocks, and a great space of stony ground, he took a river, and avoided any further chase by diving down into it, though every now and then he would show his head above water, as if to mock their skill. —*Waldron*.

Another account of the *Tarroo-Ushtey* was obtained more than a hundred years later:—

A few years ago, the farmer of Slieu Mayll, in the Parish of Onchan, was, on a Sunday evening, returning home from a place of worship, when at the *garee* of Slegaby, a wild looking animal, with large eyes, sparkling like fire, crossed the road before him and went flapping away. This he knew to be a *Tarroo-Ushtey*, for his father had seen one at nearly the same place. Over the back of this animal he broke his walking stick—so lazy was it to get out of his way. This man's brother had also seen a *Tarroo-Ushtey*, at Lhanjaghyn, in the same neighbourhood. When proceeding to the field, very early one morning in the month of June, to let the cattle out to feed before the heat of the day came on, he saw a Water Bull standing outside the fold. When the bull that was within with the cattle, perceived him, he instantly broke through the fence and ran at him, roaring and tearing up the ground with his feet; but the *Tarroo-Ushtey* scampered away, seeming quite unconcerned, and leaping over an adjoining precipice, plunged into deep water, and after swimming about a little, evidently amusing himself, he gave a loud bellow and disappeared. — *Train*.

This monster was also to be met with, according to Macculloch's *Description of the Western Isles*, in Loch Awe and Loch Rannoch. Campbell, in his tales of the *West Highlands*, says, "There are numerous lakes where Water Bulls are supposed to exist, and their progeny are supposed to be easily known by their short ears. He is generally represented as friendly to man. His name in Skye is *tarbh eithre*."

THE BUGGANE OF ST. TRINIAN'S

Was the most notorious of these fiends in Man. The following story is told of him:—This religious edifice (St. Trinian's) is said to have been erected in fulfilment of a vow made by a person when in a hurricane at sea, but, according to tradition, it was never finished. This was through the malice of a mischievous *Buggane*, or evil spirit, who, for want of better employment, amused himself with tossing the roof to the ground, as often as it was on the eve of being finished, accompanying his achievement with a loud fiendish laugh of satisfaction. The only attempt to counteract this singular propensity of the evil one, which tradition has conveyed to us, was made by Timothy, a tailor of great pretentions to sanctity of character. On the occasion alluded to, the roof of St. Trinian's Church was, as usual, nearly finished, when the valorous tailor undertook to make a pair of breeches under it, before the Buggane could commence his old trick. He accordingly seated himself in the chancel, and began to work in great haste; but ere he had completed his job, the head of the frightful Buggane rose out of the ground before him, and addressed him thus — "Do you see my great head, large eyes, and long teeth?" "Hee! Hee!" that is, "Yes! yes!" replied the tailor, at the same time stitching with all his might, and without raising his eyes from his work. The Buggane, still rising slowly out of the ground, cried in a more angry voice than before, "Do you see my great body, large hands, and long nails?" "Hee! Hee!" rejoined Tim, as before, but continuing to *pull out* with all his strength. The Buggane having now risen wholly from the ground, inquired in a terrified voice, "Do you see my great limbs, large feet, and long ——?" but ere he could utter the last word, the tailor put the finishing stitch into the breeches, and jumped out of the Church, just as the roof fell in with a crash. The fiendish laugh of the Buggane arose behind him, as he bounded off in a flight, to which terror lent its utmost speed. Looking behind, he saw the frightful spectacle close upon his heels, with extended jaws, as if to swallow him alive. To escape its fury Timothy leaped into consecrated ground, where, happily, the Buggane had not power to follow; but, as if determined to punish him for his temerity, the angry sprite lifted its great head from its body, and with great force pitched it to the feet of the tailor, where it exploded like a bomb shell. Wonderful to relate, the adventurous Timothy was unscathed; but the Church of St. Trinian remained without a roof. — *Train*.

Another *Buggane* is said to haunt the precipitous mountain of *Slieauwhallian*, whence his screams are sometimes heard; but a third fiend, of similar origin, who was formerly supposed to frequent the *Gob-ny-scuit*, "mouth of the spout," a small waterfall, in the Parish of Maughold, has disappeared. Terrible wailings were heard at times from this unfortunate spirit. Even the great fairy doctor of Ballawhane (Teare) had failed to lay it. But about 50 years ago a Manxman of a scientific and inquiring mind noticed on examining the rock, over which the water fell, that these peculiar noises proceeded from it only when the wind was blowing from a certain point. Further examination showed a narrow cleft in the rock below the fall through which the wind blew and caused the sound. Thus was the *Buggane* disposed of! — *Oral*.

LEGEND OF THE BLACK DOG, MODDEY DOO

Whence! and what art thou? — MILTON

Through one of the old churches in Peel Castle, there was formerly a passage to the apartment belonging to the Captain of the Guard, but it is now closed up. An apparition, called in the Manx language, "The Mauthe Doo," in the shape of a large black spaniel with curled shaggy hair, was used to haunt Peel Castle; and has been frequently seen in every room, but particularly in the Guard Chamber, where, as soon as candles were lighted, it came and lay down before the fire in the presence of all the soldiers, who at length, by being so much accustomed to the sight of it, lost great part of the terror they were seized with at its first appearance. They still, however, retained a certain

awe, as believing it was an evil spirit, which only waited permission to do them hurt, and for that reason forbore swearing
and all profane discourse while in its company. But though
they endured the shock of such a guest when altogether in a
body, none cared to be left alone with it. It being the custom,
therefore, for one of the soldiers to lock the gates of the Castle
at a certain hour, and carry the keys to the Captain, to whose
apartment, as I said before, the way led through a church, they
agreed among themselves, that whoever was to succeed the ensuing night, his fellow in this errand should accompany him
that went first, and, by this means, no man would be exposed
singly to the danger; for I forgot to mention that the *Mauthe
Doo* was always seen to come from that passage at the close of
day, and return to it again as soon as the morning dawned,
which made them look on this place as its peculiar residence.
One night, a fellow being drunk, and by the strength of his
liquor rendered more daring than ordinary, laughed at the simplicity of his companions, and, although it was not his turn
to go with the keys, would needs take this office upon himself
to testify his courage. All the soldiers endeavoured to dissuade
him, but the more they said, the more resolute he seemed, and
swore that he desired nothing more than that *Mauthe Doo*
would follow him, as it had done the others, for he would try
if it were Dog or Devil. After having talked in a very reprobate
manner for some time, he snatched up the keys and went out
of the Guard-room. In some time after his departure, a great
noise was heard, and no one had the boldness to see what had
occasioned it, till the adventurer returning, they demanded the
knowledge of him; but as loud and noisy as he had been at
leaving them, he was now become sober and silent enough,
for he was never heard to speak more; and though all the time
he lived, which was three days, he was entreated by all who
came near him, either to speak, or if he could not do that, to
make some signs, by which they might understand what had

happened to him, yet nothing intelligible could be got from him, only that, by the distortion of his limbs and features, it might be guessed that he died in agonies more than is common in a natural death. The *Mauthe Doo* was, however, never seen after in the Castle, nor would anyone attempt to go through that passage, for which reason it was closed up, and another way made. — This happened about 1666. — *Waldron*.

"Phantom dogs," says Campbell, "abound in Celtic stories." In many of them the hound or dog plays an important part. "Sometimes he befriends his master, at other times he appears to have something diabolical about him; it seems as if his real honest nature had overcome a deeply-rooted prejudice, for there is much which savours of detestation, as well as of strong affection. Dog, or son of the dog, is a term of abuse in Gaelic as elsewhere, though *cuilein* is a form of endearment, and the hound is figured beside his master or at his feet, on many a tombstone in the Western Isles. Hounds are mentioned in Gaelic poetry and Gaelic tales, and in the earliest accounts of the Western Isles."

GIANTS

THE SPELL-BOUND GIANT

These is an apartment in Castle Rushen "which has never been opened in the memory of man." The persons belonging to the Castle are very cautious in giving any reason for it; but the natives assign this, "*that there is something of enchantment in it.*" They tell you that the Castle was at first inhabited by fairies, and afterwards by giants, who continued in possession of it till the days of Merlin, who, by force of magic, dislodged the greatest part of them, and bound the rest in spells, which they believe will be indissoluble to the end of the world. For proof of this, they tell you a very odd story. They say there are a great number of fine apartments underground, exceeding in magnificence any of the upper rooms. Several men of more than ordinary courage have, in former times, ventured down to explore the secrets of this subterraneous dwelling-place, but none of them ever returned to give an account of what they saw; it was, therefore, judged convenient that all the passes to it should be kept continually shut, that no more might suffer by their temerity.

About some fifty or fifty-five years since (1670), a person who had an uncommon boldness and resolution, never left soliciting permission of those who had the power to grant it, to visit these dark abodes. In fine, he obtained his request, went down, and returned by help of a clue of packthread, which he took with him, which no man before himself had ever done, and brought this amazing discovery. That, after having passed through a great number of vaults, he came into a long narrow place, which the further he penetrated, he perceived he went more and more on a descent, till having travelled, as near as he could guess, for the space of a mile, he began to see a little gleam of light, which, though it seemed to come from a vast distance, yet was the most delightful sight he had ever beheld in his life. Having at length come to the end of that lane of darkness, he perceived a very large and magnificent house, illuminated with a great many candles, whence proceeded the light just now mentioned. Having, before he began this expedition, well fortified himself with brandy, he had courage enough to knock at the door, which a servant, at the third knock, having opened, asked him what he wanted. "I would go as far as I can," replied our adventurer, "be so kind, therefore, to direct me how to accomplish my design, for I see no passage but that dark cavern through which I came." The servant told him he must go through that house, and accordingly led him through a long entry, and out at the back door. He then walked a considerable way, and at last he beheld another house, more magnificent than the first, and the windows being all open, discovered innumerable lamps burning in every room. Here he designed also to knock, but had the curiosity to step on a little bank which commanded a low parlour; on looking in, he beheld a vast table in the middle of the room of black marble, and on it, extended at full length, a man, or rather, monster; for, by his account, he could not be less than fourteen feet long, and ten or eleven round the body. This prodigious fabrick lay as if sleeping, with his head on a book, and a sword by him, of a size answerable to the hand which it is supposed made use of it. This sight was more terrifying to the traveller than all the dark and dreary mansions he had passed through in his arrival to it. He resolved, therefore, not to attempt entrance into a place inhabited by persons of that unequal stature, and made the best of his way back to the other house, where the same servant re-conducted him, and informed him that if he had knocked at the second door, he would have seen company enough, but never could have returned, on which he desired to know what place it was, and by whom possessed; but the other replied that these things were not to be revealed. He then took his leave, and by the same dark passage got into the vaults, and soon after once more ascended to the light of the sun. — *Waldron*.

THE OLD MAN

Castle Rushen has long been famous in the estimation of the natives for its subterraneous passages, and there are individuals amongst them who still believe that they lead to a beautiful country underground, inhabited by giants. Many attempts, they say, have been made to explore these passages, but they have been generally unsuccessful. Once, however, a number banded themselves together, and, having armed themselves and provided torches, they descended. After proceeding some way, they came across an old man of great size, with a long beard, and blind, sitting on a rock as if fixed there. He, hearing them approach, inquired of them as to the state of the Island, and at last asked one to put forth his hand, on which one of them presented him with a ploughshare, when the old giant squeezed the iron together with the greatest ease, exclaiming at the same time, "There are yet men in the Isle of Man."— *W. Harrison.*

THE THREE-HEADED GIANT

Once upon a time there landed at The Lhane a number of Danes, who took possession of that part of the Island. Amongst them was a huge monster of a man with three heads, who officiated as their parson, and who was promptly appointed by them to the Rectory of Andreas, which chanced to be vacant at that time. He soon began to extort all he could from the people, making his bands for the tithe corn three times larger than was customary, and taking the "double penny" for every thing. For a long time he went on in this fashion, till they got used to it, and, consequently, did not grumble so much as at first. Indeed, they rather began to like him, as he often gave them a hand at busy times, when the men were for the most part away at the fishing, and was always ready to do them a good turn. So things went on till his death, when, in accordance with his wish, he was carried to the top of Karrin, and buried there under a big cairn. A long time after this, a man who had heard about this three-headed creature from the old people, and who was consumed with a desire to see him, began to open his grave. He had not dug very far, however, when he was seized with a great pain in his back, which compelled him to leave off. He managed to get home, but in three days he was dead. Since then no one has ventured to disturb the giant's remains. They say that since the days of the giant the parson of Andreas has always had three times more pay than the rest. — *Oral.*

JACK THE GIANT KILLER

The title at least of the following is clearly derived from the well known English tale: There was once a poor woman who lived in a secluded glen on the eastern side of Slieau-ny-Farrane. Her husband was a fisherman, who was frequently absent from home for long periods. The wife had, consequently, not only to attend to domestic matters, but to see after the children as well, so you may be sure the boys were left to do much as they pleased. The eldest of them, Juan, was growing into a stout lad, who was always trying to do some great feat or other. Many were the battles that he and the old gander had, to see who should be the master. As he grew bigger he extended his attacks to the cattle, so that when they saw him coming they endeavoured to get out of the way of the big stick he always carried with him. In vain did his father scold him, when he came home from the fishing on a Saturday night, for he only became the more daring. At last he began to use his stick or all, whether man or beast, that he met in those parts, and he became such a terror that they gave him the name of Jack the Giant Killer. His great strength became so notorious that many came from Laxey side to try conclusions with him, but they were always worsted. He kept his old mother well supplied with *purrs*, as they called the wild swine that were formerly found in the mountains. Now, there was an old boar *purr*, called the *Purr Mooar*, that had long been a terror to the district, so much so that it was not considered safe for any one to go alone over the Rheast, and through Druidale. Even the shepherds with their dogs were unwilling to face him. This *purr* Jack determined to kill, so he armed himself with his thickest stick, and set out in search of him. After travelling a considerable distance, he made his way down to a deep glen, through which the water was tumbling amongst the rocks below the Crammag, where he discovered the boar, it being a sultry day, luxuriating in the water. No sooner did he see Jack than he raised himself up, and, with a terrible roar, rushed out upon him. Jack, nothing daunted, received him with a severe blow upon the fore legs, which caused him to roll over. Getting up again, he rushed once more at Jack, who belaboured him with many a heavy blow, but unfortunately the boar managed to inflict a deep wound in Jack's thigh, which laid it open to the bone. Still the conflict went on till both were well-nigh exhausted and faint from loss of blood, till at last Jack with one terrible blow shattered the boar's head, and laid him dead at his feet. It was with great difficulty that he managed to crawl home, and it was long before his wounds, which were said to be of a poisonous nature, healed, and, even when they had healed, he was obliged to go about with a crutch for the rest of his life. Thus was the neighbourhood rid of two troubles—Jack and the *Purr Mooar*—for the one was now harmless and the other dead. This feat was commemorated in the saying, "Jack the Giant Killer, *varr a vuc* (*i.e.*, killed a pig) in the river."— *Oral.*

There are many other tales about giants, the accuracy of which is proved to the satisfaction of the tellers by the existence of large stones, which are pointed out in various places as having been hurled by them. There is one in particular, near Jurby Church, which is said to have been thrown by a giant from one of the mountains after a companion who had insulted him, but who contrived to escape by swimming from Jurby to Scotland. The numerous detached rocks at the southern end of Greeba are satisfactorily accounted for as being the contents of a creel which a giant had upset there. There was another giant, said to have been contemporary with St. Patrick, who by his strength and ferocity became the terror of the whole Island. He used to transport himself with great ease across the gorge between Peel Castle and Contrary Head, which is now bridged by a breakwater. On one occasion, either for amusement or in a fit of rage, he lifted a large block of granite from the Castle rock, and, though several tons weight, tossed it with the greatest ease against the acclivity of the opposite hill, about half a mile distant, where it is to be seen to this day, with a print of his hand on it. In support of such legends as these the Manx peasantry formerly showed strangers the giant's casting stones, which are two huge monoliths of clay-slate, each ten feet high, between Port St. Mary and Port Erin; the Fairy Hill; the giant's grave at the foot of South Barrule; and a green mound, thirty yards long, outside the walls of Peel Castle, having the same name.

MERMAIDS

THE CAPTURED MERMAID

A mermaid from the water rose,
A woman most fair and lovely. — SINCLAIR

Waldron was surprised to find that the Manx actually believed in mermaids, and he gave several stories that they told him about them, as follows:—"During the time that Oliver Cromwell usurped the Government of England, few ships resorted to this Island, and that uninterruption and solitude of the sea gave the mermen and mermaids (who are enemies to any company but those of their own species) frequent opportunities of visiting the shore, where, in moonlight nights, they have been seen to sit, combing their heads and playing with each other; but as soon as they perceived anybody coming near them, jumped into the water, and were out of sight immediately. Some people, who lived near the coast, having observed their behaviour, spread large nets made of small but very strong cords upon the ground, and watched at a convenient distance for their approach. The night they had laid this snare but one happened to come, who was no sooner sat down than those who held the strings of the net drew them with a sudden jerk, and enclosed their prize beyond all possibility of escaping. On opening the net, and examining their captive, by the largeness of her breasts and the beauty of her complexion, it was found to be a female. Nothing could be more lovely, more exactly formed in all parts above the waist, resembling a complete young woman, but below that all fish with fins and a huge spreading tail. She was carried to a house, and used very tenderly, nothing but liberty being denied. But though they set before her the best provision the place afforded, she would not be prevailed on to eat or drink, neither could they get a word from her, tho' they knew these creatures were not without the gift of speech, having heard them talk to each other, when sitting regaling themselves on the seaside. They kept her in this manner three days, but perceiving she began to look very ill with fasting, and fearing some calamity would befall the Island if they should keep her till she died, they agreed to let her return to the element she liked best, and the third night set open their door, which, as soon as she beheld, she raised herself from the place where she was then lying, and glided, with incredible swiftness, on her tail to the seaside. They followed at a distance, and saw her plunge into the water, where she was met by a great number of her own species, one of whom asked what she had observed among the people of the earth, — "Nothing very wonderful," answered she, "but that they are so very ignorant as to throw away the water they have boiled eggs in."

THE MERMAID'S COURTSHIP

Come to our rich and starry caves,
Our home amid the ocean waves;
ur coral caves are walled around
With richest gems in ocean found,
And crystal mirrors, clear and bright,
Reflecting all in magic light.

A very beautiful mermaid became so much enamoured of a young man who used to tend his sheep upon the rocks, that she would frequently sit down by him, bring him pieces of coral, fine pearls, and what were yet greater curiosities, and of infinitely more value, had they fallen into the hands of a person who knew their worth, shells of various forms and figures, and so glorious in their colour and shine, that they even dazzled the eye that looked upon them. Her presents were accompanied with smiles, pattings of the cheek, and all the marks of a most sincere and tender passion. One day throwing her arms more than ordinarily eagerly about him, he began to be frightened that she had a design to draw him into the sea, and struggled till he disengaged himself, and then ran a good many paces from her; which behaviour she resented so highly, it seems, that she took up a stone, and after throwing it at him, glided into her more proper element, and was never seen on land again. But the poor youth, though but slightly hit with the stone, felt from that moment so excessive a pain in his bowels, that the cry was never out of his mouth for seven days, at the end of which he died. — *Waldron*.

THE MERMAID'S REVENGE

There is a tradition that a mermaid becoming enamoured of a young man of extraordinary beauty, took an opportunity of meeting him one day as he walked on the shore, and opened her passion to him, but was received with coldness occasioned by his horror and surprise at her appearance. This, however, was so misconstrued by the sea lady, that, in revenge for his treatment of her, she punished the whole Island, by covering it with mist; so that all who attempted to carry on any commerce with it, either never arrived at it, but wandered up and down the sea, or were on a sudden wrecked upon its cliffs, till the incantatory spell or *pishag*, as the Manks say, was broken by the fishermen stranded there, by whom notice was given to the people of their country, who sent ships in order to make a further discovery. On their landing, they had a fierce encounter with the little people, and having got the better of them, possessed themselves of Castle Rushen, and by degrees of the whole Island. — (*Collins* in a note to his "Ode to Liberty.")

Of the dwellings of these creatures under the sea, and of the treasure they have accumulated there, many tales are told. The notion of a land under the waves is very widely spread, and common to many nations. Manxmen formerly asserted that a splendid city, with many towers and gilded minarets, once stood near Langness, on a spot now covered by the sea, which, in peculiar states of the atmosphere, might have been occasionally seen in all its former magnificence.

Waldron gives the following marvellous account of dwellings under the sea, stocked with treasure, which he was assured had been attested by a whole ship's crew, and happened in the memory of some then living, but at which, nevertheless, "he was exceedingly surprised":—

DWELLINGS UNDER THE SEA

There was, about some forty or fifty years since (1676), a project set on foot for searching for treasures in the sea. Vessels were got ready, and machines made of glass, and cased with a thick, tough leather, to let the person down who was to dive for the wealth. One of these ships happening to sail near to the Isle of Man, and having heard that great persons had formerly taken refuge there, imagined there could not be a more likely part of the ocean to afford the gain they were in search of, than this. They, therefore, let down the machine, and in it the person who had undertaken to go on this expedition; they let him down by a vast length of rope, but he still plucking it, which was the sign for those above to increase the quantity, they continued to do so, till they knew he must be descended an infinite number of fathoms. In fine, he gave the signal so long, that at last they found themselves out of cord, their whole stock being too little for his capacious inquisition. A very skilful mathematician being on board, said that he knew by the proportion of the line which was let down, he must have descended from the surface of the waters more than twice the number of leagues that the moon is computed to be distant from the earth. But having, as I said, no more cord, they were obliged to turn the wheel, which, by degrees, brought him up again; at their opening the machine, and taking him out, he appeared very much troubled, that his journey had so soon been stopped, at a period, telling them, that could he have gone a little further he should have brought discoveries well worth the search. It is not to be supposed but everybody was impatient to be informed of what kind they were, and being all gathered about him on the main deck, as soon as he had recruited himself with a hearty swill of brandy, he began to relate in this manner:—

After I had passed the region of fishes, I descended into a pure element-clear as the air in the serenest and most unclouded day, through which, as I passed, I saw the bottom of the watery world, paved with coral and a shining kind of pebbles, which glittered like the sunbeams reflected on a glass. I longed to tread the delightful paths, and never felt more exquisite delight, than when the machine I was enclosed in grazed upon it. On looking through the little windows of my prison, I saw large streets and squares on every side, ornamented with huge pyramids of crystal, not inferior in brightness to the finest diamonds; and the most beautiful buildings—not of stone, nor brick, but of mother of pearl, and embossed in various figures with shells of all colours. The passage which led to one of these magnificent apartments being open, I endeavoured with my whole strength to move my enclosure towards it, which I did, though with great difficulty, and very slowly. At last, however, I got entrance into a very spacious room, in the midst of which stood a large amber table, with several chairs round the same. The floor of it was composed of rough diamonds, topazes, emeralds, rubies, and pearls. Here I doubted not but to make my voyage as profitable as it was pleasant, for could I have brought with me but a few of these, they would have been of more value than all we could hope for in a thousand wrecks; but they were so closely wedged in, and so strongly cemented by time, that they were not to be unfastened. I saw several chains, carcanets, and rings, of all manner of precious stones, finely cut, and set after our manner, which, I suppose, had been the prize of the winds and waves. These were hanging loosely on the jasper walls, by strings made of rushes, which I might easily have taken down; but as I had edged myself within half a foot of them, I was unfortunately drawn back, through your want of line. In my return I met several comely mermen and beautiful mermaids, the inhabitants of this blissful realm, swiftly descending towards it, but they seemed frighted at my appearance, and glided at a distance from me, taking me, no doubt, for some monstrous and new created species.

Here he ended his account, but grew so melancholy, and so much enamoured of those regions he had visited, that he quite lost all relish for earthly pleasures, till continual pinings deprived him of his life; having no hope of ever descending there again, all design of prosecuting the diving project being soon after laid aside.

APPARITIONS

Stories of Apparitions and Spirits are common, as would naturally be expected, among such a imaginative people as the Manx. The following will suffice as specimens:—

THE APPARITION OF CASTLE RUSHEN

Be thou a spirit of health, or goblin damn'd! — SHAKESPEARE

A mighty bustle they make of an apparition which, they say, haunts Castle Rushen, in the form of a woman, who was some years ago executed for the murder of her child. I have heard, not only persons who have been confined there for debt, but also the soldiers of the garrison, affirm they have seen it various times; but what I took most notice of, was the report of a gentleman, of whose good understanding, as well as veracity, I have a very great opinion. He told me, that happening to be abroad late one night, and caught in an excessive

storm of wind and rain, he saw a woman stand before the
Castle Gate, where being not the least shelter, it something
surprised him, that any body, much less one of that sex, should
not rather run to some little porch, or shed, of which there are
several in Castletown, than choose to stand still exposed and
alone, in such a dreadful tempest. His curiosity exciting him
to draw nearer, that he might discover who it was that seemed
so little to regard the fury of the elements, he perceived she
retreated on his approach, and at last, he thought, went into
the Castle, though the gates were shut; this obliging him to
think he had seen a spirit, sent him home very much terrified;
but the next day, relating his adventure to some people who
lived in the Castle, and describing as near as he could the garb
and stature of the apparition, they told him it was that of the
woman above mentioned, who had been frequently seen, by
the soldiers on guard, to pass in and out of the gates, as well
as to walk through the rooms, though there was no visible
means to enter. Though so familiar, to the eye, no person has
yet, however, had the courage to speak to it, and as they say, a
spirit has no power to reveal its mind without being conjured
to do so in a proper manner, the reason of its being permitted
to wander is unknown. — *Waldron.*

A STRANGE APPARITION

A clergyman, accustomed to pass some hours every evening in a field near his house, indulging in meditation and
calling himself to an account for the transactions of the past
day, was in this place one night, more than ordinarily wrapt in
contemplation, he wandered, without thinking where he was,
a considerable distance farther than it was usual for him to
do; and, as he told me, he knew not how far the deep musing
he was in might have carried him, if it had not suddenly been
interrupted by a noise, which, at first, he took to be the distant
bellowing of a bull, but, as he listened more heedfully to it,

found there was something more terrible in the sound than could proceed from that creature. He confessed to me that he was no less affrighted than surprised, especially when the noise coming still nearer, he imagined whatever it was that it proceeded from, it must pass him; he had, however, presence enough of mind, to place himself with his back to a hedge, where he fell on his knees, and began to pray to God, with all the vehemence so dreadful an occasion required. He had not been long in that position, before he beheld something in the form of a bull, but infinitely larger than ever he had seen in England, much less in Man, where the cattle are very small in general. The eyes, he said, seemed to shoot forth flames, and the running of it was with such force, that the ground shook under it, as in an earthquake. It made directly towards a little cottage, and there, after most horribly roaring, disappeared. The moon being then at the full, and shining in her utmost splendour, all these passages were perfectly visible to our amazed divine, who having finished his ejaculation, and given thanks to God for his preservation, went to the cottage, the owner of which, they told him, was that moment dead. The good old gentleman was loth to pass a censure which might be judged an uncharitable one; but the deceased having the character of a very ill liver, most people, who heard the story, were apt to imagine this terrible apparition came to attend his last moments. — *Waldron.*

BEN VEG CARRAGHAN
(THE LITTE WOMAN OF CARRAGHAN.)

Once upon a time there was a poor woman of very diminutive stature, who lived in the neighbourhood of Maughold Head. She earned her livelihood with her spinning wheel, "going upon the houses" to work with it. From her cheerful disposition and readiness to do a good turn at all times, she was always welcome. She received in payment her board and lodgings, and the "bit of pence." In this way she travelled and lived for a considerable length of time, and it became notorious that she had made "a purse." Whether it was on this account or not that she was made away with, has never to this day been known; but certain it is she has been many times seen sitting on the side of Carraghan mountain with her wheel on her shoulder, and putting her head on her arm as if in great trouble. Well it is for those who have occasion to pass over this mountain that they do not come upon the apparition of this poor woman, for fear some dire calamity might befall them. A few years ago a person was returning to his home in the West Baldwin valley, about two o'clock in the afternoon, when he saw "the little woman" sitting on her favourite spot. As soon as he came in sight she rose and endeavoured to go away, but he, being determined to solve the mystery, started in pursuit with his dogs, and sent three other persons, one on each side, and one to the top of the mountain. The little woman, being thus surrounded, made many ineffectual attempts to escape, and at last came close to one of the men and the dogs. The latter could not be persuaded to touch her, but seemed in great trouble and shed tears. It had previously been noticed that, on reaching a small *gill*, she immediately vanished: and now, on reaching that spot, she disappeared, and has never been seen since. A man on the Northside afterwards affirmed that, on the same day, he had observed her hastening over North Barrule, in the direction of Maughold Head. The man who had been with the dogs and close to the woman, at once fell ill, and was not able to do any work for more than six months afterwards. — *Jenkinson*.

A LEGEND OF THE SOUND

Not far from the Sound there is a sea cave, into which one may penetrate by boat when the weather is fine. It is called *Ghaw kione doo*, "Black Head Creek." It is remarkable from a weird story being attached to it, and also from the fact (?) of an inscription of some sort being sculptured above its entrance. My informant could not point out this inscription, but said he "had heard it was somewhere about." "Once upon a time" the cave was used by a pirate as a store-place for the spoils taken in his expeditions. When he last sailed away on an expedition, from which he never returned, he left one of his crew in charge of the cave and of the treasure therein. Whether he and his crew were overwhelmed by a storm, or were suspended from a gallows, the chronicler knew not; but he proceeded to relate that, after many years of waiting, the lonely guardian of the treasure cave disappeared also. "No doubt," continued my informant, "having been taken sick in the cave he died there." At any rate he was never seen again. "An old fisherman told me," said he, "that once while he was engaged in 'laying a bolk,' close to the cave, he was surprised to see a boat, manned by six sailors in red caps, come towards land, and rowing to the mouth of the cave disappear therein. Curious to know who they were and from whence they came, he followed them into the cave, which has only one entrance, but found it quite empty."— *F. Swinnerton.*

THE CHASMS

A respectable landholder and his servant, in the neighbourhood of Spanish Head, were one day gathering their sheep, somewhere about forty years ago, when one of the best of them, to escape from a dog by which it was pursued, bounded into the mouth of that dark pit, he said, at the brink of which you were so lately standing with listless temerity. Being then young, and not easily daunted, I determined to descend for the purpose of recovering my *loughtyn* pet, notwithstanding the most urgent remonstrance on the part of my father, who was aware of many strange incidents that happened there to former adventurers. I caused myself to be let down, however, into the dark aperture in a basket attached to a rope, and every rope in the village was knotted, one to the end of another, and all used in lowering me into the pit, but just as I reached the bottom of it, I was mortified to hear the last bleat of my poor sheep, evidently struggling under the knife of the butcher. As I advanced through a spacious cavern, to a place whence the sound proceeded, I distinctly heard, in a neighbouring apartment, human voices in quick conversation, which, with the rattling of knives and forks, the drawing of corks, the decanting of liquor, and the uproarious noise which followed, tended to convince me that I was proceeding towards a company of bacchanalians, for whose gratification my poor sheep had probably been despatched. Lest, therefore, I should share the same fate, I made with all possible speed for the mouth of the cavern; but just as I had set my foot on the sward, as many angry sounds issued from the pit as if a pack of harriers had been uncoupled at my heels. My descent and retreat had evidently been discovered by the gentry below, but not till, thanks to Providence, I was out of their reach. — *Train.*

THE SPIRIT "HOA HOA"

The disturbed spirit of a person shipwrecked on a rock adjacent to this coast, wanders about it still, and sometimes makes so terrible a yelling, that it is heard at an incredible distance. They tell you that houses even shake with it; and that, not only mankind, but all the brute creation within hearing, tremble at the sound. But what serves very much to increase the shock is, that whenever it makes this extraordinary noise, it is a sure prediction of an approaching storm; nor does it ever happen, say they, but some ship or other splits, and its crew thrown up by the waves. At other times, the spirit cries out only, "Hoa! hoa! hoa!" with a voice little, if anything, louder than a human one. — *Waldron*

CHAPTER V

MAGIC, WITCHCRAFT, &C.

I T WOULD SEEM THAT THE INHABITANTS OF MAN and the other Western Isles of Scotland had acquired a reputation for magical powers at an early period. For the bard, who accompanied Hakon, king of Norway, in his expedition to these parts in 1203, wrote as follows:—"Now our deep inquiring sovereign encountered the horrid powers of enchantment and the abominations of an impious race. The troubled flood tore many fair gallies from their moorings, and swept them anchor less before the waves. A magic raised watery tempest blew upon our warriors, ambitious of conquest, and against the floating habitations of the brave."[1] Two centuries later, we are told by Ranulph Higden that "In the Ilonde of Mann is sortilege and witchcraft used; for women there sell to shipmen wynde as it were closed under three knottes of threde, so that the more wynde he would have the more knottes he must undo."[2] According to Sacheverell, Martholine, who was Governor of the Isle of Man in

1 Poem of Snorro Sturlson (Johnstone's Translation).
2 Polychronicon, A.D. 1487. Rolls Series.

1338, wrote a treatise against the practice of witchcraft then prevalent there.

A profound belief in the power of Magic was one of the charactistics of Goidelic peoples, though indeed it was formerly all but universal. Their paganism was a kind of fetichism which considered the various objects of nature, especially the sun, as malignant beings, who had to be propitiated with offerings to avert their wrath. In connection with this worship, a class of persons arose called *Druadh*, who stood between the people and their deities, and acquired great power over the former by the influence they were supposed to be able to exert over the latter by their sacrifices and magic arts. St. Patrick, who is supposed to have driven the *Druadh* from Ireland, prays in a very old hymn attributed to him, to be protected:—

> "Against snares of demons,
> Against black laws of heathens,
> Against spells of women, smiths, and *Druads*."

These Goidelic *Druadh*[1] probably belonged to the same system as the Gaulish Druids at a very remote period; but, by Julius Cæsar's time, the latter had picked up a little Greek philosophy, and were probably comparatively well educated and superior men; while the *Druadh* in Britain, and more especially in Ireland and Man, being isolated from Continental influences, had shrunk into mere Magicians and Medicine-men. It was formerly supposed that they sacrificed to *Baal* on the cromlechs within the stone circles, but more recent research has shown that these mighty stone monuments are the memorials of a pre-historic race, and that the Goidels, who, before the introduction of Christianity, worshipped the heavenly bodies, hills, fire, wells, &c., had no knowledge of the Phoenician *Baal*, or, indeed, of a personal God of any kind. With

---

1 The genitive of this word, *droata*, has been deciphered by Professor Rhs in the Ogam character on a stone at Ballaqueeney, near Port St. Mary.

the introduction of Christianity these *Druadh* disappeared, but the beliefs they had inculcated survived in other forms, as it was believed that all the powers of evil were concentrated in the devil and his myrmidons, that he could delegate his powers to human beings who sold their souls to him, and who, according to the nature of their functions or their sex, were called Magicians, Enchanters or Enchantresses, Sorcerers or Sorceresses, Wizards or Witches. By their spells, or charms, they could bring all kinds of evil on human beings, but by counter-charms they could also alleviate those evils. The Magicians, Enchanters, and Enchantresses belonged to the higher order of these beings. They had spirits or demons at their command, and were proficient in the occult sciences, but would not condescend to the petty malignity occasionally practised by the Sorcerers and Sorceresses, the Wizards and the Witches. The only Magician who is remembered by name in the Isle of Man is the famous *Manannan* (see Chapter I.) There is also the Enchantress *Tehi*, and the Sorceress, or rather Prophetess, called *Caillagh-ny-Ghueshag*, a sort of Manx Mother Shipton, who appears to have been superior to most of her kind. To the lower and much more common order of these beings belong those who practised witchcraft, which may be defined to be a supernatural power which persons were formerly supposed to obtain by entering into compact with the devil. As soon as the bargain was concluded, the devil was said to deliver to the Wizard or Witch an imp or familiar spirit, to be ready at call to do whatever it was directed. By the aid of this imp and the devil together, the Witch—who was almost always an old woman, the Wizard being comparatively uncommon— was enabled to transport herself through the air on a broomstick, and transform herself into various shapes, particularly those of cats and hares; to inflict diseases on whomsoever she chose, and to punish her enemies in various ways. The belief in witchcraft is very ancient, being common in Europe till the sixteenth century, and it maintained its ground till the middle of the seventeenth century; indeed it is not altogether extinct either in the Isle of Man, or elsewhere, at the present day. A special attribute of Sorcerers and Witches was the possession of the "Evil Eye." This was supposed to be an influence in virtue of which its possessor could injure whomsoever he or she cast a hostile or envious eye upon, and to be the cause of many things going wrong. For instance, if anyone took suddenly ill, if a cow was diseased, or any difficulty occurred in churning, if the hens did not lay well, &c., the operation of the "Evil Eye" was at once suspected. Before curing any of these complaints, it was first necessary to discover the operator. One of the most approved methods of doing this, in the case of a diseased animal, is to burn it; when, as Train remarks, "The first person that passes that way after the fire is kindled, is recognised as the witch or wizard." Fire, indeed, was considered generally efficacious against Witches and their wiles, and was used at special seasons, as we shall see later (Chapter VI.), when they were supposed to be more powerful than usual. When the possessor of the "Evil Eye" was discovered, the next step was to cure the disease, and this was frequently effected by picking up the dust from beneath the feet or from the threshold of the suspected Witch, and rubbing it on her victim.

But there were cases in which the popular and well-known methods failed, when recourse was had to the practitioners called "Charmers," or "Witch-doctors." These Charmers— *Fer-obbee*, "Men-charmers," and *Ben-obbee*, "Women-charmers," as they might be either men or women—used certain formulas and practised various ceremonies for the purpose of curing diseases, or, occasionally, of causing them; and they also made use of their powers to counteract the spells of Fairies as well as those of the malevolent Sorcerers or Witches. For diseases, in addition to using charms, they administered medicinal herbs and applied fasting spittle, in the virtues of which there was a very general belief; but to accomplish the more recondite branch of their profession they used charms and incantations[1] only. They were all more or less tainted with the suspicion of dabbling a little in sorcery and witchcraft on their own account, but, as their powers were on the whole used for good purposes, they were tolerated.

One of the best known of these Witch-doctors was Teare, of Ballawhane, who was described by Train as follows:—"The Seer is a little man, far advanced into the vale of life; in appearance he was healthy and active; he wore a low-crown slouched hat, evidently too large for his head, with a broad brim; his coat, of an old-fashioned make, with his vest and breeches, were all of *loughtyn* wool, which had never undergone any process of dyeing; his shoes, also, were of a colour not to be distinguished from his stockings, which were likewise of *loughtyn* wool." He was said to have been the most powerful of all these practitioners, and when their prescriptions had failed in producing the desired effect, he was applied to. The messenger that was despatched to him on such occasions was neither to eat nor to drink by the way, nor even to tell any person his mission. The recovery was supposed to be perceptible from the time the case was stated to him.

These powers were supposed to be hereditary, and were handed down in the same family for generations. There, is for instance, a daughter of Teare's still practising the same art, and she is resorted to by the fishermen for the sake of having their nets charmed, and so cause them to be lucky in their fishing.[2] To preserve these powers intact from generation to generation, it was supposed to be necessary to hand them down from a man to a woman, but in the next generation from a woman to a man, and so on. Having thus referred to the methods

1 Specimens of these are given at the end of this chapter.

2 Even now it is no uncommon thing for any one who has a cut, or a burn, to seek the nearest Charmer and have a charm 'put on it.'

of detecting Witches and of protecting and curing those that
were attacked by them, we will now proceed to show how they
were punished. The Law with regard to witchcraft and kindred practices was very severe in every part of Europe, and,
it is said, that in England alone, no less than 30,000 Wizards
and Witches have suffered at the stake. Blackstone writes with
regard to the law on this subject in England as follows:—"Our
law once included in the list of crime, that of actual witchcraft
or intercourse with evil spirits; and though it has now no longer a place among them, its exclusion is not to be understood
as implying a denial of the possibility of such an offence. To
deny this, would be to contradict the revealed word of God
in various passages both of the Old and New Testament; and
the thing itself is a truth to which every nation hath in its turn
borne testimony; either by examples seemingly well attested,
or by prohibitory laws, which at least suppose the possibility
of a commerce with evil spirits. * * *

By the Statute 33, Henry VIII., all witchcraft and sorcery
were declared to be 'felony without benefit of clergy,' and by I.
Jac. I., 'all persons invoking any evil spirits, or consulting, cov-
enanting with, entertaining, employing, feeding or rewarding
any evil spirit; . . . for killing, or hurting any person by such
infernal arts; should be guilty of felony and suffer death; and
if any person should attempt, by sorcery, to discover hidden
treasure, or to restore stolen goods, or to provoke unlawful love,
or to hurt any man or beast, he, or she, should suffer imprisonment and pillory for the first offence, and death for the second.'
These acts long continued in force, to the terror of all antient
females in the kingdom; and many poor wretches were sacrificed thereby to the prejudice of their neighbours and their own
illusions; not a few having confessed the fact at the gallows."
In the Isle of Man, too, legislation on this subject was not neglected, for we find, by the 50th Spiritual Law, that "all such
as are suspected for sorcerie and witchcraft are to be presented

to the Chapter Quest, then the Ordinary in such cases finding any suspicion is to impannel a jury of honest men within
the same parish and the party suspected in the meantime to
be committed to the Bishop's Prison, and all the offences and
crimes the jury doth find the Ordinary shall write, and if the
jury can prove any notorious fault or crime done by the same
person, then the Ordinary to deliver him out of the Bishop's
Prison to the Lord's Jail and Court." It is supposed that in old
times the usual result of the legal procedure against Witches was
that they were subjected to two so-called forms of ordeal, but
which were really means of putting them to death, as, if they
survived the first, the second would almost certainly prove fatal,
for they were said to have been thrown into the middle of the
Curragh Glass, or "green bog" pool, in the valley below Greeba
mountain. If they sank, their bodies were taken out of the water, carried home, waked, and received a Christian burial; but
if; to save themselves from drowning, they managed to paddle
to either side, they were instantly declared guilty of the crime of
which they were charged, and were consequently either burned
alive as unconvicted witches or rolled from the top of *Slieau
Whuallian* in spiked barrels, Thus literally was followed the
Scripture maxim, "Thou shalt not suffer a witch to live."

The following extracts from the Manx Episcopal and Civil
Records show, however, that our forefathers dealt with these poor
creatures in the seventeenth century, and later, in a milder fashion
than they did, according to tradition, at an earlier date:—

1638. — Whereas Jony Tear hath been presented by the Chapter Quest upon information given them that she was seen together
with an Irish woman in a gill pulling strange herbs, and whereas
the said Jony Tear hath cleared herself, her slanderers had to ask her
forgiveness before the congregation.

The following entry, taken from the *Liber Scaccar*, or
Exchequer Book, appears in the Malew Register in 1659. It

affords an instance of the enforcement of Church discipline by the temporal ruler who took the Bishop's place during the time of the Commonwealth:—

Bishop's Court, 30th September, 1659. — Whereas Mrs Jane Cesar hath been accused upon suspicion of witchcraft, charminge or sorscerie, where upon certaine examinacons have been taken. And the said case being putt to the triall of a jurie, they the said jurors (after examinacon of the business) have this day cleared and acquitted ye said Jane Cesar of the accusacon aforesaid as by theire Answere may appeare. Nevertheles that the said Jane Cesar may declare her inocencie of such practizes and that shee doth renounce the same as diabolicall and wicked; she is hereby ordered to acknowledge the same before the Congregacon off (sic.) Kk. Malew Parish on the next Lord's day to the end that others may be admonished to relinquish detest and abhor such delusions which are of great inducement to greater temptacons and are too frequently practised in this Island as is dayly observed. Of which if any one shall be hereafter accused and the same lawfully proved such persons are to be severely fined and punished, or otherwise proceeded against accordinge as the law doth provide in such cases.

(Signed) Jam. Chaloner.

To Sr. Tho. Parr minister of Kk Malew who is to read ye before his Congregacon the next Sabbath in English and Manxe and to return this Order with the acknowledgment made as aforesaid into the Comptrouleres office afterwards. True Coppie agreeinge with ye originall.

October the 2th, 1659

(Signed) J. Woods.

It is certainly remarkable that this unfortunate woman, after being acquitted by the jury of the offence alleged against her, should be ordered "to acknowledge the same before the congregation," and at the same time "to declare her innocencie."

The following, in 1690, is from the Archideaconal Register:—

We, whose names are hereunder written, being sworn in a jury of inquiry to take evidence in some difference between Gilbert Moore and John Steon about witchcraft, picking of herbs, and strikening them unknown, do give in our verdict as followeth:—Ann Callister, alias Karran, and Grace Cowley, being sworn and examined say that John Steon said unto Ann Callister thou b—— and w—— that little fat that thou has gotten upon thee I will take it oft thee in a short time, and since that time she has lost very many of her goods, and furth: saith not, Ann Callister further saith that John Steon's wife said unto her that she knew an herb, that if a man drank of the drink of it he would forget himself, but if one drank of it twice he would forget himself for ever—and further saith not. John Corlet and William Tear swore that Daniel Quayle told them that John Steon gave him an herb to put to his eyes and he never saw afterward, and further saith not. Gilbert Callister and Ann Callister declared that the said Daniel Quayle's wife told them the same words, and further saith not. Dollin Gawn sworn, examined, saith that himself and John Steon chid (sic) and the said John Steon promised to give him loss, and shortly after he received it, & furth: saith not, Dollin Gawn's wife sworn, examined, saith that the same John Steon told her that he knew that none of her children should inherit that little place they had, and since that time one of her child[n] dyed and another is now a cripple at her fire side, and furth: saith not. Adam Callister sworn, examined, saith that he came with John Corlett and John Steon from church and John Corlett told Steon he would present him to the great inquest, and the said Steon answered that he could not tell whether he would be able to do so, but that he might be sick and have need to be washed in tobacco water and swines broth, and further saith not. Ann Cowle sworn, examined, saith that John Steon said unto her he would deceive her and blind her, and strike her unknown. Adam Callister sworn, examined, saith that the said Steon told him that he would strike him unawares, and John Corlett declared that that was the common report he had heard of John Steon that he would strike people unknown and furth: saith not. Gilbert Moore sworn, examined, saith that the said Steon came to his house and said to his wife and children that he would strike them unawares so that they should not know of it, and since that time he lost abundance (sic) of his goods, and furth: saith not. Gilbert Moore likewise and Pat. Cowley sworn, examined, say John Steon came to the plough to Gilbert Moore for the lone (sic) of a Manks spade, and the said Moore denyed him, whereupon Steon told him he would do him a mischief and that shortly and within a while after one of his oxen were struck lame so the said Moore sent to Steon to come to see the Ox, and Steon coming spit upon the Ox and handled him and he recovered, and further saith not. Mrs. Nelson sworn, examined, saith that John Steon told her that he knew she would be willing to deliver up her land unto Grinsey and Richard Cannell, and the said Mrs. Nelson asked him how did he know, whereupon the said Steon replyed that he knew she would be willing to give them payment for taking it from her and they would not accept of it, and further saith not. Pat. Cannell sworn and examined saith that he came upon John Steon's daughter picking of herbs in the Court land where corn was sowen on our Lady day in Lent a little after break of day. Ellin^r Cannell sworn, examined, saith as aboves^d, Jaine Quayle examined saith that she saw an herb with John Steon's daughter, and asked what that was for and she said to preserve her from the flux and seeing something else with her she said it was to preserve her from the feaver.—Having taken the above depositions we find said Steon to be guilty, and leave him to the discretion of the Court for fine and punishment. Jo. Quayle his m^{k.} X, Gilb^{r.} Callist^r his m^{k.} X, Pat, Caine his m^{k.} X, and Wm. Quayle his m^{k.} X.

At Kirk Michael, July 31, 1712, one Alice Knakill, *alias* Moor, of Kirk Lonan, confessed to a charge of having taken up some earth from under a neighbour's door, and burnt it to ashes, which she gave to her cattle, "with an intention, as she owns, to make them give more milk. Also another woman declares that the said Alice Knakill cut a piece out of her petticoat and burnt it to powder, which she drank with a design, as she confessed, to recover her health, and procure sleep. Both which charms she owns to have been taught her by an Irishwoman." She was sentenced to three Sundays' penance in the neighbouring churches. In the following year, Alice Cowley, of Ballaugh, a regular dealer in charms, and known as such far and wide in the Island, was brought before the Consistory Court. It was then deposed that this old crone, "addressed herself to a youth, and told him, if he would give her a ninepenny piece, she would give him something that would make a young woman fall in love with him, which proves to be a powder in a paper, which he believes to be the powder of some of the bright stones that are at Foxdale." Her dealings with married women, under the pretence of removing barreness; with farmers for procuring a crop of corn, or making the herd fruitful; with young women for procuring lovers; and with parents for the recovery of a sick child were also deposed to; the mischief in each case being implied to be the Witch's doing, and thought to be remedied by drawing blood from her. All these charges were proved, and Alice was sentenced, by the Bishop and Vicars-General, to "thirty days' imprisonment, and before releasement to give sufficient security to stand two hours in a white sheet, a white wand in her right hand, and these words, 'for charming and sorcery,' in capital letters on her breast, in the four market towns of this Island, at the public cross, in the height of the market; and afterwards to do penance in Ballaugh Church."

In 1716, a woman from Jurby complained to Vicar-General Walker that she and her husband had been "suspected to have been out early in the morning last May-day, walking on the dew in their neighbours' fields, with a design to prejudice them in the increase of their crop," and that though this calumny had been disproved by evidence, it was still repeated. It was, therefore, ordered by the Court, in order "to discourage such vile and unchristian thoughts of one neighbour receiving damage from another, by any trivial, foolish customs of that kind, which betray great weakness of faith and trust in God," that a fine of £3, and imprisonment for forty days, besides further punishment at the Ordinary's discretion, should be imposed on anyone reviving the story.

Bishop Wilson evidently viewed the practice of charming with abhorrence, as we find him writing about it, in 1741, as follows:—"There is a cursed practice carried on secretly by Satan and his instruments, which I beseech you, my brethren, take this proper occasion[1] to speak upon: both to terrify those that practice it, and to confirm people's faith in God, against any hurt the devil or his agents can do them. Many complaints have been brought into our courts against people using foolish and wicked charms and arts, either to injure their neighbour in his goods, or to transfer them to themselves, to the great dishonour of God, who alone can increase the fruits of the earth to our comfort, or withhold them for our sins; and, indeed, it is for want of a true faith in God's power and goodness that makes men afraid of what such wretched instruments of Satan can do . . ."

There are many other similar presentments to be found in the Records during the seventeenth and eighteenth centuries, but we will content ourselves with mentioning two cases which have come into the Courts in the present century. In the *Manx Sun* newspaper of the 5th of January, 1838, it is reported that "a case of sorcery was recently brought into and solemnly heard in one of the Courts of Law." About the same time the then Deemster McHutchin was applied to for a warrant against a Witch on the charge of depriving cows of their milk, and causing them to sicken. He, however, wisely asked

---

1 During the perambulations of the parishes on Ascension Day.

a veterinary surgeon to supply a remedy, and thus put a stop to the prosecution.

The following account was published in the *Mona's Herald* newspaper of the 10th of January, 1844, concerning the proceedings against a suspected Witch:—A farmer in the parish of Marown, having lost in succession, a heifer, a cow, and a horse, attributed the death of these animals to the influence of witchcraft. Consequently he obtained a trespass warrant from one of the Deemsters, under authority of which a jury was sworn, and a number of persons summoned as witnesses and examined. Such questions as the following were put: 'Did you ever witch Quine's cattle?' 'Do you bear malice against Quine?' 'Did you hear anybody talking about Quine before his cattle died, and seeming to grudge him what he possessed?' Among those who were sworn was Quine's sister-in-law, and on being asked if she ever came *in any shape or form* to do Quine or his goods an injury, she confessed 'that she had once passed through Quine's fields without leave.' The poor woman was frightened into paying the costs in consequence of this. While the case was going on someone let loose a wild rabbit in the room. On the appearance of this unexpected visitor all became terrified, crying, 'The Witch, the Witch!' This continued for several minutes, till one of the party, more courageous than the rest, seized the supposed Witch, and, while depriving the harmless creature of existence, triumphantly exclaimed, 'You shall not trouble poor Quine again.'"

The stories which follow relate to the various practices of MAGIC, ENCHANTMENT, SORCERY, and WITCHCRAFT. A list of the CHARMS most in vogue is also given.

THE MAGICIAN'S PALACE

In visionary glory rear'd,
The gorgeous castle disappear'd;
And a bare heath's unfruitful plain
Usurp'd the wizard's proud domain,

WARTON

In the days of enchantment a certain great magician had, by his art, raised for himself the most magnificent palace in the Isle of Man that eye ever beheld; but none who, either out of curiosity or a desire of being entertained there, went to it but was immediately converted into stone, or at least had the appearance of it, so implacable an enemy was the wicked master of it to all his own species, being served only by infernal spirits. He became at length so much the terror of the whole Island that no person would venture to live or pass within several leagues of his habitation, so that all that side of the country was in a manner desolate, to the great loss and detriment of the place in general. This had continued for the space of three years, when an accident, or rather the peculiar direction of divine providence, was pleased in mercy to deliver them from the terror of so cruel a neighbour.

A poor man, whom one may justly term a pilgrim, having nothing to subsist on but what he procured by imploring the charity of those able to afford him succour, happening to travel on that side of the Island, not knowing anything of the fame of this enchanter, and perceiving no house inhabited, nor any cottage even, where he might get a lodging, and it growing dark, he was in terrible apprehensions of being under the necessity of taking up his lodgings on those bleak mountains, yet wandering on as long as light permitted, in hopes of better fortune, he, at last, came within sight of this palace, which filled his heart with much joy. Coming near it, he beheld large piazzas, which surrounded that magnificent building, and believing these might serve him for a resting-place, without being troublesome to any of the servants, whose churlish disposition in other places did not always afford a ready welcome to strangers, he chose rather to content himself with resting his wearied limbs on the marble floor than entreat a reception into any of the barns, which, perhaps, might be denied. In a word, he sat down on a bench in one of these piazzas, and, finding himself hungry, he took out of his pouch a piece of meat and bread, which he had begged at the last town he had passed through. He had also a little salt, which, by dipping his meat in the dark, he happened to spill some on the floor, on which he presently heard the most terrible groans to issue from the earth beneath, vast winds seemed to be let loose from every quarter of the element, all the face of heaven was deformed with lightning, the most dreadful thunder rattled over his head, and in less than a moment this fine palace, with all its proud and lofty piazzas, porticos, and brazen doors, vanished into the air, and he found himself in the midst of a wide, desert, mountainous plain, without the least appearance of anything he had formerly seen. Surprised as he was, he instantly betook himself to his prayers, nor removed from his knees till day began to break, when, after thanking God for bringing him safe through the dangers of the night past, he made what speed he could to the next village, and relating the adventure just as it was to the inhabitants, they could not at first give credit to what he said, but, going in great numbers towards the place where the palace of the necromancer had stood, they were convinced, and all joined in prayer and thanksgiving for so great a deliverance.

It was presently concluded, from what the pilgrim said, that the salt spilt on the ground had occasioned this dissolution of the palace, and for that reason salt has ever since been in such estimation among them that no person will go out on any material affair without taking some in their pockets, much less remove from one house to another, marry, put out a child, or take one to nurse, without salt being mutually interchanged; nay, though a poor creature be almost famished in the streets, he will not accept any food you will give him unless you join salt to the rest of your benevolence. — *Waldron*.

Salt has borne a conspicuous part in many superstitious ceremonies. The high priest of the Jews was ordered to season all offerings with salt.[1] The Egyptians and Romans also used it in their sacrifices. In Ireland, before the seed is put into the ground, salt is sent into the field for the purpose of counteracting the power of the witches and fairies. So in the Isle of Man, salt was placed in the churn lest the fairies should prevent the production of butter. Salt was formerly placed on the breast of a corpse in the Isle of Man, as elsewhere, as an emblem of the immortality of the soul. The dread of spilling salt was a general superstition.

ORIGIN OF KING WILLIAM'S SANDS

They tell you that the Island was once much larger than it is at present; but that a magician, who had great power over it, and committed many wonderful and horrible things, being opposed by one who was a friend to the place, and at length, overcome by him, he, in revenge, raised a furious wind, not only in the air, but also in the bosom of the earth, which, rending it, tore off several pieces, which, floating in the sea, in process of time were converted into stone, and became those rocks which are now so dangerous to shipping. The smaller fragments, they say, are sands, which, waving up and down, are at sometimes to be seen, and at others, shift themselves far off the coast. They maintain that it was on one of these that the late King William had liked to have perished, and strengthen this suggestion by the trial of the pilot, who must infallibly have been hanged, if on strict examination of all the charts there had been in any of them the least mention made of any such sands, but, however, these floating ruins have ever since remained, and from thence are called, King William's Sands. — *Waldron.*

THE DEVIL'S DEN

"Deeper than plummet ever sounded."— SHAKESPEARE

About a league and a half from Barrule, there is a hole in the earth, just at the foot of the mountain, which they call

1 Leviticus ii., 13.

"The Devil's Den." They tell you, that, in the days of enchantment, persons were there confined by the magicians, and that
it now contains a very great prince, who never knew death,
but has for the space of six hundred years been bound by
magic spells; but in what manner he lies, or in what form,
none had ever courage enough to explore. They add, that if
you carry a horse, a dog, or any other animal to the mouth
of this hole, its hair will stand on end, and its eyes stare, and
a damp sweat cover its whole body. Strange noises are also
said to have been heard to issue from this place, and I knew
a man once, who positively averred that his great-grandfather
saw a huge dragon, with a tail and wings that darkened all the
element, and the eyes that seemed two globes of fire, descend
swiftly into it, and after that, heard most terrible shrieks and
groans from within. — *Waldron*.

THE SUBMERGED ISLAND

There was supposed to be a submerged island near Port
Soderick which appeared every seven years. Train relates
the story of one of these appearances as follows:—"Many
a time and oft had Nora Cain heard her old grandsire relate the tradition of the enchanted island at Port Soderick,
while sitting spinning by the turf fire on a winter's evening. It was in the days of the Great Fin MacCooil, that
mighty magician, who, for some insult he had received
from the people who lived on a beautiful island, off Port
Soderick, cast his spell over it, and submerged it to the
bottom of the ocean, transforming the inhabitants into
blocks of granite. It was permitted them, once in seven
years, to come to the surface for the short space of thirty
minutes, during which time the enchantment might be
broken if any person had the boldness to place a Bible on
any part of the enchanted land when at its original alti-
tude above the waters of the deep.

On one occasion, it was about the end of September, on a fine moonlight night, Nora was sauntering along the little bay in sweet converse with her lover, when she observed something in the distance which continued to increase in size. It struck her to be none other than the enchanted isle she so often had heard of. It continued gradually rising above the surface of the water, when, suddenly disentangling herself from the arm of her lover, she hastened home with all the speed she could, and rushed into the cottage, crying out, and breathless with her haste, "The Bible, the Bible, the Bible!" to the utter amazement of the inmates, who could not at the moment imagine what had possessed her. After explaining what she had seen, she seized hold of the coveted volume and hastened back to the beach, but, alas! only just in time to see the last portion of the enchanted isle subside once more to its destined fate of another seven years' submersion.

From that night poor Nora gradually pined away, and was soon after followed to her grave by her disconsolate lover. It is said from that time no person has had the hardihood to make a similar attempt, lest, in case of failure, the enchanter in revenge might cast his club over Mona also.

TEHI-TEGI, TEH ENCHANTRESS

> "With lips of rosy hue,
> Dipp'd five times over in ambrosial dew,
> She led them to their destruction."— OLD POET

A famous enchantress, sojourning in this Island, had by her diabolical arts made herself appear so lovely in the eyes of men that she ensnared the hearts of as many as beheld her. The passion they had for her so took up all their hearts that they entirely neglected their usual occupations. They neither ploughed nor sowed, neither built houses, nor repaired them; their gardens were all overgrown with weeds, and their once fertile fields were covered with stones; their cattle died for want of pasture; their turf lay in the bowels of the earth undug for, and everything had the appearance of an utter desolation, even propagation ceased, for no man could have the least inclination for any woman but this universal charmer, who smiled on them, permitted them to follow and admire her, and gave everyone leave to hope himself would be at last the happy He. When she had thus allured the male part of the Island, she pretended one day to go a progress through the provinces, and being attended by all her adorers on foot, while she rode on a milk-white palfrey, in a kind of triumph at the head of them. She led them into a deep river, which by her art she made seem passable, and when they were all come a good way in it, she caused a sudden wind to rise, which, driving the waters in such abundance to one place, swallowed up the poor lovers, to the number of six hundred, in their tumultuous waves. After which, the sorceress was seen by some persons, who stood on the shore, to convert herself into a bat, and fly through the air till she was out of sight, as did her palfrey into a sea hog or porpoise, and instantly plunged itself to the bottom of the stream.

To prevent the recurrence of a like disaster, it was ordained that the women should go on foot and follow the men hence forth, which custom is so religiously observed, that if by chance a woman is seen walking before a man, whoever sees her cries out immediately, "Tehi! Tegi!" which, it would appear, is the name of the enchantress who occasioned this law. — *Waldron.*

CAILLAGH-NY-GHUESHAG

Caillagh was the name given to an old woman, and, from the ugliness associated with old women, it came to mean a hag or witch. The most famous *Caillagh* was an old woman called *Caillagh-ny-Ghueshag*, "old woman of the spells," or the Sorceress. She was an adept at chiromancy—*Faaishlaght*—and could perform a charm or incantation—*pisag*; but her posthumous reputation arose mainly from her having foretold certain things, which, she said, were to happen before the end of the world. Such of her predictions as have been recorded certainly related to very trifling events. There was a small treen chapel called *Cabbal-keeill-Vout*, between the Foxdale river and Slieau-whallin, concerning which she is said to have predicted as follows

> *Tra Vees Cabbal-keeill-Vout ersooyl lesh-y-hooilley,*
> *Cha bee cleïn Quirk Slieau-whallin veg sodjey.*

i.e., "When the Chapel Keeil-Vout shall be taken away by the flood the Quirk family will be no longer in Slieau Whallin." It is said that about 70 years ago the last fragment of the chapel and the last of the Quirks of Slieau Whallin disappeared simultaneously. The following sayings are also attributed to her:—*Dy beagh chimlee caardagh ayns chooilley hie roish jerrey yn theill*— "That there would be a smithy chimney in every house before the end of the world;" and that *Dy nee ass claghyn glassey yoghe sleih nyn arran*— "People would get their bread from grey stones." Like many other prophecies, these decidedly require an interpreter! Another saying that was attributed to her was that "the Manx and the Scotch will come so near as to throw their beetles at each other." Certainly, the Point of Ayre is extending slowly towards Scotland, but thousands of years would have to elapse, even if the same process continued steadily, before it could get there. — *Harrison.*

THE GLENCRUTCHERY WELL

A story is told of a girl who was going to the Glencrutchery well for water, and met an old man, who had the reputation of being a sorcerer,[1] on her way. He asked her where she was going. "Going to your well for water," she said. "Is there no water in your well?" said he. She replied that there was, but that her mistress had sent her to get water from his well. He then

---

1 There seems to be practically no distinction between Sorcery, when deprived of the prophetic element, and Witchcraft.

gave her some money, and told her to take the water out of their own well. The girl took the money, which confirmed the charm, and went to the fair, which was going on that day, after fetching the water home. When she returned home in the evening her mistress asked her where she had got the water, as she had been churning all day without getting any butter. — *Oral.*

THE EFFIGY

In a lonely part of the northern district of the Island stood the cottage of an old woman, who had been long suspected of being a practitioner of the "black art,"to the detriment of many of her neighbours. A person of great courage having had occasion to pass that remote dwelling one night, at a late hour, and seeing a strong light within, on peeping through a chink in the door, perceived distinctly the old beldame busily turning an image before a large fire, and sticking pins into it occasionally, on which she muttered a cabalistic rhyme which he could not understand. Next morning, on hearing that the minister had been suddenly seized by a chronic disease on the preceding evening, which lasted till midnight, the man who had seen the crone at work at the very time the minister was tortured by racking pains, publicly charged her of being the sole cause of his indisposition, which was seemingly confirmed by the Captain of the Parish finding in her possession the image or supposed effigy of the minister, with an old bladder containing rusty nails, pins, and skewers. After having been tried and found guilty, she walked seemingly quite unconcerned to the common place of execution, and just before she was bound to the stake, confessed the crime for which she was about to suffer. — *Train.*

THE WITCH OF SLIEU WHALLIAN

They say,
Lamentings heard i' the air! strange screams of death. — SHAKESPEARE

About two miles from Peel, opposite to the Tynwald Mount, there is a hill called Slieu Whallian, said to be haunted by the spirit of a murdered witch, but, however, it does not appear to mortal eyes, but every night joins its lamentations to the howling winds. This woman was put into a barrel with sharp iron spikes inserted round the interior, pointing inwards, and thus, by the weight of herself and the apparatus, allowed to roll from the top of the hill to the bottom.

Many other persons have suffered here in a similar manner, one of whom was a man named Thomas Carran, who died protesting his innocence of the crime of which he was accused. In proof of this, as he is said to have predicted, a thorn-tree has since grown, and marks the fatal spot on the summit of the hill, where the cask, in which he was enclosed, in fulfilment of the sentence awarded against him, was pushed over the brow, to roll, and bound, and dash with headlong speed to the plain below. — *Train.*

THE BURNT BESOM

The following story was told last year by a man who is now living:—One morning as he was returning from courting— courting it should be mentioned was, and still is in the country districts, carried on at night—he saw a woman, who was a reputed Witch, at the four cross-roads, near Regaby, sweeping a circle round her as large as that made by horses when threshing. He kicked her, and took her besom (broom) from her, and hid it till mid-day, when he and some boys collected some dry gorse, fired it, and put the besom on top. Wonderful to relate, when burning it made reports like guns going off, which could be heard at Andreas Church. This besom had on it "17 sorts of knots." Soon after its destruction the woman died. — *Rhys.*

BUTTER BEWITCHED

One day a woman who was a reputed Witch, called at the door of a neighbouring farm-house when churning was going on, and asked the dairymaid for some buttermilk. Not having any, she refused and went on churning; but from that moment it was of no avail, as the butter refused to come, and she got none at all, while the Witch, who kept only one cow, took sixteen pounds of butter to sell, the produce of her dairy, which was a common event with her when the farmers near her were unsuccessful. — *Oral*.

The following extract from a poem by the Rev T. E. Brown, of Clifton, entitled "The Manx Witch," gives an excellent idea of the usual Manx notions about these creatures:—

THE MANX WITCH

A wutch[1], of coorse she was a wutch,
And a black wutch, the wuss that's goin'—
The white is—well, I'm hardly knowin'.
Is the lek in[2]: but these ould things
That's sellin' charms to sailors—rings,
Papers, ye know . . .
I spose the most of ye's got the lek
Somewhere hung about your neck.
But there's odds of charms; for some is just
A sort of a blessin'; but some is a cuss,
Most bither—brewed in the very gall
Of spite and hate, and'll creep and crawl
Over your body and over your sowl,
Aye, man! aye! at laste so I'm tould;
And through and through, and making you sick,
And making you mad—aw, they know the trick!
Cussin' your fingers and cussin' your toes,
Cussin' your mouth and cussin' your nose,
Every odd jint, and every limb,
And all your inside—that's the thrim—
Cussin' your horse and cussin' your cow,
Cussin' the boar and cussin' the sow—
Everything that's got a tail.
Aye, and your spade, and your cart and your flail,
Plough and harras[3], stock and crop,
Nets and lines—they'll navar stop.
. . . You'll be passin' by,
And not a word, but the evil eye.—
There ye are! Your stuck, they've done ye!
They've got ye—you're tuck! they've put it upon ye!

1 Witch.

2 If the like exist.

3 Harrows.

>   .   .   .   And harbs! they picks them
> The right time of the moon, and they'll take and mix them.
> Divils! divils! that's what they are!
> And should be tuk and burnt the way
> They used to be.

The following stories refer to the popular antidotes to the effects of witchcraft, which, as stated above, are mainly the use of fire and dust, the former being used partly as a preventive to witchcraft, and partly as a means of detecting the Witch, while the latter is an antidote only. The sacrifice of cattle by burning, as a means of preventing witchcraft, has been common even in the present century, and is secretly practised in the remote districts even now:—

The cattle of a farmer, in the Parish of German, having been, in about 1834, attacked by a kind of murrain, which he attributed to witchcraft, he sought to stay the spreading of the disease by offering up a living calf as a burnt sacrifice. The ashes of this unfortunate beast were collected and applied to the rest of the herd. A small chapel was afterwards built near the spot where this disgusting sacrifice took place, and was consequently called *Cabbal yn oural losht*, "Chapel of the burnt offering."— *Oral.*

A similar case occurred near the Union Mills in 1843.

The *Manx Sun* newspaper describes the sacrifice of a calf in the Parish of Maughold, in 1853, as follows:—"The calf was dragged to an eminence not far from the highway, a large quantity of peat and straw was provided, and, a light having been applied, the calf and pyre were consumed."

There was an *oural losht* in the Parish of Jurby in 1880, and even within the last five years there have been several sacrifices, but it is difficult to obtain any particulars. One of them was that of a young horse which was supposed to have been bewitched to death, which was burned in order to see the Witch come by, and she was, accordingly, seen through the smoke.

Some thirty years ago, cattle which were afflicted with "black-leg" were thrown into the sea at the *Lhen-vuirr*, in the hope that, as the tide carried them out, so would the disease be prevented from seizing their fellows.

It was not only on land that burning some animal or thing to detect or exorcise witchcraft was resorted to, but at sea also, for when a boat was unsuccessful during the fishing season. the cause was ascribed by the sailors to witchcraft, and, in their opinion, it then became necessary to exorcise the boat by burning the Witches out of it. Townley, in his journal, relates one of these operations, which he witnessed in Douglas harbour in 1789, as follows:—"They set fire to bunches of heather in the centre of the boat, and soon made wisps of heather, and lighted them, going one at the head, another at the stern, others along the sides, so that every part of the boat might be touched." Again he says, "there is another burning of witches out of an unsuccessful boat off Banks's Howe—the flames are very visible to the top of the bay." Feltham, writing a few years latter, also, mentions this practice.

We now come to some stories relating to the use of dust, the great antidote to the effects of witchcraft. "If a person," says Train, "wishes to purchase an animal, but will not give the price demanded, the disposer lifts earth from the print made by the person's right foot on the ground, where he stood to drive the bargain, and rubs the animal all over with it, to prevent the effects of what is called by the Islanders, 'overlooking.'" The following stories will illustrate this:—

A farmer and his neighbour were in treaty for the purchase of a pony; but, differing about the price, his neighbour, vexed at his disappointment, put an evil eye upon the beast, who instantly, and without visible cause, became so lame as to be wholly useless, and so continued for twelve months; when, by extraordinary good luck, another person called on him, who had on his part the power to discern these unrighteous influences, and to do away with them by a counter-charm. No sooner had this man cast his eye on the animal than he pronounced his lameness to have originated with the malignant purchaser, and, after performing certain ceremonies, he assured the farmer that the spell was broken, and that within a few hours, the pony would be restored to perfect soundness and strength, all which, in course, happened as foretold. — *Waldron.*

A farmer in the parish of Braddan sold a calf to a Douglas butcher; but his wife, not being aware of this, had sold the same calf to another person of the same trade, who, upon concluding the bargain, paid the price agreed on, and then took away the calf and killed it. As soon as the farmer discovered the mistake made by his wife, he called on the butcher to whom he had sold the calf; and, after explaining the circumstances, offered to refund the price which his wife had received from the other butcher, which was more than the price which the first butcher had agreed to pay. This he not only refused; but instituted an action against the farmer for the unlawful disposal of his property. During the continuance of this law suit, the mother of the disputed calf ceased to give milk, and became hide-bound, as did all the rest of the farmer's cows. This led to the belief that they were all bewitched, and they were not cured till a servant maid was obtained, from the north of the Island, who was skilful in applying the antidotes to witchcraft. — *Train.*

Mr. Karran, the late Captain of the Parish of Marown, had a fine colt, to which a person in Baldwin took a particular fancy, and was very anxious to purchase it, though Mr Karran had no intention of parting with the animal. On the evening of the last refusal, the colt became suddenly ill; and although every possible means were resorted to for its recovery, it continued to grow worse. On the third day, a friend accidentally called at Mr Karran's house, and on being told the circumstance thus related of the colt, undertook the cure of it. He immediately started off for Baldwin, in the hope of meeting the person whose *evil-eye* had infected it; he did so; and when the person with the evil eye had passed Mr Karran's friend, the latter gathered the dust of the road out of his footsteps, and returned with it in his pocket-handkerchief. On rubbing the colt all over with the dust, it presently partook of food and rapidly recovered, to the surprise of the proprietor and many of his neighbours. — *Train*.

In the following there is no purchase:—A hare, or rather a Witch in the shape of a hare, was crossing a field and stood still to stare at a team of horses employed in ploughing, when, to the horror of the ploughman, they instantly dropped dead on the ground. Fortunately, however, he retained his presence of mind, and, remembering that what had occurred was doubtless the result of the "Evil Eye," he collected some of the dust from where the hare had stood and threw it over the horses, who were at once restored to life. — *Oral*.

The use of dust against the influence of the "Evil Eye" has not been uncommon during the last fifty years. Quite recently a man on the south side of the Island, finding his calf suddenly taken ill, and observing an old woman crossing a field where it was, hurried after her, took up the dust from the place where she had passed, and then rubbed the calf with it till it recovered. It should be remembered that touching or lifting the earth was in many countries considered a remedy for diseases, especially for those of the eye. Earth taken from the spot where a man was slain was prescribed in Scotland for a hurt to an ulcer.

Having given an account of the remedies against witchcraft made use of by amateurs, we will now proceed to describe the skill of the regular practitioners, or Charmers, in the same direction. The two following stories relate to two of the best known of them, the first being about the famous Teare, of Ballawhane:—

In the spring, when the doctor is called professionally to more places than he can accomplish in the time required, many respectable farmers will suspend for days the operation of sowing, although the land should be fully prepared, and even in the most precarious weather, rather than run the risk of committing the seed to the soil without his accustomed benediction. Seer Teare had power over the birds of the air as well as over the beasts of the field. In July, 1833, the great Fairy Doctor had just entered the house of Mr Fargher, innkeeper, of Laxey, and seated himself in an old arm-chair, when he was greeted by the landlord, "Well, Ballawhane, I am glad to see you; my little field of wheat is nearer ripe than any grain in the glen, and the sparrows feed on it in such flocks, notwith-standing all I can do to prevent them, that they will have all the grain carried away before the straw is fit for the sickle." "I am quite aware of that," replied Mr Teare, "and I am just come to try if I can put them away for you." After returning from the cornfield, where he had performed some ceremoni-ous rites, he remarked to the innkeeper "these sparrows know well to take advantage of corn that has not been seen by me before it was sown, but I have sent them all away now, and I think they will not again venture into your field this season." This singular exorcism of the sparrows soon became known throughout Laxey; the paper-makers and the miners in the neighbourhood were the only persons who had any doubt as to the doctor's power in such matters, and, for the purpose of satisfying themselves, they narrowly watched the field during the remaining part of the season. To their great surprise, how-ever, though the sparrows flocked round Mr Fargher's field in greater numbers than before, casting many a wistful eye to the waving grain, yet not one of them dared to enter the charmed precincts. — *Train.*

Another of these Charmers, who lived in Ballaugh, was specially noted for his skill in bringing luck in fishing to those who applied to him. One of these was told by the old fellow that he could not put the fish in their nets; but he could remove anything that might cause him to be unsuccessful. He then gave him a lot of herbs, which he was to pound and boil, and mix with a pint of whisky. Of this compound, a glass was first to be taken by the captain of the boat, and then by each man in it, and the rest was to be sprinkled over the boat and nets. On one occasion he was sent by his fellows, after a spell of ill-luck in the fishing, to see the old charmer; but, being somewhat sceptical, he spent the charmer's fee in drink, and compounded the nostrum himself; though quite ignorant of the proper herbs, the result was a magnificent haul that night; but he never dared tell his comrades of the trick he had played on them. — *Rhys*.

But these powers may be taken away for having been made use of when unnecessary, as witness the following story:—A man near Laxey had the power of being able to stop any effusion of blood by a charm he possessed. On one occasion he was taunted by an unbeliever with being unable to stop the bleeding of a pig which he was about to kill. The moment the creature's throat was cut, the incantation was pronounced; but the power of the charmer was gone from henceforth. — *Oral*.

We now append a list of such of the charms as we have been able to discover.

CHARMS

YN CHIED PHISHAG DY GHEDDYN FUILL

Farraneagh yn uill ghoo, myr doo naght jiarg; goym's eh, as bee eh aym, as cha derrym geill da ny smoo.

THE FIRST CHARM TO GET BLOOD

"The black blood running, as black as red; I will take it, and it shall be mine, and I will take no further heed of it."

YN NAH PHISHAG

Phillip va Ree ny Shee, as Bahee yn yen echey; yinnagh ee Brearey gys Jee, nagh beagh dy bragh lackal er aeg ny shenn.

Goym's spyrryd firrinagh, as jiooldym voym yn doo spyrryd; as goym's eh, as bee eh aym, as cha beem dy bragh yn drogh spyrryd.

THE SECOND CHARM

"Philip was the king of peace, and Bahee his wife; she would vow to God, that there never would be want to young or old. I will take the true spirit, and cast from me the black spirit; and I will take it, and it shall be mine, and I shall never be the evil spirit."

A CHARM TO STAUNCH THE HORSE'S BLOOD

Three Moirraghyn hie dyn Raue, ny Ke imee as ny Cughtee, Peddyr as Paul, dooyrt Moirrey jeu, shass, dooyrt Moirrey jeu, shooyl, dooyrt Moirrey elley, Dy gast yn uill shoh, myr chast yne uill haink as lottyn Chreest: mish dy ghra eh, as mac Voirrey dy chooilleeney eh.

"Three Maries went to Rome, the Spirits of the Church stiles and the Spirits of the houghs,[1] Peter and Paul, a Mary of them said, stand; a Mary of them said, walk; the other Mary said, may this blood stop as the blood stopped which came out of the wounds of Christ: me to say it and the son of Mary to fulfil it."

A CHARM TO BANISH ALL EVIL SPIRITS

The following is a printed form having blank spaces for the insertion of names by the Charmer:—

PISHAG DY STHAPPAL ROIE FOALLEY

Three deiney chranee haink voish y Raue—Chreest, Peddyr, as Paul. Va Creest y Chrosh, yn uill echey shilley, as Moirrey er ny glioonyn yn ec liorish. Ghow for jeu yn er-obbee ayns e lau yesh, as hayrn Creest crosh[2] harrish eh. Three mraane aegey haink harrish yn ushtey, dooyrt unnane jeu, seose, dooyrt, nane elley, fuirree— dooyrt yn trass-unnane sthappyms fuill dooinney ny ben. Mish dy

---

1 Or, cliffs by the sea.

2 Or, heal.

ghra eh, as Chreest dy yannoo eh, ayns ennym yn Ayr, as y Vac as y spyrryd Noo.

N.B. — On repeating "crosh," you are to draw a cross with the thumb of your right hand over the bleeding part.

CHARM TO STOP BLOOD

"Three godly men came from Rome—Christ, Peter, and Paul. Christ was on the cross, his blood flowing, and Mary on her knees close by. One took the enchanted one in his right hand, and Christ drew a cross over him. Three young women came over the water, one of them said, "up," another one said, "stay," and the third one said, "I will stop the blood of man or woman." "Me to say it, and Christ to do it, in the name of the Father, and the Son, and the Holy Ghost."

PHISHAG SON Y ROIG

Ta mee dy rheynn eh ayns ennym yn Ayr as y Vac as yn spyrryd Noo, eddyr eh ve roig shee, ny roig Ree, dy jean yn chrou rheynnit shoh skeayley'n dourin shoh er geinnagh ny marrey.

CHARM FOR THE KING'S EVIL

"I am to divide it in the name of the Father, and of the Son, and of the Holy Ghost; whether it be a sprite's evil, or a King's evil, may this divided blemish banish this distemper to the sand of the sea."

TO CURE THE TOOTHACHE

The following charm, written on a scrap of paper or parchment, and stitched securely into the inner garments, is a certain means of prevention as well as cure:—

Saint Peter was ordained a saint
Standing on a marble stone,
Jesus came to him alone,
And saith unto him, "Peter, what makes thee shake?"
Peter replied, "My Lord and Master it is the toothache."
Jesus said, "Rise up and be healed, and keep these words for

my sake,
And thou shalt never more be troubled with toothache."

A CHARM TO STOP BLEEDING

Sanguis mane in te,
Sicut Christus in se;
Sanguis mane in tuâ venâ,
Sicut Christus in suâ pœnâ;
Sanguis mane fixus.
Sicut erat Christus,
Quando fuit crucifixus.

The consequence of interpreting this would be that its efficacy would be lost for ever! The same charm was in use in the West of England, and is to be found in Pepys's Memoirs.

CHARM TO REMOVE NUMBNESS OR "SLEEP" IN THE FEET

(This is called in Manx, *Cadley-Jiargan*.)
"Ping, ping, prash,
Cur yn cadley-jiargan ass my chass."
A translation of this would spoil the effect.

Another charm to stop blood is as follows:—*O Hiarn eaisht rish my phadjer! Ayns dty ynrickys cur geill da my aghyn! As ayns dty ynrickys jean hoilshaghey mieys; son cha vel dooiney bio oddys ayns dty hilley's ve ynrick as er ny heyrey gys yn jerrey*. Ta mee credjal dy ren Adaue as Eve chur er hoshiaght yn cheid peccah. Ayns ennym Adaue ta mish eisht cur fo harey dagh giarey as bine jeh fuill yn,* {dooiney/ben} *shoh dy scuirr Amen. Amen.*

"O Lord hear my prayer! In Thy faithfulness give heed to my petitions! And in thy faithfulness manifest goodness; for no man living in Thy sight can be perfect and justified to the end. I believe Adam and Eve did begin the first sin. In Adam's name I then do charge each gash and drop of this {man's/woman's} blood to stop. Amen. Amen."

A CHARM AGAINST THE FAIRIES

Shee Yee as shee ghooinney,
Shee Yee er Columb-Killey[1]
Er dagh uinnag, er dagh ghorrys,
Er dagh howl joaill stiagh yn Re-hollys.
Er kiare corneillyn y thie
Er y voayl ta mee my lhie
As shee Yee orrym-pene.

"Peace of God and peace of man,
    Peace of God on Columb-Killey,
    On each window and each door,
    On every hole admitting moonlight,
    On the four corners of the house,
    On the place of my rest,
    And peace of God on myself."

NOTE. — It will be observed that in this charm the name of the famous St. Columba, Columcille or Columb-Killey, is mentioned. There are two *Keeills* dedicated to him in the Island.

One of the most efficacious charms to prevent milk being bewitched, was to place a branch of the *cuirn*, or mountain-ash, in the cow-house on May-eve. Written charms were believed to prevent people from taking diseases if they were carried about sewn in the clothes. Great virtue was supposed to attach to red flannel for curing coughs. The virtue lay in the colour, not in the flannel.

The following charms are for curing warts:—Take a halfpenny and smear it over with fat bacon; then rub the wart with the halfpenny; after doing this, bury both the bacon and the halfpenny, and by the time the bacon has decayed the wart will have passed away.

Procure a piece of woollen thread and tie as many knots upon it as there are warts. Throw it away, or bury it in some

1 These words are almost identical with those of the first two verses of the 143rd Psalm.

place that the patient is ignorant of; and as the thread rots, the warts will die away. It is essential that no tie of blood exist between the operator and the patient.

Steal (the stealing is necessary) a piece of raw beef, and rubbing it nine times backwards over the warts, secretly bury it in a dry sandy place, when, as the beef decays, the warts will disappear; but perfect secrecy must be preserved, not even the patient's wife is to receive a hint of it, if a successful result is desired.

The following case of a successful "charming" operation was reported in the *Mona's Herald* newspaper, in 1853:—A man named John Kaighan, employed at the landing pier works, was hammering an iron rod, when he missed his stroke, and the iron rod pierced one of the arteries in his left arm. The blood flowed freely from the wound, and he was taken to the hospital; but all efforts to stop the flow of blood were fruitless, and it was feared the man would bleed to death. In this state of affairs, his relatives had recourse to a certain person who bears the reputation of being a blood charmer; and when this person had repeated his incantation over the wound, strange to say the flow of blood shortly afterwards ceased.

The following extraordinary charm emanated from a woman who was much better educated than such practitioners usually are. She lived at Ballasalla, fifty years ago, and produced a number of religions pamphlets, which for the most part consisted of wild prognostications, and of invocations to the Deity. Her mind seems to have been affected, and she was at times subject to hallucinations. She was called the Prophetess of Ballasalla, and was much respected and feared by her neighbours:—

"WHERE is the JEHOVAH ELSHADDAI, the LORD GOD of ELIJAH?" See 2d. Kings, 2d. Chapter, 14th Verse.

"Behold, I give you power to tread on serpents and scorpions," and over all the power of the enemy: and nothing shall by any means hurt you."— See Saint Luke, 10th Chapter, 19th Verse.

"And, Lo, I am with you alway, even to the end of the world. Amen." See Saint Matthew, 28th Chapter, 10th Verse.

In the Name of the FATHER, and of the SON, and of the HOLY GHOST, In the Name of GOD the FATHER, and of GOD the SON, and of GOD the HOLY GHOST, the most HIGH GOD HELION ELSHADDAI, Whose Name alone is JEHOVAH, and through the GRACE, and by the POWER of our LORD JE-SUS CHRIST, I, a Baptised Papist, and a poor unworthy Servant of the LORD JESUS CHRIST, do now command all devils, and all damned spirits, and all evil, wicked and bad spirits, and all Fair-ies, and all Wizards, and all Witches, and every evil eye, and each, all and every evil bad devilish satanick power and powers of evil whatsoever, Not to hurt, Not to harm. Not to injure, Nor do any devilish evil bad wicked mischief in anywise whatsoever unto thee [Margaret C—— alias C——, Nor unto thy Husband, Nor unto any one of all your Children,] Nor unto any thing that ever did, or that now doth, or that hereafter shall and may both Justly and Law-fully belong in any-wise whatsoever unto thee [Margaret, or unto Thy Husband, or unto your Children, (And now especially) as unto Thy Child Elizabeth Anna C——] so long as the *Almighty Lord Jesus Christ, the Holy Son of God with Power*, Liveth and Reigneth *God over all, God* blessed for evermore. Amen. even so *Lord Jesus*, Amen; if it be Thy *Holy Godly Blessed Will*; for the alone sake of Thy most Holy Atoneing, Redeeming Propitious Blood, and justi-fying Righteousness, and Holy Sanctifying saving Grace of *God* the *Holy Ghost*, the Blessed gift of *God* the *Father Jehovah*, To them that believe through saving Grace.—Wherefore, none of all the powers of evil, shall not again be able to hurt thee [Margaret,] in anywise whatsoever, so long as thou believeth in the *Lord Jesus Christ*, to be the *Son* of *God*, with Power. Amen. *Lord Jesus*, Amen. For thy great Almighty Name's sake.

May *Jesus* Help thee [Margaret, and Help all of Them.] May *Je-sus* Save thee, [and Save all of Them;] and, O, May *Christ the Lord Je-sus*, both Bless, Prosper, and Keep thee, both now and forever more, even forever. Amen. *Lord Jesus Christ*, our *God* and only *Saviour*. Let it be so, according to Thy Promise, and our Faith in Thee; and give us Faith alone in Thee. Amen, Almighty *Lord Jesus Christ*.

CHAPTER VI

CUSTOMS AND SUPERSTITIONS CONNECTED WITH
THE SEASONS

I N THE ISLE OF MAN, as elsewhere, many customs and superstitions, as well as much weather-lore, have attached themselves to the different seasons of the year. Both the Celts and Norsemen, before the introduction of Christianity, held high festival at the beginning of summer and winter, the mid-winter and mid-summer feasts being more especially of Scandinavian origin. When Christianity was introduced, its ministers, unable to do away with these feasts, wisely adopted their periods as Christian festivals, and so they have continued semi-pagan in form till the present day. Such ancient observances as perambulating the parish bounds, were also christianised by being associated with Divine worship; and the wells, which the people were wont to visit, were dedicated to the Saints and Martyrs of the Church. After the Reformation, the practice of visiting these holy wells, and of frequenting the tops of the mountains at Lammas, was denounced as superstitious and wicked, but in vain, as, even at the present day, it can scarcely be said to have altogether ceased.

The various customs and superstitions will he considered in the order of the Calendar:—

January 1, New Year's Day, formerly called *Laa Nolick beg*, "Little Christmas Day," was the occasion for various superstitions. Among these was that about the "first foot." The "first foot," called the *qualtagh* in Manx, is defined as follows by Kelly in his Dictionary: "The first person or creature one meets going from home. This person is of great consequence to the superstitious, particularly to women the first time they go out after lying-in." The *qualtagh* (he or she) may also be the first person who enters a house on New Year's morning. In this case it is usual to place before him or her the best fare the family can afford. It was considered fortunate if the qualtagh were a person (a man being preferred to a woman), of dark complexion, as meeting a person of light complexion at this time, especially if his or her hair is red, would be thought very unlucky. It is curious that the superstition in Scotland is the exact reverse of this—*i.e.*, to meet a light complexioned person was fortunate. If the *qualtagh* were *spaagagh*, or splay-footed, it would be considered very unfortunate. It was important, too, that the *qualtagh* on New Year's Day should bring some gift, as if he or she came empty-handed, misfortunes would be sure to ensue. To meet a cat first on this day was considered unlucky. It was supposed to be necessary to exercise great care to sweep the floor of the house on New Year's morning from the door towards the hearth, so that the dust should go towards the hearth, for, if this were not done, the good fortune of the family would be considered to be swept from the house for that year.

It was formerly the custom for a number of young men to go from house to house on New Year's Day singing the following rhyme:—

> *Ollick ghennal erriu, as blein feer vie;*
> *Seihll as slaynt da'n slane lught thie;*
> *Bea as gennallys eu bioyr ry-cheilley,*

Shee as graih eddyr mraane as deiney;
Cooid as cowryn stock as stoyr.
Palchey puddase, as skeddan dy-liooar;
Arran as caashey, eeym as roauyr;
Baase myr lugh ayns ullin ny soalt,
Cadley sauchey tra vees shiu ny lhie,
Gyn feeackle y jiargan, cadley dy mie.

"A merry Christmas, and a very good year to you;
Luck and health to the whole household,
Life, pleasantness and sprightliness to you together,
Peace and love between men and women;
Goods and riches, stock and store.
Plenty of potatoes and herring enough;
Bread and cheese, butter and beef.[1]
Death like a mouse in a barn haggart
Sleeping safely when you are in bed,
Undisturbed by[2] the flea's tooth, sleeping well."

Nothing should he lent on this day, as anyone who does so will be lending all the year. In old times, when tinder and flint were used, no one would lend them on this day.

SEASONS

January 6, or *Twelfth-day*, was the thirteenth or last day of Yule in the Northern Calendar. It was one of the days on which no one might borrow fire, but had to purchase it. After the introduction of Christianity, it became a Church festival in commemoration of the Manifestation of Christ to the Gentiles. Bishop Phillips, in the Manx Prayer Book[3] written by him early in the seventeenth century, calls it *Shen lail chibbert ushtey*, 'old feast-day of the water-well,' the meaning of which is not clear. It was formerly a day of much festivity in the Isle of Man, being called *Laa giense* 'dance or revel day.' Among the games then played were "Cutting off the Fiddler's Head," "The Lackets," and "The Goggans."

---

1 The meaning of this is, probably: may death, when it comes upon you, find you as happy and comfortable as a mouse in a well-stocked barn.

2 Literally "without."

3 This, we hope, will shortly be published by the Manx Society.

The Cutting of the Fiddler's Head is described by Waldron as follows:—"On Twelfth-day the Fiddler lays his head in some one of the wenches' laps, and a third person asks who such a maid or such a maid shall marry, naming the girls then present one after another, to which he answers according to his own whim, or agreeable to the intimacies he has taken notice of during this time of merriment. But whatever he says is as absolutely depended on as an oracle; and if he happens to couple two people who have an aversion to each other, tears and vexation succeed the mirth. This they call *Cutting of the Fiddler's Head*, for after this, he is dead for the whole year." The *Lackets, Legads*, or 'valentines,' was the name of a game which was played as follows:—A *mainster*, or master of ceremonies, was elected, who then proceeded to appoint a *legad* to every man of the party from among the girls present in the following words: *Eaisht-jee, as clasht-jee, as cur-jee myner; ta N. as M. legadyn son y vlein shoh, as ny sodjey, my oddys ad cordail. Moylley as soylley, jingey as pronney daue, &c.* "Listen, and hear, and give heed; N. and M. are valentines for this year, and longer, if they be agreeable. Praise and joy, peace and plenty to them, &c." (The remaining words are lost.) Doubtless, the appointments of the *mainshter*, who probably had a shrewd idea which of the young people were attached to each other, were the cause of much merriment. It would seem that these entertainments were usually held at a public-house, whose landlord would be elected as the *mainshter*. After the *legads* had all been appointed, the whole party sat down to supper, each man paying for his own legad, or valentine. During the supper the *laare vane*, or white mare,[1] was brought in. This was a horse's head made of wood, and so contrived that the person who had charge of it, being

---

1 This was probably a harvest custom originally. See Chapter VII, where an attempt is made to explain the origin of all customs associated with the animal or vegetable kingdom.

concealed under a white sheet, was able to snap the mouth. He went round the table snapping the horse's mouth at the guests who finally chased him from the room, after much rough play. A similar custom is mentioned by Dr. Johnson as taking place on New Year's Eve, in Scotland: One of the company dressed himself in a cow's hide, upon which the rest of the party belaboured him with sticks. They all then left the house and ran round it, only being re-admitted on repeating the following words, which are still preserved in St. Kilda: "May God bless this house and all that belongs to it, cattle, stones and timber. In plenty of meat, of bed and body clothes, and health of men, may it ever abound." Each then pulled off a piece of the hide, and burnt it for the purpose of driving away disease. The Manx custom was probably formerly the same as this.

The *Goggans*, or *Noggins*, were small mugs filled with symbols of various trades, thus—water, for a sailor; meal, for a farmer, &c. These were laid in front of the hearth, and then, when the girls had gone outside, they were changed. The girls were then brought back, and, according to the *goggan* they laid their hands upon, so was the trade of their future husband.

It was supposed that the weather on the twelve days after "Old Christmas Day," indicated the weather of each month in the following year.

January 25, *Laa'l Noo Phaul*,[2] "St. Paul's Feast-day," is a church festival in commemoration of the conversion of St. Paul. There seems to have been a very general superstition throughout Western Europe that, from the state of the weather on this day, the whole character of the year

2 The word *laa'l* appears to be a contraction of *Lau-feaill* 'feast day.' F is a weak consonant in Manx, and when aspirated it loses all its force. Phillips, in his Prayer book of the early seventeenth century, spells this word *lail*, which shows its origin more distinctly.

following might be predicted. We have, for instance, the old Latin distich:—

> *Clara dies pauli bona tempora denotat anni,*
> *Si nix vel pluvia, designat tempora cara;*
> *Si fiant nebulæ, pereunt animalia quæque;*
> *Si fiant venti, design at prælia genti.*

An English version of which is:—

> If St Paul's day be fair and clear,
> It does betide a happy year;
> But if it chance to snow or rain,
> Then will be dear all kinds of grain;
> If clouds or mists do dark the skie,
> Great store of birds and beasts shall die;
> And if the winds do flie aloft,
> Then war shall vex the kingdom oft.

The Manx version is as follows:—

> *Laa'l Paul ghorrinagh as gheayagh,*
> *Ghenney er-y-theill as baase mooar sleih;*
> *Laa'l Paul aalin as glen,*
> *Palchey er y-theill dy arroo as mein.*

> Paul's day stormy and windy,
> Famine on the earth and much death on people;
> Paul's day beautiful and fair,
> Abundance on the earth of corn and meal.

February 1, *Laa'l Breeshey* "Bridget's Feast-day," when the festival of this famous Irish saint was celebrated. A parish church, a nunnery, and no less than seven of the ancient *keeills* or cells are named after her in the Isle of Man, where she seems to have been a great favourite. An old custom on this day was to gather rushes, and standing with them on the threshold, to invite St. Bridget to come and lodge there that night, saying "*Brede, Brede, tar gys my thie, tar dys thie ayms noght. Foshil jee yn dorrys da Brede, as lhig da Brede cheet stiagh.*" "Bridget, Bridget, come to my house, come to my house to-night, open the door to Bridget, and let Bridget come in." After these words were repeated, the rushes were strewn on the floor by way of a carpet or bed for her. It is said also that straw was sometimes used, instead of rushes.

A similar custom is described by Martin,[1] as practised in some of the other Sodor Isles:—"The mistress and servants of each family take a sheaf of oats and dress it up in woman's apparel, put it in a large basket and lay a wooden club by it, and this they call Briid's bed, and then the mistress and servants cry three times, 'Briid is come, Briid is welcome.' This they do just before going to bed, and when they rise in the morning, they look among the ashes expecting to see the impression of Briid's club there, which, if they do, they reckon it a true presage of a good crop and a prosperous year, and the contrary they take as an ill omen."[2]

There were various weather sayings with regard to this day, thus:—

> *Laa'l Breeshey bane.*
> *Dy chooilley yeeig lane.*
> Bridget's Feast-day white, every ditch full.

i.e.. If snowy on St. Bridget's day, there will be a wet mild spring.

Choud as hig y skell ny-gall-ghreinney stiagh Laa'l Breeshey, hig y sniaghtey roish Laa Boayldyn. "As long as the sunbeam comes in on Bridget's Feast-day, the snow comes before May Day." *i.e.,* If mild on St. Bridget's day, there will be a cold spring.

February 2. — The festival of the Purification of the Virgin Mary, or Candlemas-day, called in Manx *Laa'l Moirrey ny gianle*, "Mary's Feast-day of the Candle," seems, since St. Bridget has been forgotten, to have taken the place of the festival of the Irish saint, as the prognostics founded on the state of the weather on this day are practically identical with those derived from St. Bridget's festival. There is a universal superstition throughout Christendom that good weather on this day indicates a long continuance of winter and a bad crop, and that

---

1 Western Isles, p. 119.

2 See Chapter VII.

its being foul is, on the contrary, a good omen. Sir Thomas Browne, in his *Vulgar Errors*, quotes a Latin distich expressive of this idea:—

> *Si sol splendescat Maria purificante,*
> *Major erit glacies post festum quam fuit ante;*

Of which the Scotch version is:—

> If Candlemass day be dry and fair,
> The half o' winter's to come and mair;
> If Candlemass day be wet and foul,
> The half o' winter's gane at Yule.

The Manx proverb corresponding with this conveys a caution to the farmers:—

> *Laa'l Moirrey ny gianle,*
> *Lieh foddyr as lieh traagh.*

"Candlemas-day (or Mary's Feast-day of the Candle), half straw and half hay."

i.e. — In the probable event of a mild Candlemas, half the stock of fodder should still be unconsumed, as much wintry weather will probably follow.

Shrove Tuesday, in Manx *Oie Ynnyd*, "Eve of the Fast," seems to have been observed in the Isle of Man in much the same way as in England. It was formerly the custom to have *sollaghan*, which is made of oatmeal and gravy, for dinner on this day, instead of at breakfast as usual, while the supper consisted of meat and pancakes. The following Manx saying is, we suppose, a warning against relying on the continuance of such sumptuous fare:—

> *Ec shibber Oie Ynnyd my vees dty volg lane;*
> *My jig Laa Caisht yiow traisht son shen.*

> "At Shrove-Tuesday supper if thy belly be full;
> Before Easter-day thou mayest fast (hunger) for that."

February 6. — A fair, called *Periwinkle* Fair, was held on this day till 50 years ago. It took place on the shore at *Pooyl-Vaa-ish*, where cattle, horses, and sheep were bought and sold as usual, and fairings sold, among them periwinkles. Hence the name. The 6th was St Dorothy's day, but there seems to be no trace of any special celebration on this day elsewhere.

March — There are various weather sayings about this month:—

Share craagh ve 'sy cheer, na mee ny Vayrnt cheet stiagh meein. "Better a slaughter in the country than the month of March should come in mild."

Sheeu hishan dy yoan Mayrnt maaill bleeney Vannin. "A peck of March dust is worth a year's rent in the Isle of Man."

Ta'n Vayrnt chionney as yn nah bee fanney. "March tightens and the next month skins." This refers to the characteristics of these two months—dry, with cold winds.

There is an old superstition that a Saturday's new moon was unlucky, and, if it occurred in March, it was still more so. Hence the saying:—*Ta eayst jesarn 'sy Vayrnt dy-liooar ayns shiaght bleeantyn.* "A Saturday's noon in March is enough in seven years."

March 17 is *L'aal Pharick*, "Patrick's Feast-day," when a fair was held. This famous Irish saint and missionary has three churches and seven *keeills* dedicated to Lim in the Isle of Man. This day was also called *Patermas*, "Patrick's Mass," and on it the saint's staff was carried in procession by some one who was paid by the owner of the saint's staffland, who also had to keep in order and renew the staff itself; for there are two small properties, one in the parish of Patrick and the other in the parish of Maughold, which seem to have been held on this tenure. The former of them, first mentioned in a Papal Bull of 1231 as *terram de baculo Sti. Patricii*, "The land of the Staff of St Patrick," has long since disappeared as a separate property; the latter, which is part of the Barony of St. Bees, still survives under the name of The Staffland. This place is considered to be freehold, inasmuch as no rent or service is rendered in respect of it to the lord.[1] The service of the Staff of St. Patrick seems

---

1 It will be seen that these tenures are not peculiar to the Isle of Man from the following:

to have been commuted for a money-rent at the time of the Reformation, while the Staffland in Maughold fell into the hands of the Christians of Milntown.

There is an old saying: *Laa'l Pharick arree, yn dow gys e staik as y dooiney ass e liabbee.* "Patrick's spring Feast-day, the ox to his stake, and the man from his bed." It thus seems to indicate the time when active farming operations (March 17) should begin. Seed-sowing is usually begun in the Isle of Man about this time.

April — There is the following weather saying about the month of April:—

> *Tra heidys Avril dy-bing e charyn,*
> *'Sy theihll vees palchey traagh as oarn.*

When April shall shrilly sound his horn,
On earth there will be plenty of hay and corn (barley).

i.e., A dry April is good for the crops.

Good Friday. — *Jy-heiney chaist*, or, as Bishop Phillips has it, Jy-heny-ghayst, "Easter Friday," was a day on which several superstitious customs were observed. No iron of any kind was to be put into the fire, and even the tongs were laid aside, lest any person should unfortunately stir the fire with them, a stick of the mountain-ash (*cuirn*) being used as a substitute. To avoid placing the

---

'Grant of lands in Free Alms in the Isle of Linsmore, with the custody of the Staff of St. Moloc.'

DEED OF CONFIRMATION

To all and singular, etc. We, Archibald Campbell, feudatory, Lord of the lands of Argyle, Campbell, and Lorn, with the consent and assent of our most dear father and guardian, Archibald, Earl of Argyle . . . have granted, and as well in honour of God omnipotent, of the Blessed Virgin, and of our holy Patron Moloc, and have *mortified*, and by this present writing have confirmed to our beloved John McMolmore, and the heirs male of his body lawfully begotten or to be begotten, all and singular our lands . . . in the Isle of Linsmore . . . with the Custody of the Great Staff (Baculi) of St. Moloc, as freely as the . . . other predecessors of the sd John had from our predecessors . . . in pure and free alms.' (Dated 9th April, 1544).

iron griddle on the fire, a large thick cake, called a *soddag*,[1] which is triangular in shape, was baked on the hearth. It was also a custom for people to go to the shore on this day to gather shell-fish.

Easter Sunday. — It was believed that anyone who went up to the top of a high hill on this morning to watch the sunrise would see the sun bow two or three times, as if in adoration to the risen Saviour. The superstition that the sun bowed or danced on this day was once very prevalent in England, and was embodied by Sir John Suckling in the following verses on a belle of the day:—

> Her feet beneath her petticoat
> Like little mice peep'd in and out,
>   As if they feared the light!
> And oh! she dances such a way
> No sun upon an Easter Day
>   Were half so fine a sight.

April 25 is now best known as *Laa'l Noo Markys-yn-sushtallagh*, "St. Mark the Evangelist's Feast-day"; but it was formerly connected with the famous Manx saint, Maughold, to whom a parish church is dedicated. He had two days in the year, this, the first and more important, being called *Laa'l Maghal toshee*—Maghold's chief Feast-day. The superstitions formerly practised on the eve of this day were the same as those belonging to the eve of St. Mark in England. If a person on the eve of this day were to watch in the churchyard from eleven in the evening till one in the morning he would see the wraiths of those who are to be buried there during the year.

May 11 — *Oie Voaldyn*, or May-day Eve—was the occasion of many superstitious observances. On this evening the Fairies were supposed to be peculiarly active. To propitiate them, and to ward off the influence of evil Spirits and Witches, who were also active at this time, green leaves or boughs and *sumark*, or primrose flowers, were strewn on the threshold, and branches of the *cuirn*, or mountain-ash, were made into small

---

1 See Chapter VII.—Similar cakes were made in the little island of St. Kilda, but on "All Soul's Day," November and not Good Friday.

crosses without the aid of a knife, which was on no account to be used, and stuck over the doors of the dwelling-houses and cow-houses. Cows were further protected from the same influences by having the *bollan-feaill-Eoin*[1] (John's-feast wort) placed in their houses. This was also one of the occasions on which no one would give fire, and on which fires were and are lit on the hills to drive away the Fairies, Witches, &c., and also to purify the fields, cattle, and horses by the smoke passing over them. It is said that a handful of gorse was formerly lit in each field to purify it.

With reference to the practice of not giving fire, Waldron remarks that there was not one of the native families "but keeps a small quantity of fire continually burning, no one daring to depend on his neighbour's vigilance in a thing which he imagines is of such consequence: everyone consequently believing that if it should ever happen that no fire were to be found throughout, most terrible revolutions and mischiefs would immediately ensue;"— and, as to the lighting of fires, Kelly says that "the inhabitants kindle fires on the summits of the highest hills, in continuation of the practice of the Druids, who made the cattle, and probably the children, 'to pass through the fire,' using certain ceremonies to expiate the sins of the people; but the northern practice is for each *balla* or town to kindle a fire, so that the wind may drive the smoke over their cornfields, cattle, and habitations. . . . The inhabitants dress their houses with flowers, and before every door a considerable space is strewed with primroses. . . . On this eve also the damsel places a snail between two pewter dishes, and expects to find next morning the name of her future husband in visible characters on the dish; but the success of this depends on her watching till midnight, and having first purified her hands and face by washing them in the dew of the wheat."[2]

1 See Chapter VII.

2 Kelly: Manx Dictionary, p. 15. Manx Society: vol. XIII.

Fifty years ago the celebration of May-day Eve was still very general, as will be seen from the following account extracted from the *Mona's Herald* newspaper of the 5th of May, 1837; but now it has almost died out:—"On May Day eve the people of the Isle of Man have, from time immemorial, burned all the whin (gorse) bushes in the Island, conceiving that they thereby burned all the witches and fairies which they believe take refuge there after sunset. The Island presented the scene of a universal conflagration, and to a stranger, unacquainted with our customs, it must appear very strange to see both old and young persons gathering particular herbs, and planting them at their doors and in their dwellings for the purpose of preventing the entrance of the witches."

It is thus clear that the Manx people placed very great reliance on the influence of fire in protecting them from the powers of evil. This influence was also made use of—or would seem to have been made use of—by sacrificing animals as propitiatory offerings to the powers above mentioned. Such a method would naturally be supposed to have belonged to past ages only if there was not evidence that lambs have been burnt on May-day Eve or May-day—*son oural*—for a sacrifice within living memory. Such sacrifices seem to have been distinct in their purpose from the burning of animals already mentioned (in Chapter V) for discovering Witches or driving away disease.[3]

May 12. — *May-Day*, or *Laa-Boaldyn*, the *Beltaine*, as it was called in Irish, was the fire of the great Celtic feasts, and was held at the opening of the summer half of the year. Cormac, in his Glossary, says that this name, *Beltaine*, arose "from two fires which the Druids of Erinn used to make with great incantations"; and he adds that cattle used to be brought to these fires and driven between them, as a safeguard against

3 See Chapter VII.

diseases. According to Jameson, "the Gaelic and Irish word, *Beal-tine* or *Beil-tine*, signifies Bel's fire; as composed of *Baal* or *Belis*, one of the names of the sun in Gaelic, and *tein*, signifying fire;" but, as a matter of fact, this is all pure guess-work, no one having given a satisfactory derivation of the name.[1]

At an early hour on this morning the maidens went forth to gather the dew, and wash their faces in it, as it was supposed to ensure a good complexion, as well as to render the hostility of the Witches innocuous. At an equally early hour, horns were blown to prevent the Fairies from enticing children away. Later on in the day a Queen of the May was chosen, according to Waldron, in the following fashion: "In almost all the great parishes they choose from among the daughters of the most wealthy farmers a young maid for the Queen of May. She is dressed in the gayest and best manner they can, and is attended by about twenty others, who are called maids of honour, she has also a young man, who is her captain, and has under his command a great number of inferior officers. In opposition to her is the Queen of Winter, who is a man dressed in women's clothes, with woollen hoods, fur tippets, and loaded with the warmest and heaviest habits one upon another; in the same manner are those who represent her attendants dressed; nor is she without a captain and troop for her defence. Both being equipped as proper emblems of the beauty of the spring and the deformity of the winter, they set forth from their respective quarters; the one preceded by violins and flutes, the other with the rough music of tongs and cleavers. Both companies march till they meet on a common, and then their trains engage in a mock-battle. If the Queen of Winter's forces get the better, so far as to take the Queen of May prisoner, she is ransomed for as much as pays the expenses of the day. After this ceremony, Winter and

---

1 Kelly's (see Manx Dictionary) notion of a connection with the Phoenician God *Baal* is an evident absurdity.

her company retire and divert themselves in a barn, and the others remain on the green, where, having danced a considerable time, they conclude the evening with a feast, the queen at one table with her maids, the captain with his troop at another. There are seldom less than fifty or sixty persons at each board." For the seizure of her majesty's person, that of one of her slippers was substituted more recently, which was in like manner ransomed to defray the expenses of the pageant. The procession of the summer, which was subsequently composed of little girls, and called the *Maceboard*, outlived that of its rival, the winter, some years. The Maceboard went from door to door, inquiring if the inmates would buy the queen's favour, which was composed of a small piece of ribbon; this has also fallen into disuse.

This custom was evidently derived from the Northmen, whose proceedings on this day are thus described by Olaus Magnus, who wrote in the sixteenth century:—"The Southern Swedes and Goths that are very far from the Pole, have a custom, that on the first day of May, when the sun is in Taurus, there should be two horse troops appointed of young and lusty men, as if they were to fight some hard conflict. One of these is led on by a captain, chosen by lot, who has the name and habit of Winter. He is clothed with divers skins, and adorned with fire torks, and casting about snow balls and pieces of ice, that he may prolong the cold, he rides up and down in triumph, and he shows and makes himself the harder, the more the icicles seem to hang from their stoves (?) The chieftain of the other is for summer, and is called Captain Floria, and is clothed with green boughs and leaves and summer garments that are not very strong. Both these ride from the fields into the city, from divers places, one after another, and with their fire spears they fight, and make a public show, that Summer hath conquered Winter. Both sides striving to get the victory, that side more forcibly assaults the other which on that day seems to borrow more force from the air, whether temperate or sharp. If the winter yet breathes frost, they lay aside their spears, and riding up and down, cast about upon the spectators ashes mingled with live sparks of fire taken from the graves or from the altar; and they, who in the same dress and habit are auxiliary troops, cast fire-balls from their horses. Summer, with his band of horse, shows openly his boughs of birch, or tiel-tree, which are made green long before by art, as by the heat of their stoves and watering them, and privately brought in as if they newly came from the wood. But because nature is thus defrauded, those that fight for winter press on the more, that the victory may not be got by fraud; yet the sentence is given for summer by the favourable judgement of the people, who are unwilling to endure the sharp rigor of winter any longer; and so summer gets the victory with the general applause of them all, and he makes a gallant feast for his company, and confirms it by drinking cups, which he could scarcely win with spears. This is the custom of driving away the winter, and receiving of summer."

The Welsh story of the contest of Gwyn, as representing the powers of darkness, and Gwythur, as representing the summer sun, makes them fight for the possession of a beauteous damsel on the first of May. Gwythur gains the victory, which symbolises the recovery by the Sun-God of his bride at the beginning of summer, after his antagonist had gained possession of her at the beginning of winter.

The 12th of May is still the general day for letting houses, paying house rents, and taking grazing cattle, and also for farm girls going to their places; but the distinctive observances connected with it have died out.

On the 10th of this month was the Church festival called *Laa'l Spitlin souree*, "Spitlin's summer Feast-day," after a Saint now unknown.

PERAMBULATIONS OF PARISH BOUNDARIES. — On the Monday, Tuesday, or Wednesday, before Ascension Day it was

an ancient custom in the Isle of Man, as in England, to per-
ambulate the boundaries of the parishes. In Roman Catholic
times, this perambulation was a matter of great ceremony, and
banners, handbells, and lights enlivened the procession. In
Queen Elizabeth's reign it was ordained that the people should,
once in a year, make a circuit of the parish with the curate,
who was to admonish the people to give thanks to God, as
they beheld his benefits, and for the increase and abundance
of the fruits upon the face of the earth. This custom seems to
have been derived from the Roman *Terminalia* and *Amberval-
ia*, which were festivals in honour of the god Terminus, and
the goddess Ceres. In England, and, as we shall see, in the Isle
of Man also, it has likewise a twofold object, firstly to preserve a correct knowledge of the bounds of the parishes, and
secondly to supplicate the divine blessing on the fruits of the
earth. How this custom was performed in the Isle of Man will
be seen from the following injunction by the Bishop, Henry
Bridgeman, in 1677:—"Upon a solemn and tedious audience
of the tennants of my Ld Bp's demesne together with most or
many of the most aged and most substantiall parishioners of
the parish and parish Church of St Mary of Ballaugh, in the
Isle of Mann, concerning the performance of parochiall rights
and the payment of Parochiall duties betwixt the s^d tennants
and the rest of the parishioners aforesaid, which difference hath
now continued to be agitated betwixt them for many years. It
was finally sentenced and determined upon the second day of
February, 1677, by the Right Revd Father in God, Henry, Ld
Bp of this Isle, before whom it was clearly proved by the oaths
of Thomas Craine, of the Glaick, in Ballaugh, aged 71 years
or thereabouts, and of Thomas Kinred, of Ballaterson, in the
same parish of Ballaugh, aged about 60 years, and of Thomas Cowley, of Knockan, in the psh aforesaid, aged about 55
years. Many other aged persons of the said parish being ready
to confirme the same by their respective oaths had they been

thereunto admitted or required, which was forborne for the said Ld. Bp's tenants did before his L'sp then and there confesse and acknowledge the verity of their assertions vidt. That they had for severall years known the respective parsons of Ballaugh and vicars of Kirk Michaell meet upon severall ascension dayes together with their respective parishes at the gate of B'sp's Court, and in their perambulation goe into the Chappell of the said Ld. Bp., and there unanimously agree that the upper or East end thereof did stand, and was of antient time held to be within the præcints of the Parish of St. Mary, of Ballaugh, and the tower or West end of the said Chappell was of ould time accounted and esteemed to be within the site and præcints of the parish of Kirk Michaell and that the said respective Parsons and Vicars did severally officiate divine service, the one at the one side or end of the said Chappell, and the other at the other side or end of the same Chappell alternately upon the said same dayes of perambulation. The Parsons of Ballaugh coming down by a well called Aulcaugh als Phinlowes' well and so along by the river or milne-dam of the said Ld. Bp's demesne up to the said Chappell: and from thence with a considerable part of his meadow called Ballaugh-third, conterminating upon the middle-third of the said meadow, and thence to a parcell of land called John Gawn's Croft, and so to Brough-garge's lands, which goes along the Strand or seaside whereby it did evidently appear unto the said Ld Bp that all his tenants upon the Demesne aforesaid which were inhabitants within the said perambulation of the Parson of Ballaugh were and ought to be esteemed, and are now by his Lp accordingly adjudged to be parishioners of the parish and Church of St. Mary, of Ballaugh, and so subject and liable to all parochial duties and performances unto ye said church as the rest of the parishioners of the said parish are (excepting *onely* the payment of such tythes as now are and of ould usually have been due and payable unto the Ld Bp. And more particelarly yt it is incumbent upon them (as such) to make their proportionable part of the Churchyard hedge or ditch of the said parish of St. Mary's of Ballaugh, according as it is apportioned them in ye Register Book of the s^d church in the year 1660, and it is now ordered and decreed by the said Ld Bp that henceforth all the said tenants shall repaire unto divine service and all the offices of the Holy Church upon every Ld^s Day, every holy day, and other extraordinary dayes of public fasts and thanksgivings unto the said church of St. Marie's, as to their sole proper parish church; and yt if they shall absent themselves frequently from the same upon such dayes (without a lawfull and sufficient cause and reason to be allowed by the s^d Ld Bp and his successors or his Vic^r Gen^{le}) that they shall be presented by the churchwardens of the said parish for the time being (whose consciences are hereby onerated to deall faithfully therein) unto the Bp or his Vic^r Gen^{le} that they may be punished or fined 12d apiece for every such dayes absence whereof they cannot give a reasonable and satisfactory account. Provided always that ye decree be no longer of force after they shall produce an antient, sufficient and legall execution, which some of them seem to pretend unto, but are not or have not yet been able to produce or make good, and in the intervine (*sic*) they are hereby required to yield punctual submission and obedience hereunto upon pain of excommunication. Given under the Episcopal Seal of the said Ld Bp this second day of February, in the seventh year of his consecration and in the year of Our Lord, 1677.

JOHAN ALLEN, Actuar
a Secretis D^{mi} Epi.

A copy whereof is hereby enjoyned to be entered in the several registers of both parishes, and the original to be kept in the Ld Bp's records. }

The following is taken from the Parochial Register of Lezayre, Anno. 1715:—"The Revd. Mr. Wm. Walker, Vicar

Genl. and Rector of Ballaugh, and the Revd. Mr. Henry Allen, Vicar of Kirk Christ, Lezayre, together with several of the ancients of both parishes, having met this day at a place called Cottier's platt in order to determine Boundaries of the two Parishes from the place aforesaid unto the High-road leading from Bishop's Court to Ramsey: and both Parties having agreed to leave it to me to hear what can be sayd on both sides, and to put a final end to all controversies for the future concerning the said Boundary, I, therefore, having heard all that hath been sayd by both Parties, and having carefully viewed and walked the ground, do adjudge and declare that a straight line drawn from the East side of the platt aforesaid, betwixt two remarkable trees growing in the Highway aforesaid, and betwixt two large white stones on the other side of the said Highway to the end of an Hedge leading from thence to the mountains, shall ever hereafter be looked upon and be the true Boundary of the two Parishes, with which both sides being entirely satisfied, I do hereby require that nobody do presume presumptuously to cut down the trees or to remove the stones aforesaid; and that a true copy of this determination be preserved in the Registers of both Parishes, as an end of all strife on this account. Given under my hand and seal at Bishop's Court the day and year above written.   (Signed) THO: SODOR AND MAN."

A letter of Bishop Wilson's, on the subject of perambulations follows:—"To the Reverend the Archdeacon and the rest of the Clergy of the diocese of Sodor and Man: My brethren,—The last Convocation but one, you were put in mind of a very considerable ommission, in not going every Holy Thursday the boundary of your severall Parishes or some part of such as are large which hath been practised till of late, time out of mind. In order, therefore, to the keeping of this laudable custom, you are hereby required to give notice to your Parishioners on Rogation Sunday, May 3rd, that you purpose (God willing) to walk the boundarys of your Parish, or some considerable part of them, on Holy Thursday following, and desire the people to meet you at prayers and to accompany you. And that they may be better dispos'd to do so, you shall inform them that besides the great advantage of settling and securing the boundarys of Parishes, the great design is to give publick and national acknowledgement and thanks to God for all his blessings both by sea and land, and especially for the fruits of the earth which at this time begin to appear, as also to beg of God to send us such seasonable weather, as that we may receive the fruits thereof, to our own comfort, and for the relief of those that are in want, and lastly to beseech God of his mercy to preserve us from all infectious diseases and un-usual mortality amongst men and beasts and from the rage of enemies. You shall further inform them, how necessary this is to keep up a constant sense of our dependence upon Almighty God, for every blessing we enjoy or hope for, whether peace or plenty, or security from our enemies, or health to enjoy these blessings. Now, the manner of observing this laudable custom has been at certain places to read distinctly the 103rd Psalm, by the Minister only, and in other places to pronounce openly the curse set down in Deut. 27, 17—'Cursed is he that removeth his neighbour's landmark,' that is, who defrauds his neighbour of any of his rights, either by fraud or force, or going to law without just cause. At the same time people should be exhorted to beware of the great sin of covetousness, and to be content with the blessing God has given to their own honest labours. That 'better is the little that the righteous have,' such as they have gotten by righteous ways, than 'great riches of the ungodly,' which they have gotten wrongfully, and that God will never bless such possessions as are gotten, or defended, or kept by unjust means. Here also it will be very becoming a clergymen against the great sin of Litigiousness by which Christian love and charity are broken, and men hazard the loss of a heavenly inheritance to gain some trifle often in this world. — Dated at Bishop's Court, the 24th April. 1741. (Signed) THO: SODOR AND MANN." Below this he appends the proper "Collects to be used on the perambulation: Quinquagesima Sunday; Third Sunday in Lent; Septuagesima Sunday; The Prayer for Rain, if then needful; In time of Death and Famine; In time of Warr; In the Litany, the last two petitions, viz., That it may please Thee to give and preserve to our use, &c., 'That it may please Thee to forgive us all our sins,' and the Prayer in Mr Nelson's book for Rogation Week."[1] These Perambulations have not yet fallen entirely into disuse.

The festival on June 24th, *Midsummer-day*, and on its eve, *Midsummer-eve*, kept since the change in the Calendar on July 5th and July 4th, seems to have been of Scandinavian origin, for, among the ancient Celts, the longest day, as far as is known, was of no especial account. But to people living within the Arctic circle, who for months in the winter were altogether deprived of the sun, his ascent and descent were naturally of greater importance than to people living further south. This festival was probably originally in honour of Balder, the northern Sun-God, who at Midsummer attained his greatest splendour and duration, and from thence began to decline.[2] The beginning of his declination was commemorated by the lighting of his funeral pyre, which the modern bonfires have perpetuated. Of the later celebration of this eve and day in Scandinavia, Vigfusson writes:—"St. John Baptist's Day is in the northern countries a kind of Midsummer Yule, and was in Norway and Sweden celebrated with bonfires, dance, and merriment; and tales of fairies and goblins of every kind are connected with St. John's Eve in the summer as well as Yule-eve in winter." And with regard to its origin, he

1 These extracts about Perambulations were taken from the Ballaugh *Parochialia*, by the permission of its compiler, the late Rev. W. Kermode.

2 See Chapter VII.

says:—"The origin of this feast is no doubt heathen, being a worship of light and the sun, which has since been adapted to a Christian name and a Christian Calendar."[3] Very similar are the observances of this eve in Man. Bonfires were lit on the hills, and blazing wheels were formerly rolled from their tops, probably originally with the intention of typifying the beginning of the sun's declination.[4] Cattle were also driven between or over fires to keep them from disease, and men and boys leaped over the flames. Train says that "on the eve of St. John the Baptist, the natives lighted fires to the windward side of every field, so that the smoke might pass over the corn; they folded their cattle and carried blazing furze or gorse round them several times."

These fire observances were in fact the same as on May-day Eve, and they seem to have been designed as Charms to secure as much sunshine as possible, which, considering our dull and cloudy climate, is not to be wondered at; and they were at one time connected with human sacrifices.[5] There was also a notion that the corn would grow well as far as the bonfires were seen, and, therefore, numerous bonfires were lit on these occasions, and it was supposed that the height of the straw depended on the height that the men jumped over the flames.

Fairies are supposed to be especially powerful on this eve, and Witches are said to hold a saturnalia.

A curious belief that the souls of all people left their bodies when asleep on this night, and wandered to the place where they would die was formerly prevalent, and from this probably arose the custom of sitting up to watch, and so avoiding such an occurrence. Those who watched in the church porches were

3 Cleasby and Vigsusson, Icelandic Dictionary.

4 See story of "Origin of Arms of the Island." Chapter III. This custom of rolling down wheels was formerly practised in Bohemia and central France.

5 See Chapter VII.

rewarded with the sight of those who would die in the year, as on St. Mark's eve and Hollantide eve. On this eve, too, was gathered the *Bollan-Feaill-Eoin*, "John's Feast-day wort" (mugwort), which was made into wreaths to be worn on the heads of man and beast to protect them from witchcraft.

The next morning the great *Tinwald Court*,[1] corresponding to the Icelandic *Althing*, was held, when the laws were promulgated, and the festival proper, all Witches and evil Spirits having been disposed of on the previous evening, began. At this festival, which probably lasted a fortnight in old times, there took place not only the Court, but probably a religious feast and merry-makings of all kinds, such as hurling and football, match-making, feasting, and, above all, recitals of legends and traditions. As regards Man, however, we have no definite information about the observance of this day from tradition, except that there was a fair, which still continues; and from written sources there is only preserved a letter written, in 1636, by Bishop Parr to Archbishop Neile, in which he states that on St. John Baptist's day he found the people in a chapel dedicated to that Saint "in the practice of gross superstitions," which he caused "to be cried down," and, in the place of them, "appointed Divine services and sermons." We can only wish that the good Bishop had informed us what these "gross superstitions" were. We have already seen (Chapter I) that Manannan received his tribute of rushes on this day, and it is curious that the pathway leading up to the chapel is still covered with rushes supplied by a small farm close by, which is held on the tenure of doing this service.

As we have already seen from the name, St, John, the Church adopted this heathen festival as that Saint's feast, *Feaill Eoin*, "John's-Feast," as it is called in Manx. It has been ingeniously

---

1 The date of this Court has only been changed to the 5th of July since the alteration of the Calendar. For a full description of it see "Manx Names."

suggested by Mr. Tylor that this adoption, or rather adaptation, may have arisen from the same train of symbolism which adapted the heathen Midwinter solar festival to the Nativity of our Lord, *i.e.*, from our Lord's own words "He must increase, but I must decrease." It seems, however, much more probable that St. John was merely substituted for Balder, as our Saviour was substituted for him in other portions of the northern faith.

The following proverb attached to St. John's Day probably refers to the desirability of having rain to bring on the straw of the corn crops at this time rather than later, when it would interfere with the maturing of the grain: *Lane croie cabbyl dy ushtey L'aal Eoin feeu mayl Vannin*, "A full horse-shoe of water (on) John's Feast-day is worth the rent of Man."

July 13 was dedicated to the Saint called German, after whom the Cathedral on Peel Island is supposed to be named.[2]

August 1st, kept since the change in the calendar, on August 12th, is called *Laa Luanys*, or *Laa Lunys*, "Luanys's Day." This name was probably originally associated with the Celtic god *Lug*, or *Lleu*, as he is called in Wales, who, as he was said to have been brought up at the court of Manannan, was closely connected with Man.[3] In Ireland, his festival, called the *Lug-nassad*, or the wedding of Lug, was celebrated on this day by a fair, at which games and sports took place. In Man, too, there was, within living memory, a great fair in the parish of Santon, on the same day. This festival was, according to Professor Rhys, "the great event of the summer half of the year, which extended from the calends of May to the calends of winter. The Celtic year was more thermometric than astronomical; and the *Lugnassad* was, so to say, its summer solstice."[4] The fair has disappeared; but the ancient custom of visiting the highest

2 Manx Names.

3 See Chapter I.

4 The Hibbert Lectures, 1888, p. 149.

hills and the sacred wells on this day, cannot be said to be altogether extinct. These wells are usually found near old ecclesiastical sites, as the holy recluses would naturally build their *keeills* near springs, where they would construct wells both for their own personal convenience as well as for baptizing their disciples. Some of these wells were formerly much venerated, as their waters were supposed to possess sanative qualities, and to be of special virtue as charms against witchcraft and Fairies. The devotees would drop a small coin into the well, drink of the water, repeat a prayer, in which they mentioned their ailments, and then decorate the well, or the tree overhanging it, with flowers and other votive offerings, usually rags. They believed that when the flowers withered, or the rags rotted, their ailments would be cured. These rites have been observed in the Isle of Man within the memory of those now living. There is a well on Gob-y-Vollee, called Chibber Lansh (where the meaning of *lansh* is uncertain), consisting of three pools, which was formerly much resorted to for the cure of sore eyes. The cure could only be effective if the patient came on Sunday, and walked three times round each pool, saying in Manx, *Ayns enym yn Ayr, as y Vac, as y Spyrryd Noo*, "In the name of the Father, and of the Son, and of the Holy Ghost," and then applied the water to his or her eye. Many of these wells, however, together with the sacred tree which overshadowed them, were certainly objects of veneration long before the days of the recluses and their religion.[1]

The Church attempted to put an end to this custom, and failed, but contrived to give it a religious character by changing the date of its observance from the first day of August to the first Sunday in that month.[2] The following representation made to the Ecclesiastical Court by the curate and wardens of

1 See Chapter VII.

2 *i.e.*, after the change of the calendar to the first Sunday after the 12th of August.

the parish of Lonan, in 1732, will show that this custom was prevalent at that time:—

"The curate and wardens represent to the Court that there is a superstitious and wicked custom, which is yearly continued and practised in this and the neighbouring parishes by many young people (and some of riper years) going to the top of Snaefell Mountain upon the first Sunday in August, where (as they are informed) they behave themselves very rudely and indecently for the greater part of that day. Therefore, they crave that the Rev. Court may be pleased to order what method must be taken to put a stop to this profane custom for the future." The Court (consistorial), in consequence of this order, ordained "that publication be made yearly on the two last Sundays in July, by the minister for the time being, after the Nicene Creed, that whoever shall be found to profane the Lord's Day after this wicked and superstitious manner shall be proceeded against with severe ecclesiastical censures; and the minister and wardens are hereby required to do their utmost in discovering the persons guilty in this particular, and to make presentment thereof."

But such methods did not avail against this "superstitious and wicked custom" and in vain, too, did Bishop Wilson fulminate against it, as it was quite common 70 years ago, and is not quite extinct yet. It is said that, about 1820, a preacher, named Gick, went up South Barrule and denounced it, and that consequently it has since then almost ceased, though a few people still ascend the mountains on the first Sunday after the 12th of August, pretending that they do so to search for blaberries; and a few may be seen lurking in the vicinity of the wells. There is now an idea prevalent that this custom of ascending the hills is in commemoration of Jepthah's daughter going forth on the hills, with the daughters of Israel following her, an idea which has probably been promulgated by the preachers with a view of causing a heathen superstition to be superseded by a Christian ceremony.

HARVEST. — When the landlord, or farmer, entered for
the first time the field where harvesting operations went on, it
was customary to bind him with *sugganes*, or straw ropes, and
not to release him till he paid a forfeit.

The harvest festival is called in Manx *yn mheillea*, or *yn
meailley*, 'the harvest home,' "though," says Gill,[1] "more strictly it is the name of the garland made of the last handful of
corn which is shorn and formed into the shape of that which
is borne by Ceres. This figure, dressed with ribbons, is carried
before the reapers, and is called, together with the procession,
yn meailley, or *meilley*, 'the reapers feast,' from *meail*." "*Meail*,"
he adds, "is the whole gang of reapers." This figure, somewhat
obscurely described by Gill, was called *yn moidyn*, 'the maid-
en,' and was made of straw, decorated with ribbons and wild
flowers. It was carried by the Queen of the *Meailley*, a girl
elected from among the female workers, though usually the
youngest of them, to the highest part of the field where it was
placed and saluted with hearty cheers. It was also a custom to
cut off a bunch of ears from this last sheaf of corn, with about
12 inches of straw attached. This bunch of corn, called *baban
ny mheillea*, 'the doll of the harvest,' or simply, *yn mheillea*, 'the
harvest,' which was usually about 4 inches in diameter, was
dressed up to represent a woman, from the neck downwards,
the ears doing duty for the head and face. It was then placed
on the chimney piece in the kitchen of the farm house, and
was not removed till the following harvest, when its place was
taken by a similar successor. This custom has not long died
out, and indeed the small sheaf, though not dressed, may still
be seen in many a farm house. The large sheaf previously referred to was taken from the field, when the last load of corn
was carried and placed on top of it, together with the *moidyn*.[2]
It was then deposited in the barn with much clamour and

1 Kelly's Manx Dictionary, p. 129.

2 See Chapter VII.

rejoicing, and was kept there till the following harvest. After this they all adjourned to the supper, which it was usual for the farmer to provide on these occasions, and which was a scene of great joy and merriment, the *Laare-vane*, as on twelfth-day, being a conspicuous feature (see p. 104). The carrying of the 'maiden' has now fallen into desuetude, so that the name is now associated with the harvest supper only.

October 25th. — *Laa'l Maghal*, 'Maughold's Feast-day,' the second of the two days dedicated to this Saint.

October 31st and November 11th are the present and past dates, in accordance with the change in the Calendar, of the eve of the Church festival called "All Hallow Mass," or "All Saints' Mass" (Middle English *halowe* 'a saint'). The eve of this day, Hallowe'en in English, is called *Oie houiney* in Manx, and is still kept in the Isle of Man on the 11th of November. The day itself is called *Sauin*, *Souin* or *yn Tauin*, corresponding with the Irish and Scotch *Samhain*, though the English "Holland-tide" is the name now usually given to the season and to the fair held on the 12th of November.

This day was formerly the first day of the first month of winter, and also the first day of the Celtic year. A tradition to the effect that it was the first day of the year still obtains among the Manx, who are accustomed to predict the weather for the ensuing year from that on the 12th of November, and this is emphasised by the fact that, as we shall see later, the ceremonies now practised on New Year's Eve, were, within living memory, practised on the 11th of November. Among the Norsemen, the first night of winter, which they celebrated by a feast, was the 14th of October, but winter would come earlier in their more Northern clime. According to the ancient Irish, Samhain Eve was the proper occasion for prophecies and unveiling mysteries. In Wales, within almost recent times, women congregated in the parish churches on this eve to learn their fortune from the flame of the candle each one held in her hand, and to hear the names or see the coffins of the parishioners destined to die in the course of the year. The Scotch believed that all the Warlocks and Witches assembled in force at this season, and perpetrated all sorts of atrocities. Similar beliefs to the above prevailed in the Isle of Man. It was, therefore, very necessary to propitiate the Fairies, who alone were amenable to such attentions, on this night in particular. The leavings of the supper of the family were consequently not removed, and crocks of fresh water were placed on the table, so that 'the little People' might refresh themselves. Professor Rhys says that the reason why this night was regarded as "the Saturnalia of all that was hideous and uncanny in the world of spirits" was because "it had been fixed upon as the time of all others when the Sun-God, whose power had been gradually falling off since the great feast associated with him on the first of August, succumbed to his enemies, the powers of darkness and winter. It was their first hour of triumph after an interval of subjection, and the popular imagination pictured them stalking abroad with more than ordinary insolence and aggressiveness."[1] It was, in fact, the time when the result of the combat which took place in May was reversed; then the powers of light gained the ascendency, now the powers of darkness. Bonfires were lit on *Oie Houiney*, as on *Oie Voaldyn*, and for the same reason.

The following custom, which survived till recently, has now died out. Mummers went from house to house shouting the following curious refrain, the meaning of which can only be conjectured. The portion now in English was, of course, formerly in Manx:—

> *Hog-annaa*—This is old Hollantide night:
> *Trolla-laa*—The moon shines fair and bright.
> *Hog-annaa*—I went to the well,
> *Trolla-laa*—And drank my fill;
> *Hog-annaa*—On my way back

---

1 Rhys' Hibbert Lectures, 1886; pp. 516-17.

Trolla-laa—I met a witch-cat;
Hog-annaa—The cat began to grin,
Trolla-laa—And I began to run.
Hog-annaa—Where did you run to?
Trolla-laa—I ran to Scotland.
Hog-annaa—What were they doing there?
Trolla-laa—Baking bannocks and roasting collops.
Hog-annaa—*Trolla-laa!*
If you are going to give us anything, give us it soon,
Or we'll be away by the light of the moon—*Hog-annaa!*

Professor Rhys came across a different and seemingly more rational version of this Hollantide rhyme in the South of the Island last year:—*Oie Houna*—"Hollantide Eve." *Shibber ny gauin(a)*[2]—"Supper of the heifer." *Cre gauin marr mayd?*—"Which heifer shall we kill?" *yn gauin veg vreac*—"The little spotted heifer." There were more lines, but his informant had forgotten them.

The first line of this song was formerly "*Hog-annaa*—Tonight is New Year's Night,"[3] which is another proof that this was the last night of the year; and it is significant, also, that the customs of raking out the ashes from the fire and placing ivy in water, now practised on the 31st of December, were practised on this night within living memory. These facts, combined with the recollection of the 12th being considered New Year's Day by old persons (as previously mentioned), may be considered to settle the question. But, in addition to this, the words of the chorus, *Hog-annaa, trollalay*, are probably identical with *Hogmanaye, trollalay*, the words of a Scotch song which is sung on New Year's Eve—*Hogmanaye*, according to Jamieson, being either the last day of the year or the entertainment given to a visitor on this day. In France, too, there is a similar custom and word, as *En Basse Normandie les bauvres le dernier jour en demandant l'aumosne, disent Hoguinanno*. "In Low Nor-

---

2 This looks like reminiscence of sacrifice and feasting. See Chapter VII.

3 Kelly, Manx Dictionary, p. 24.

mandie, the poor, the last day (of the year), in demanding alms, say *Hoguinanno*." We may, therefore, conclude that this was undoubtedly the last night of the year. As to the meaning of this word, *Hog-annaa*, *Hogmanaye*, or *Hoguinanno*, we may venture to suggest that, supposing the Scotch form to be the most accurate, both it and trollalay are of Scandinavian origin, and refer to the Fairies and the Trolls. We know that on this night it was considered necessary to propitiate the dwellers in fairy-land, who, with the Phynnodderees, Witches, and Spirits of all kinds, were abroad and especially powerful. We may, therefore, perhaps translate *Hog-man-aye* into *Hanga-man-ey*—"mound-men (for) ever," the Fairies being considered as dwellers in the *hows* (or *tumuli*, or green mounds)—and *trollalay* into *trolla-á-lá*, "trolls into the surf." The Fairies, who were considered the most powerful of these creatures, being thus propitiated, would then protect their suppliants against the rest. The boys, who went round singing this song, carried big sticks with cabbages or turnips stuck in the top, and with these they knocked at people's doors till they received herrings and potatoes and such-like gifts. The usual supper on this night consists of potatoes, parsnips and fish, pounded together and mixed with butter; and a cake is made, called *Soddag valloo*, or dumb cake. "Every woman is obliged to assist in mixing the ingredients (flour, eggs and eggshells, soot, &c.), kneading the dough and baking the cake on the glowing embers; and when it is sufficiently baked, they divide it, eat it up, and retire to their beds backwards without speaking a word, from which silence the cake derives its name, and in the course of the night they expect to see the images of the men who are destined to be their husbands."[1] The following is another Hollantide recipe for dreaming of a future husband:—Take a salt herring from a neighbour's house without the consent or knowledge of the owner. Be sure to capture it in the dark, and

---

1 Kelly, Manx Dictionary, p. 14.

take the first that comes to hand. Then take it home, and roast it in its brine upon the cinders. Maintain strict silence, both while eating it and afterwards, and carefully consume every scrap—bones and all. On the stroke of midnight retire to bed backwards, undress in the dark, and avoid touching water. If these instructions are properly carried out, the future husband will appear in a dream, and will present a drink of water. Yet another recipe was, for the girls to fill their mouths with water, and hold a pinch of salt in each hand. Thus equipped they went to a neighbour's door, and listened to the conversation within, when the first name mentioned would be that of their future husband. There are various customs practised on this evening in Man, which are almost identical with those in all other parts of the United Kingdom. Of these, the burning of nuts for purposes of divination, is one of the most popular. It is described by Burns for Scotland; and by Brand, in his "Popular Antiquities," for Ireland, in words which we quote, as they are precisely applicable to what takes place in Man:—

> The auld guidwife's well hoordit nits[2]
> Are round and round divided,
> And mony lads' and mony lasses' fates
>   Are there that night decided:
> Some kindle couthie[3] side by side,
>   An' burn thegither trimly,
> Some start awa' wi' saucy pride,
>   And grimp out owre the chimlie
>   Fu' high that night.
>
> Jean slips in twa wi' tentie e'e;[4]
>   Wha 'twas she wadna tell;
> But this is Jock, and this is me,
>   She says in to hersel;
> He bleez'd owre her, an' she owre him,
>   As they wad ne'er main part!

---

2 Nuts.

3 Lovingly.

4 Watchful eye.

Till fuff! he started up the lum,[1]
An Jean had e'en a sair heart
To see't that night.

"It is a custom in Ireland, when the young women would know if their lovers are faithful, to put three nuts upon the bars of the grate, naming the nuts after the lovers. If a nut cracks or jumps, the lover will prove unfaithful, if it begins to blaze or burn, he has a regard for the person making the trial. If the nuts named after the girl and her lover burn together, they will be married."

Much amusement is also derived from the custom of setting apples afloat in a tub of water from which they have to be extracted by the teeth. The pouring of molten lead into water, where it takes various fantastic shapes from which the future vocation of the person who pours is divined, is still a favourite pastime. The popular belief ascribes to children born on Hallowe'en the possession of the mysterious faculty of perceiving and holding converse with supernatural beings.

The following day, the first of November, according to the present reckoning, is the church Festival of All Saints, *Laa'l Mooar ny Saintsh* "Great Festival of the Saints," as it is called in Manx.

The twelfth of November is the general day for letting lands, payment of rent, and for men-servants taking their places for the year. The largest fair of the year is still held on this day. It is considered as the beginning of the winter half of the year.

November 18. — *Laa'l Spitlin Geurey*, "Spitlin's Winter Feast-day," the second feast of this unknown Saint.

December 6th. — *Laa'l Catreeny*, "Catherine's Feast-day" (old style). On, or about, this day possession must be taken on the South side of the Island of lands, when there is a change of occupier. A fair was held on this day

---

1 Chimney.

in the Parish of Arbory, when the following curious distich was repeated:—

> *Kiark Catreeny maroo,*
> *Gow's y kione,*
> *As goyms ny cassyn,*
> *As ver mayd ee fo'n thalloo.*
> Catherine's hen is dead,
> Take thou the head,
> And I will take the feet,
> And we will put her under ground.

If any one got drunk at the fair he was said to have
"plucked a feather of the hen."

December 11th. — *Laa'l Andreays*, "Andrew's Feast-day."
On, or before, this day possession must be taken on the North
side of the Island, under similar circumstances.

December 21. — *Laa'l Thomase*, "Thomas's Feast-day,"
formerly *Laa'l Fingan*, "Fingan's feast-day," St. Fingan, or Fin-
nian, was the first of the great Irish scholars, being especially
devoted to the study and exposition of Scripture. The following saying has reference to the eve of this day: *Faaid mooar son
Oiel Fingan*, "A large turf for Eve of Fingan's Feast." It probably means that, as the Christmas festivities were drawing near,
it was necessary to have an extra large turf to cook the fare for
that feast. There is a weather saying with reference to this time
of the year, that "if the frost will bear a goose before Christmas, it will not bear a duck after Christmas." *Ny nee yn rio
gymmyrkey guiy roish yn Ollick cha nymmyrkey e thunnag lurg
yn Ollick.*[2]

December 24. — Christmas-eve, in Manx *Oie'l Verrey*, a
corruption of *Oie feaill Voirrey*, "Eve of Mary's Feast." It was the
custom for the people to go in crowds to the Parish Churches
on this evening to attend a service, the main feature of which
was the singing of Carols, called in Manx *Carvals*, many of
which were of portentous length. Each one brought his or her
own candle, so that the Church was brilliantly illuminated.

2 This is identical with an English proverb.

The decorations were of a very primitive kind, mainly consisting of huge branches of *hullin* (holly), and festoons of *hibbin* (ivy). After the prayers were read, and a hymn was sung, the parson usually went home, leaving the Clerk in charge. Then each one who had a carol to sing would do so in turn, so that the proceedings were continued till a very late hour, and sometimes, also, unfortunately became of a rather riotous character, as it was a custom for the female part of the congregation to provide themselves with peas, which they flung at their bachelor friends. On the way home, a considerable proportion of the congregation would probably visit the nearest inn, where they would partake of the traditional drink on such occasions, viz., hot ale, flavoured with spice, ginger, and pepper. After this, the parting song commencing with:—

> *Te traa goll thie dy goll dy thie,*
> *Te taern dys traa ny lhiabbagh &c.*
>
> It is time to go home to go to lie down,
> It draws towards bed-time, &c.

would be trolled out, and the last of the revellers would depart. The *Oie'l Verree* services are still continued, but are entirely shorn of all their riotous accompaniments, while ordinary hymns, or short carols sung by the choirs, have taken the place of the lengthy solos of the past. Carols are also sung by bands, who go from house to house during the week before Christmas, and receive a small Christmas-box, or some refreshment, in return for their entertainment.

It was formerly the custom for fiddlers to go round in this way before Christmas. They stopped and played at the houses where they thought they were likely to receive a fee, wished the inmates individually "good morning," called the hour, and reported the state of the weather. The custom of mumming at this season, formerly common, is now almost moribund. The mummers, or as they are called in Man, "The White Boys," perform the time-honoured legend of "St. George and the Dragon," which has, however, became considerably modified.

Both in England, Scotland, and Ireland, it has been from an early day amongst the most popular amusements of Christmas, and, till recently, continued to be so in Man. The plot everywhere seems to be pretty nearly the same, though scarcely any two sets of performers render it alike, as they constantly mix up extraneous matter, often of a local nature, and frequently allude to the passing events of the day, making the confusion of character in all the versions very great.[1]

In this Isle the *dramatis personæ*—St. George, Prince Valentine, King of Egypt, Sambo, and the Doctor—are attired in white dresses, showing their shirt sleeves, fantastically decorated with ribbons, fancy-coloured paper, beads, and tinsel. They wear high caps or turbans of white pasteboard similarly decked out, with a sprig of evergreen or "Christmas" stuck in them, and each carrying a drawn sword in his hand. The "Doctor" is in full black, with face and cap of the same, armed with a stick, and a bladder tied to the end, with which he belabours those who press too close upon the performers. He generally carries a small box for the contributions, and is a kind of Merry-Andrew to the play, which, if it happens to fall in the hands of a sprightly wag, causes some amusement to the audience, who, somehow or other, generally appear more frightened than pleased with the rest of the characters. The performance is often wound up by a song. The following was taken down by W. Harrison as it was recited in his house at Christmas, 1845.[2]

---

1 This play is mentioned by Davies Gilbert, F.R.S., as being popular in the West of England in his *Ancient Christmas Carols*, London, 1822.

2 Manx Society, vol. XVI., pp. 166-171.

THE WHITE BOYS

Dramatis Personæ.

ST. GEORGE	PRINCE VALENTINE
KING OF EGYPT	SAMBO

A DOCTOR

Enter SAMBO

It is here by your leave, Ladies and Gentlemen,
We will act a sporting play;
We will show you fine diversion,
Before we go away.
It is room, room, brave gallant boys!
Give us room to rhyme,
We will show you fine diversion
In this Christmas time.
It is room, room, give us room to sport,
This is the place we wish to resort—
To resort and to repeat our pretty rhymes,
Remember, good folks, it is the Christmas times.
This Christmas time as we now appear,
We wish to act our merry Christmas here;
We are the merry actors that travel the street,
We are the merry actors who fight for our meat,
We are the merry actors who show pleasant play;
Enter in the King of Egypt—clear the way!

Enter THE KING OF EGYPT

I am the King of Egypt, and so boldly do appear,
And St. George, he is my son, my only son and heir!
Step forth, my son, St. George! and act thy part with ease,
Show forth to all the living company thy praise.

Enter ST. GEORGE

I am thy son St. George, and from England have I sprung,
Many are the noble deeds and wonders I have done.
Full fourteen years in prison I was kept,
And out of that into a cave I leap't,
From thence I went into a rock of stone;
'Twas there I made my sad and grievous (sic) moan.
Many were the lions that I did subdue,
I ran the fiery dragon through and through;
With a golden trumpet in my mouth
I sounded at the gates divine, the truth.
It's here to England, right from Egypt's station,
It is here I draw my bloody weapon.
Show me the man that dare before me stand;

I'll cut him down with my courageous hand!
Or, who dare challenge me to fight, and I so great?
I who have fought Lords, Dukes, and made the earth to quake!

Enter PRINCE VALENTINE

ST. GEORGE—Who art thou? poor silly fellow?
VALENTINE—I am a Turkish champion, from Turkish land I came,
I came to fight that valiant knight, St. George they call his name;
For it is hereby my name is written, Prince Valentine,
Descended from a hardy race and of a noble line.
And soon St. George I'll make thy lofty laurels flee,
It shall not be said by all that I did yield to thee!
Well fight it out most manfully. Draw!

[They Fight.

ST. GEORGE—The point of my sword is broke.
VALENTINE—It happens so indeed! this night
    St. George is beat, he dare not fight!
ST. GEORGE—Beat by thee! thou poor silly rook!
VALENTINE—Fall in, Prince Actor.

[They fight; St. George falls on one knee.

KING OF EGYPT—O mortal stars! and skies of heaven above!
What a thing it is for a man to lose his love!
To strike that val'rous champion from the helm,
And cursed be he, that did him overwhelm.
O Sambo! Sambo! help me now in speed
For never was I in a greater need.
SAMBO—O yea, my master! I soon will thee obey,
With sword in hand I hope to gain the day.
Art thou the knave that singly standest there?
That slew my master's only son and heir?
VALENTINE—He challenged me to fight, and why should I deny!
He cut my coat so full of rents and made my buttons fly,
And if the rascal had had the honour to obtain,
Why, sir! he would have served you the same.
SAMBO—I'll try if thou art born of noble race;
I'll make thy blood come trickling down thy face;
And if thou dost another word against my master say,
Right through thy yellow body I'll make an open way.

[They fight; and Valentine falls.

KING OF EGYPT—O guards! come, take this dismal corpse away,
For in my sight it shall no longer stay,
O Doctor! Doctor! is there a doctor to be found,
Can cure St. George of his deep and deadly wound?

Enter DOCTOR

Oh yes! master, yes, there is a doctor to be found,
Can cure St. George, thy son, of a deep and deadly wound.

KING OF EGYPT—From whence come ye?
DOCTOR—From France, from Spain, from Rome I came,
    I've travelled all parts of Christendom.
SAMBO—Well spoken, Doctor!
KING OF EGYPT—What can you cure?
DOCTOR—All sorts of diseases,
        Whatever you pleases.
        All pains within, all pains without,
        The plague, the palsy, and the gout.
        The itch, stich, and molly-grubs.
        I can cure all these deeds.
        All big-bellied maids,
        And such like jades.
        Likewise, I will pledge my life,
        I can cure a scolding wife;
        Let them be curst or ever so stout,
        If the devil's in, I'll blow him out.
KING OF EGYPT—What is your fee?
DOCTOR—Twenty pounds down is my fee,
        But half of that I'll take from thee,
        If it is St. George's life I save,
        That sum this night from you I crave.
KING OF EGYPT—What medicine do you carry, Doctor?
DOCTOR—I carry a little bottle in my pocket of rixum-raxum, prix
    um-praxum, with I-cock-o'-lory—a little of this to his nostrils.
        Rise up St. George! and fight again!

        [*The Doctor performs his cure, and St. George rises.*
ST. GEORGE—Oh horrible! terrible! the like was never seen,
    A man drove out of seven senses into seventeen,
    And out of seventeen into seven-score,
    Oh horrible! terrible! the like was ne'er before.
    It was neither by a bull, nor yet by a bear,
    But by a little devil of a rabbit there.

        [*The Doctor performs the cure on Valentine, who rises.*
VALENTINTE—It is a kind of rough tough, coming up like a fly,
    Up the seven stairs, and down the lofty sky.
    My head is made of iron, my body made of steel,
    My legs are made of pipe-shanks, I'll cause you all to yield.
[*Valentine and Sambo fight, when the King of Egypt interposes.*
KING OF EGYPT—Oh! oh! we are all brothers,
    Why should we be all through others?
    Put up your swords and fight no more,
    No longer in this house adore.
DOCTOR—My box it is dumb and cannot speak,
    Please give us something for Christmas sake.
        [*Exeunt omnes.*

It is said, that on this Eve, at midnight, all the bullocks of seven years old or more fall on their knees and utter a sort of groan, and, that at the same time, the myrrh plant bursts into flower and so continues for one hour, when it disappears again. My informant is positive that he saw this latter phenomenon last Christmas Eve (1890).

To the superstitious Manx, one pleasant feature of this sacred season generally, and of Christmas-eve and Christmas-day in particular, was that they were able to pass any haunted glen or road in perfect safety, as, owing to the beneficent influence of Christ, no Phynnodderee, Buggane, Witch, or evil creature of any kind could harm them.

Christmas-day, called *Laa Nollick* or *Laa Nullick*, in Manx, where *Nollick* is probably a corruption of the latin *Natalicium* "birthday," is observed in the Isle of Man in much the same way as in England, Scotland, and Ireland.

It is interesting to note that the church festival of Christmas was placed at the same time as the Pagan feast of the winter solstice, which was called the *Saturnalia* by the Romans, and Yule by the Scandinavian nations, with whom the Isle of Man was closely connected. The meaning of the word *Yule* has given rise to considerable controversy, the most probable interpretation being that of Ficke;[1] who explains it to mean "noise," or "cry," especially the loud noise of revelry and rejoicing. The heathen *Yule* was certainly a great time of merrymaking, and lasted for thirteen days, inclusive of the 6th of January. This merrymaking was to express their joy at the days having reached their shortest limit on the 21st of December, when the sun recommenced his upward course. The Church attempted to change the heathen ceremonies into the solemnities of the Christian festivals, of which it put as many as possible at this season. The result was, the strange medley of Christian and Pagan rites, especially with regard to the

1 Indogermanischen Sprachen, vol. III., p. 245.

mistletoe and the *Yule* log, which contribute to the festivities of the modern Christmas.

"As soon as the prayers at the *Oiel Verrey* are over," says Waldron, "Christmas begins, and there is not a barn unoccupied for the whole twelve days—every parish hiring fiddlers at the public charge; and all the youths, nay, sometimes people in years, make no scruple to be among these nocturnal dancers."

Every family that could afford it, had a special brewing called *Jough-y-Nollick*, "drink of Christmas;" and as one brewing kettle generally served a whole neighbourhood, it was in great request at this time, hence the Manx proverb, "To go about like a brewing pan." The weather saying for this season is: *Ollick fluigh, Rhullick vea*, "Wet Christmas, rich churchyard," *i.e.*, wet weather at this time is considered unhealthy.

December 26. — *Laa'l Steaoin*, Stephen's Feast-day. On this day the cruel but curious custom of Hunting the Wren is kept up. The unfortunate bird was stoned to death; and there is, therefore, an appropriateness in the Church festival commemorating the stoning of St. Stephen being on the same day. This stoning of the wren, however, if Waldron is to be believed, seems to have taken place on Christmas morning 160 years ago, as he says, "on the 24th of December, towards evening, all the servants in general have a holiday; they go not to bed all night, but ramble about till the bells ring in all the Churches, which is at twelve o'clock; prayer being over, they go to hunt the wren, and after having found one of these poor birds, they kill her, and lay her on a bier with the utmost solemnity, bringing her to the parish church, and burying her with a whimsical kind of solemnity, singing dirges over her in the Manx language, which they call her knell, after which Christmas begins." A writer of the early part of the present century gives the following account of the origin of the hunting of the wren:—

"It has been a pastime in the Isle of Man from time immemorial to hunt the wren. It is founded on a tradition that in
former times a fairy of uncommon beauty exerted such undue
influence over the male population, that she at various times
seduced numbers to follow her footsteps, till, by degrees, she
led them into the sea, where they perished. This barbarous
exercise of power had continued for a great length of time,
till it was apprehended the Island would be exhausted of its
defenders, when a knight errant sprung up, who discovered
some means of countervailing the charms used by this syren,
and even laid a plot for her destruction, which she only escaped at the moment of extreme hazard, by taking the form
of a wren. But though she evaded instant annihilation, a spell
was cast upon her, by which she was condemned on every
succeeding New Year's Day, to reanimate the same form, with
the definitive sentence, that she must ultimately perish by a
human hand. In consequence of this *well authenticated* legend, on the specified anniversary, every man and boy in the
Island (except those who have thrown off the trammels of superstition), devote the hours between sunrise and sunset, to
the hope of extirpating the Fairy, and woe be to the individual
birds of this species, who show themselves on this fatal day to
the active enemies of the race; they are pursued, pelted, fired
at, and destroyed, without mercy, and their feathers preserved
with religious care; it being an article of belief that every one
of the relics gathered in this laudable pursuit is an effectual
preservation from shipwreck for one year; and that fishermen
would be considered as extremely foolhardy who would enter
upon his occupation without such a safeguard."— (*Bullock*,
History of the Isle of Man, 1816.)

Kelly's description of this custom at about the same period
is as follows:—"It is the custom of the inhabitants of the several parishes to catch a wren, on this day, and parade with flags
flying and music, with the wren fixen upon the point of a long

pole; and they oblige every person they meet to purchase a feather,[1] and to wear it in their hats for the day; in the evening they inter the naked body, with great solemnity; and conclude the evening with wrestling and all manner of sports. This is supposed to be in memory of the first martyr."

The manner of celebrating this custom 50 years ago was described by William Harrison as follows:—"This custom is still kept upon St. Stephen's Day, chiefly by boys, who at early dawn sally out armed with long sticks, beating the bushes until they find one of these birds, when they commence the chase with great shoutings following it from bush to bush, and when killed it is suspended in a garland of ribbons, flowers, and evergreens. The procession then commences, carrying that 'King of birds,' as the Druids called it, from house to house, soliciting contributions, and giving a *feather* for luck; these are considered an effectual preservative from shipwreck, and some fishermen will not yet venture out to sea without having first provided themselves with a few of these feathers to insure their safe return. The "*dreain*," or wren's feathers, are considered an effectual preservative against witchcraft. It was formerly the custom in the evening to inter the naked body with great solemnity in a secluded corner of the churchyard, and conclude the evening with wrestling and all manner of sports."[2]

Barrow gave the music of the song which follows in his *Mona Melodies*, published in 1820, and the words were taken down by William Harrison from a company of "Wren boys," in 1843:—

1 See Chapter VIII, and Manx Dictionary, p. 116.
2 Mona Miscellany Manx Society, vol. XXI.

HUNT THE WREN. 135

MANX AIR.

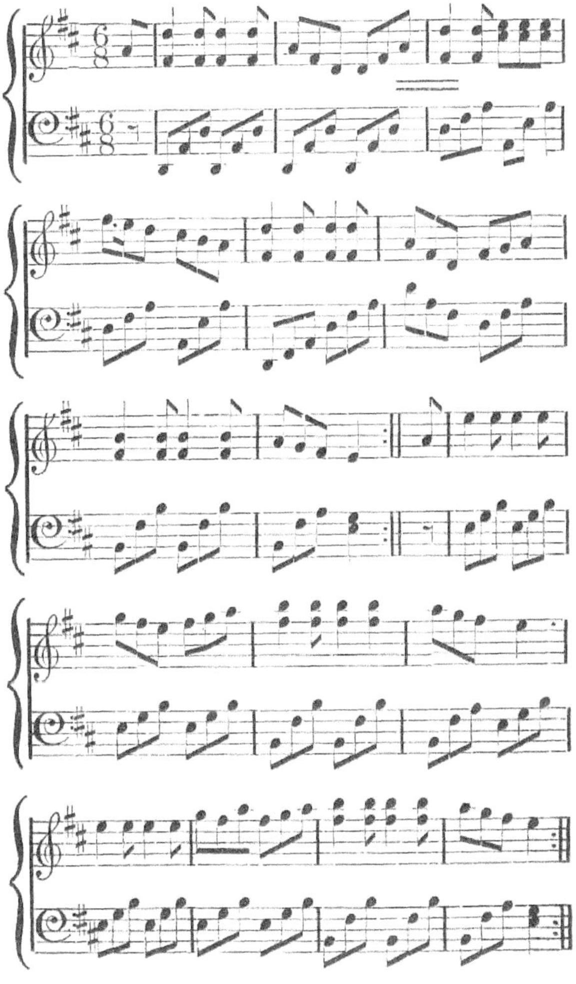

THE HUNTING OF THE WREN

We'll away to the woods, says Robin to Bobbin.
We'll away to the woods, says Richard to Robin;
We'll away to the woods, says Jack of the Land,
We'll away to the woods, says every one.

What shall we do there? says Robin to Bobbin.
                              Repeat, etc.
We will hunt the wren, says Robin to Bobbin.
                              Repeat, etc.
Where is he? where is he? says Robin to Bobbin.
                              Repeat, etc.
In yonder green bush, says Robin to Bobbin.
                              Repeat, etc,
I see him, I see him, says Robin to Bobbin,
                              Repeat, &c.
How shall we get him down? says Robin to Bobbin.
                              Repeat, etc.
With sticks and stones, says Robin to Bobbin.
                              Repeat, etc.
He is dead, he is dead, says Robin to Bobbin.
                              Repeat, etc.
How shall we get him home? says Robin to Bobbin.
                              Repeat, etc.
We'll hire a cart, says Robin to Bobbin.
                              Repeat, etc.
Whose cart shall we hire? says Robin to Bobbin.
                              Repeat, etc.
Johnny Bill Fell's, says Robin to Bobbin.
                              Repeat, etc.
Who will stand driver? says Robin to Bobbin.
                              Repeat, etc.
Filley the Tweet, says Robin to Bobbin.
                              Repeat, etc.
He's home, he's home, says Robin to Bobbin.
                              Repeat, etc.
How shall we get him boil'd? says Robin to Bobbin.
                              Repeat, etc.
In the brewery pan, says Robin to Bobbin.
                              Repeat, etc.
How shall we get him in? says Robin to. Bobbin.
                              Repeat, etc.
With iron bars and a rope, says Robin to Bobbin.

Repeat, etc.
He is in, he is in, says Robin to Bobbin.
Repeat, etc.
He is boil'd, he is boil'd, says Robin to Bobbin.
Repeat, etc.
How shall we get him out? says Robin to Bobbin.
Repeat, etc.
With a long pitchfork, says Robin to Bobbin.
Repeat, etc.
He is out, he is out, says Robin to Bobbin.
Repeat, etc.
Who's to dine at dinner? says Robin to Bobbin.
Repeat, etc.
The King and the Queen, says Robin to Bobbin.
Repeat, etc.
How shall we get him eat? says Robin to Bobbin.
Repeat, etc.
With knives and forks, says Robin to Bobbin.
Repeat, etc.
He is eat, he is eat, says Robin to Bobbin.
Repeat, etc.
The eyes for the blind, says Robin to Bobbin.
Repeat, etc.
The legs for the lame, says Robin to Bobbin.
Repeat, etc.
The pluck for the poor, says Robin to Bobbin.
Repeat, etc.
The bones for the dogs, says Robin to Bobbin;
The bones for the dogs, says Richard to Robin;
The bones for the dogs, says Jack of the land;
The bones for the dogs, says every one.
The wren, the wren, the king of all birds,
We have caught, St. Stephen's Day, in the furze;
Although he is little, his family's great,
I pray you, good dame, do give us a treat,

And so on, always chorusing with affected labour and exertion, "Hoist! Hoist!"

Colonel Vallancy, in his *Collectanea de Rebus Hibernicis*, says, "The Druids represented this as the king of all birds. The superstitious respect shown to this little bird gave offence to our first Christian missionaries, and by their commands *he is still hunted and killed by the peasant on Christmas Day*, and on the following (St. Stephen's Day) he is carried about hung by the leg in the centre of two hoops, crossing each other at right angles, and a procession made in every village of men, women, and children, singing an Irish catch, importing him to be the king of all birds. In several European languages his name imports the same—as, Latin, *Regulus*; French, *Reytelet*; Welsh, *Bren*, king; Teutonic, *Konig-Vogel*, king-bird; Dutch, *Konije*, little king."[1]

This kingly dignity is accounted for in the following curious traditional tale, which is current in the West Highlands and in Skye, and is also related in Grimm's story of "King Wren":—"In a grand assembly of all the birds of the air, it was determined that the sovereignty of the feathered tribe should be conferred upon the one who would fly highest. The favourite was, of course, the eagle, who at once, and in full confidence of victory, commenced his flight towards the sun; when he had vastly distanced all competitors, he proclaimed with a mighty voice his monarchy over all things that had wings. Suddenly, however, the wren, who had secreted himself under the feathers of the eagle's crest, popped from his hiding-place, flew a few inches upwards, and chirped out as loudly as he could, 'Birds, look up and behold your king;' and was elected accordingly." The meaning of the Manx, *Dreain*, is uncertain, though Kelly[2] boldly derives it from *druai-eean*, "the druid's bird."

Aubray relates in his *Miscellanies* that, after a battle in the north of Ireland, "a party of the Protestants had been surprised sleeping by the Popish Irish were it not for several wrens that had just wakened them by dancing and pecking on the drums as the enemy were approaching. For this reason the wild Irish mortally hate these birds to this day, calling them the devil's

---

1 Indeed the wren was called "King of birds" by almost every European nation.

2 Manx Dictionary, p. 67.

servants, and killing them wherever they can catch them: they teach their children to trust them full of thorns; you'll see sometimes on holidays a whole parish running like madmen from hedge to hedge a *wren-hunting*." This is not the case in England, where a kind of reverence is paid to these birds, for it is considered unlucky to kill them or to destroy their nests, and it is supposed that anyone doing so would infallibly, within the course of the year, meet with some dreadful misfortune. This feeling is expressed by the distich:—

> A robin and a wren,
> Are God Almighty's cock and hen.

and an old poet says:

> I never take away their nest, nor try
> To catch the old ones, lest a friend should die;
> Dick took a wren's nest from his cottage side,
> And ere a twelvemonth past his mother dy'd!

W. Harrison, who gives the above quotations, adds:—"In the version as printed of this song, it is given as recited at the time, but evidently there are several expressions not in unison with the Manx idiom, which only shows the difficulty of preserving in their original purity these orally delivered songs, for each batch of minstrels are constantly introducing something of their own. Thus, 'Robin *to* Bobbin,' and 'Jack *of the* Land,' should certainly be 'Robin *the* Bobbin,' and 'Jackey *the* Land,' being the particular designation by which they were known, similar to what may be met with in many instances at the present day, as 'Billey the Bo,' 'Jackey the Cook,' 'Tom the Rock,' etc. Other minor expressions might be noticed as 'he is' for 'he's,' but the last verse is evidently belonging to an Irish version. The Manx song terminates generally after 'The bones for the dogs' with:—

> He's eat, he's eat, says Robin the Bobbin,
> He's eat, he's eat, says Richard to Robin,
> He's eat, he's eat, says lackey the Land,
> He's eat, he's eat, says every one.

I have never met with a copy of dirges in the Manx lan-guage, said to have been sung over the body at the interment, as is recorded in Waldron's History.[1]

In Essex, the wren was killed and carried about in furze bushes, the boys asking a present in these words:—

> The wren! the wren! the king of birds,
> St. Stephen's Day was killed in the furze;
> Although he be little, his honour is great,
> And so, good people, pray give us a treat.

The following wren song is also met with at Waterford:—

> On Christmas Day I turned the spit,
> I burned my fingers—I feel it yet;
> Between my fingers and my thumb,
> I ate the roast meat every crumb.
>   Sing, hubber ma dro my droleen.
>
> We were all day hunting the wren,
> We were all day hunting the wren;
> The wren so cute, and we so cunning,
> She stayed in the bush while we were a-running.
>   Sing, &c.
>
> When we went to cut the holly,
> All our boys were brisk and jolly;
> We cut it down all in a trice,
> Which made our wren boys to rejoice.
>   Sing, &c.

This custom is also found in Pembrokeshire, where it is prac-tised on 12th day, and at several places in the south of France on the first Sunday in December. It is very remarkable that though in many counties it was reckoned unlucky to kill the wren, yet it was killed ceremonially once a year. This, taken into connec-tion with the value set upon the possession of a feather from the slain bird, points to a sacrificial custom.[2] In Man at the present day the bush decorated with ribbons and flowers still survives, and the wren is occasionally found ensconced within it, but the song has dwindled to a mere fragment.

---

1 "Mona Miscellany," Manx Society, vo. XVI.

2 See Chapter VII.

December 27th, *Laa'l Eoin Nollick*, "John's Christmas Feast-day," and December 28th, *Laa'l ny Macain*, "Feast-day of the Children (or Innocents)," are Church Festivals.

December 31st — On the Eve of New Year's Day it was a custom to fill a thimble with salt and upset it on a plate, one thimble for every one in the house. The plate was then carefully put by and examined next morning; if any of the little heaps of salt had fallen or looked untidy, then the person whom it represented would die during the year.

"In many of the upland cottages," writes Train, "it is yet customary for the housewife, after raking the fire for the night, and just before stepping into bed, to spread the ashes smooth over the floor with the tongs, in the hope of finding in it, next morning, the track of a foot; should the toes of this ominous print turn towards the door, then, it is believed, a member of the family will die in the course of that year; but, should the heel of the fairy foot point in that direction, then, it is firmly believed, that the family will be augmented within the same period." Another means of prying into futurity made use of on this evening was to put the leaves of *hibbin* or ivy in water. Each of these leaves were marked by a member of the family, and, if any one of the leaves was withered in the morning, it would mean death to its owner during the year. It would seem probable, however, that the chance of any of the leaves withering under the circumstances was a very remote one. (See November 11th)

It may be mentioned here that Tuesdays and Thursdays were considered lucky days, and Fridays unlucky. A search through the Parish Registers will show that weddings usually took place on Tuesday or Thursday, and hardly ever on Friday. Nothing would induce the fishermen to go to sea on Friday.

CHAPTER VII

SUPERSTITIONS CONNECTED WITH THE SUN, ANIMALS, TREES, PLANTS, SACRED EDIFICES. &C.

THERE IS BUT LITTLE TRACE OF SUPERSTITIONS connected with the great objects of Nature, the mountains, rivers, glens, sea, &c., which were probably regarded by the ancient inhabitants of Man merely with dumb awe and reverence. But of their adoration of the Heavenly Bodies which supplied them with light, and of the animals, trees, and plants, which supplied their daily needs, there are significant traces.[1] Their religion, like those of all primitive races, was, in effect, a vague worship of the phenomena of nature, which they regarded as living powers. Now, of all the phenomena which are visible to man, the Sun is at once the most awful, beneficent, and mysterious. It is the source of light and warmth, and, when it departs, darkness and cold follow. With darkness, fear and death are associated, and with light, joy and

---

1 The question of the real origin and significance of the ideas of primitive Man on these subjects is still obscure, and the views given must be regarded as merely tentative. For an able account of this question see "The Golden Bough," by J.G. Frazer, M.A. (Macmillan & Co.), from which the writer has derived some valuable hints.

life. And as the sun is the source of light, it was considered the originator and generator of life. The worship of the sun was a very widely extended cult, a cult of which we have remains, even at the present day, in the ceremonial observances at no less than four festivals during the year. Of these, the one perhaps most distinctly connected with solar adoration is the procession to the tops of the highest hills on *Laa Lunys* (the first of August); and as the connection between the sun and fire is naturally intimate, so it is not improbable that the fires called bonfires, which still light up the hill-tops on the eves of the great festivals of *Boaldyn*, of Midsummer, and of *Sauin*, have some connection with sun worship. A further reason in support of this contention is afforded by the undoubted fact that the practice of lighting these fires at such a time is evidently a very ancient one, as in the eighth century, when the Christian synods vainly endeavoured to put it down, it is described as having been in vogue from a remote period. We have (in Chapter VI) also referred to the practice of leaping over these bonfires, and of driving cattle through them; of rolling the fire-wheels, and of lighting fires to the windward of fields. We have given the popular notion that these ceremonies were performed with a view to driving away Fairies, Witches, and all evil influences; and have alluded to the wide-spread notion of the purifying power of fire. But, as we have just indicated, it is probable that their object, in the earliest times, was the worship of the sun; and it would seem that primitive man imagined that he could thus influence or charm the sun into providing him with a due amount of sunshine for his own welfare and that of his animals and crops; and it would seem, also, that as the flames of these bonfires mimicked the sunshine, they were supposed to promote fertility, for, as we have already seen (in Chapter VI) the crops were supposed to flourish only as far as the bonfires were visible. These bonfires, according to the testimony of Julius Cæsar, were used by the

ancient Celts for sacrificing human beings; and from another source we learn that it was considered that the fertility of
the year would be in accordance with the number of victims.
The funeral pyre of Balder, himself the sun-god, being lit on
Midsummer-eve, is significant of the same custom among the
Scandinavians; and, when we remember that the Gaelic High-
landers, as late as the middle of last century, pretended to burn
a man on their *Need*-fires, a sign of the reality of the burning
at an earlier epoch, we may conjecture that a similar practice
once prevailed in Man.

The Moon and the Stars, as mitigators of darkness, were
also recipients of adoration, but in a much less degree. As regards the moon, with the exception of the belief that too much
gazing at it would deprive those who did so of their senses, the
only superstitions left are in connection with amatory questions. For it was supposed that, if the new moon were invoked
in due form, the applicant would learn in a dream the identity
of his or her future partner. But it was absolutely necessary
that this invocation, the words of which are unfortunately
lost, should be addressed to the moon in the open air, as, if it
passed through glass, there would be no response. It was also
supposed that the best time for marrying, or engaging in any
important undertaking, was when the moon was full.

As regards Animals, Trees, and Plants when, in previous
chapters, any mention has been made of the superstitions
connected with them, we have for the most part merely given
the popular explanation of the sacrifice of the former, and
the use of the latter, on such occasions as the eves of *Boaldyn*,
Sauin, and Midsummer, *i.e.*, as being charms to ward off the
influence of Fairies and Witches, or to expel disease; and,
in the absence of such explanation, we have refrained from
giving one of our own. But in this chapter, where all the superstitions on this subject have been brought together, we
propose to briefly investigate their true primary connection,

which, as already stated, is probably with the earliest known form of religion, *i.e.*, that of the worship of the phenomena of nature.

It seems highly probabl e, indeed, that the belief in the efficacy of such charms against Fairies and Witches, was encouraged by the early teachers of Christianity as a means of diverting the minds of their converts from their worship of nature or its spirit, personified by animals and trees. Animal worship was at one time prevalent in every part of the world; and it is clear that man considered some animals at least superior to himself. A mild and distant reflex of this opinion may possibly be found in the popular modern belief that some animals "are wiser than Christians." Dogs, for instance, are supposed to be able to forecast a coming death, to recognise Witches, when men cannot, and to understand human speech; and horses are accredited with seeing ghosts when invisible to men. The luckiness or unluckiness connected with certain animals is also possibly a remnant of this belief. It was unlucky to meet a cat on New Year's morning, but on other occasions there seems to have been no particular significance attached to this animal, though there was a hazy notion that it was, especially if black, the companion of Witches. Magpies were lucky or unlucky, according to the number of them that were seen. The popular distich on this subject is:—

> One for sorrow, two for death,
> Three for a wedding, and four for a birth.

Ravens, too, had an uncanny reputation, but this may have been, originally, because they were supposed to be Odin's messengers; while to see a hare cross a road was deemed very unlucky.

It is also possible that a survival of a belief in animal superiority may have originated the confidence which still exists in their weather wisdom. After what we have stated with reference to the idea of the superiority of some animals entertained by primitive man, the undoubted fact that he sacrificed them will seem very curious at first sight. But when we learn that this was thought to be the very highest honour he could pay them, and the greatest kindness he could do them, the aspect of the question is changed. It is true, of course, that there were animals worshipped by some tribes which its members would not venture to kill. This cult is called *Totemism* as each tribe is supposed to be of the kindred of its *totem* or sacred animal, and to kill, or kill and eat it, would be the height of impiety. On the other hand, there were animals which were worshipped on account of their being killed and eaten. But they were not killed and eaten on ordinary occasions, but only on certain festivals. And, as they thought that all things must die, the gods included, they supposed that they did particular honour to and conferred a benefit upon the victims they sacrificed, by relieving them from the suffering and weakness attendant upon old age; while the benefit to themselves was gaining a communion with the Deity by eating his body and drinking his blood. A remnant of this form of sacrificial worship perhaps occurs in the Manx custom of "hunting the wren." For we have seen that this bird was highly honoured, being called almost universally the "king of birds," and yet once a year it was ceremonially slain, and its feathers distributed, so that each might receive some benefit from its divine virtue. This divinity of the wren is also indicated by the former practice of the Manx fishermen not to go to sea without a dead wren to protect them from storms.

The procession of the *laare vane*, "white mare," on twelfth-night, and at the harvest festival,[1] may also have some connection with animal worship. For it seems probable that in Man as in St. Kilda, the "mare" once possessed a hide, that pieces of this hide were plucked off like the feathers of the wren, and that they were supposed to have similar virtues. On Hollan-

---

1 Thus it was taboo for Cuchullin to eat his namesake, the dog.

tide-eve, too, the last night of the old year, a calf was sacrificed, as we have learned from the old ballad sung on that occasion. And the bonfires at *Boaldyn*, Midsummer, and *Sauin* formerly consumed sacrifices either of men or of beasts. But we have not to go to tradition for instances of animal sacrifices, or even to such ceremonies as the slaying of the wren, of which the symbolical meaning has been lost; for we know, on the testimony of those now living, that lambs were burnt in Man less than 50 years ago, and that not even according to popular superstition for the discovery of Witches or the expulsion of disease, but, in the words of the informants, *son oural*, "for a sacrifice." It seems possible, too, that the practice of burning animals to discover Witchcraft, &.c., really originated from their being burnt for sacrificial purposes. In all these sacrifices the notion of laying the sins of the people on the sacrificed was probably present, and we have this more nearly represented in the recent custom already alluded to, of throwing diseased cattle, like scapegoats, out to sea, so as to ward off the disease from their fellows.

The curious superstition about the unluckiness of letting blood, especially that of a king or person of high rank, fall on the ground, may also have some sacrificial meaning. We have a historical instance of this in Man, for it is remembered to this day that when *Iliam Dhone*, William Christian, was shot at Hango Hill in 1662, blankets were spread where he stood, so that not one drop of his blood should touch the earth.

The equally curious notion that all nail and hair cuttings should be carefully destroyed may have some connection with this species of superstition, though the reason popularly assigned for this precaution is that it is to prevent the Witches getting hold of them, and so gaining power over their owners. Hair was formerly supposed to have great sanative virtues, but why it was formerly considered obligatory to hang a criminal by a hair rope, as the following story related to Train will show, does not appear:—

"A malefactor, who had been condemned to suffer the extreme penalty of the law, was taken from Castle Rushen to the place of execution, where a great concourse of people were assembled from all parts of the Island to witness a spectacle of rare occurrence. By an old customary law, it was ordained that a person convicted of felony should be hanged by the neck in a hair rope; but in the case alluded to one of the constituted authorities had given orders privately that a hempen halter should be substituted. The innovation was discovered by some of the spectators just as the convict was suspended from the fatal tree. The populace instantly became so infuriated. . . . . that they not only had well-nigh killed the executioner for not publicly resisting such an infringement of the ancient statute, but also, having cut down the felon in the agonies of death, they even . . . again hung up the dead body in a hair halter."

The prevalence of superstitions connected with Trees in past ages will not be wondered at when we remember that Europe was formerly almost all one vast forest. Its primitive inhabitants lived in small clearings in this forest, and they must have been greatly impressed, not only by the immensity of their surroundings, but by the great changes produced in them by the seasons. The first approach of Spring, with its budding leaves, must have filled them with wonder and joy, and the approach of Winter, and the consequent decay of vegetation, must have inspired them with equal wonder and sorrow. We cannot be surprised then if they adored their mighty surroundings, and attributed their natural changes to the agency of Deities or Spirits. In the Isle of Man, trees seem always to have been rare, and perhaps this is why there are so few tokens of any tree worship, though there are some signs of an adoration of the reproductive power of Nature. Thus the invitation to Bridget, on the first of February, to repose upon a rush or straw couch, is probably the remains of some ceremony connected with the first revival of vegetation in Spring. On May-day, as we have seen, branches of trees, especially of the mountain ash, were strewed upon the thresholds, a custom which is now supposed to be practised as a protection against Fairies and Witches, but which was probably formerly a method of invoking the reproductive power of Nature. For trees were supposed to produce fertilising effects on both women and cattle, and, according to Camden, the Irish "fancy a green bough of a tree fastened on May-day against the house will produce plenty of milk that summer."[1] We have already seen that the *Cuirn* tree, or Mountain-ash, was regarded with special veneration. It was planted, in common with the Thorn and the Ash (*unjin*), by the sacred wells in Man. Some of these trees are still to be found in these positions, and votive offerings have, within living memory, been placed on them. The *Cuirn* tree was considered an antidote to witchcraft, though this scarcely explains why a stick of it was substituted, on Good Friday, for the ordinary iron poker. Another significant ceremony, as showing the adoration of nature, was the combat between winter and summer which took place on May day (*Laa-boaldyn*); the latter, which was represented by a young girl, decorated with leaves, being victorious, and thus typifying the victory of Nature's reproductive power. In the Isle of Man winter was represented by a man in winter garb, but in some countries the defeated champion was dressed to represent death, so that the contest was still more significant of the triumph over decay. The Midsummer celebrations seems also to have been connected with Nature as well as Sun

---

1 It seems probable that the practice of making these branches into crosses is probably of Christian origin, and, therefore, comparatively speaking of recent date, though it must be remembered that the symbol of the cross was known before Christianity existed.

worship, being intended as charms to promote the fertility of the crops. The sacrifice of Balder, too, who was both Oak-god and Sun-god, as typified by the bonfires which were formerly made of oak wood, is significant of this connection; as is also the probability that this was the day on which the *Druadh* cut the mistletoe, and thus enabled Balder to be slain.[1] For the oak which was thus burned was universally considered the noblest of trees, and we have seen that the object of ceremonial sacrifice received adoration. But it is in our harvest festival that we have retained the most characteristic survival of the adoration of the reproductive power of nature, or of its spirit. For the last sheaf, called the maiden, and the little sheaf taken from it, called the harvest doll, were the objects of much ceremony, and the fact of their being preserved till the following harvest would seem to indicate a belief that the corn's life could thus be continued from one harvest to the next, and so ensure lasting fertility. It may be noted, too, that the ceremony of the *laare vane*, or white mare, may have had some connection with the last sheaf, as this sheaf is in some counties in England and Wales to this day called "The Mare."

The following superstitions about Animals and Plants are probably not, except as regards the Weather-Lore to be derived from them, connected in any way with Nature worship, so that the popular explanation of their origin will suffice:—

The Hedge-hog and the Hare were tabooed, from their supposed connection with Witches, who took their forms upon them. The former animal was supposed to draw milk from cows, and the latter had a very bad reputation, though no specific misdeeds were attributed to it.

Mr. P. M. C. Kermode writes as follows concerning superstitions about the Hare:—"Here, as elsewhere, it is the object of superstition, and seems to be a favourite form to be as-

---

1 According to the well-known myth, the beloved Balder was invulnerable till pierced by the mistletoe.

sumed by a Witch. Thus, while labourers have been at work in a field they would see the dogs pursuing a hare which would presently be lost to sight, in a few moments the dogs would be observed to bark and whine around a man well-known to all and suspected of being a Witch. Of course it was he who was pursued, and, being hard-pressed, was forced to assume his normal form, to the mystification of the dogs. Again, a man whose cattle were suffering from some unknown cause would learn that a hare might be seen at a certain hour every day in a particular spot. Suspecting the meaning of this he would load his gun, having as the only sufficient bullet a broken silver coin, and go in pursuit. Having shot the hare, he would follow his dogs, and find them howling by the side of a stream, while an ugly old crone would be seated on a boulder in the midst of it nursing her broken leg and muttering curses. Again, dogs will give chase to a hare, and, upon approaching it, stop suddenly and refuse to go further, even though encouraged to do so. This, of course, is because they recognise a Witch."[2] This belief that a Witch when she had turned into a hare could only be shot with a silver bullet was very general. The following incident, which is said to have occurred about 30 years ago, will illustrate this:—A suspected Witch was successfully convicted in the parish of Andreas by a sportsman, who, seeing a hare crossing a field, fired and wounded it, and, when getting over a hedge to secure his prey, he found that he had shot an old woman, who was a reputed Witch. — *Oral*.

At table, no one will turn a Herring; but, when one side is eaten, the bone is taken away, so that the rest can be eaten: for to turn the Herring would be tantamount to overturning the boat into which it was drawn from the ocean if it then chanced to be at sea. When a Cow had newly calved, she was driven over a burning turf to protect her from evil influences. Anyone removing into a new house formerly put in a Cock before taking possession, in order to thwart any bad wishes that may have been expressed by the last inhabitant. There was a superstition to the effect that the cross-bone of the head of a *Bollan-fish* would prevent anyone from straying from the most direct road to any place to which he wanted to proceed, either by day or night. Manx sailors seldom went to sea without one of these bones in their pocket to direct their course at night or in hazy weather.

There is a firmly-rooted belief in the weather wisdom of animals; and, apart from superstition, there is some reason for supposing that their faculties in this respect are mote acute than men's. It is said that, during the earthquake in the Riviera, in 1887, animals—especially dogs and cats—were seen stealing out of the towns before the first shock was felt. But, on the other hand, they frequently make mistakes, as, for instance, when birds nest in an inclement spring, and consequently lose their offspring. The following weather prognostics from animals are still esteemed in the Isle of Man.[1] We may divide them into prognostics of Storm, Rain, and Fine weather. *Storms* will ensue when Seagulls come inland and Rooks fly to the mountains; when Cattle and Sheep seek shelter, and when the Porpoise,[2] or Herring-hog, is seen gambolling round ships at sea. *Rain* will follow when Sparrows chirp, when Rooks and Herons[3] fly low, when Rats and Mice are restless, and when many Bees return to the hive and none leave it. *Fine weather* is certain when Bats fly about at sunset, when Rooks, Herons, and Larks fly high, when Seagulls fly out to sea, when Bees are seen far from their hives, and Spiders spin their webs in the open air. The few remaining weather prognostics from other sources may be also conveniently discussed here. If the Hawthorn and Blackthorn have many berries the ensuing winter is expect-

1 NOTE.—It will be noticed that most of them are common to many countries.

2 *Yn Pherkin vooar* in Manx.

3 *Coar-ny-hastan*—"Crane of the eel" in Manx.

ed to be severe. Clover is supposed to close up its leaves at the approach of a storm. A clear Sunrise betokens fine weather, and so does a red Sunset; but a pale Sunset is a sign of rain. The old Moon in the arms of the new is a certain forerunner of storms. A Halo round the moon means rain. When the Cumberland mountains are clearly seen, rain is expected.[4]

The following quaint tales about animals, though they do not come strictly under the head of Superstitions, may certainly be considered as belonging to Manx Folk-Lore:—The *Ushagreaisht*, or Mountain-plover, is a favourite both in song and legend. The following ballad about it has been sung by Manx nurses as a lullaby, to the same tune as that of "Here we go round the Mulberry Bush," for many generations:—

> *Ushag veg ruy ny moanee doo*[5]
> *C'raad chaddil oo riyr syn oie?*
> *Chaddil mish riyr er baare y dress,*
> *As ugh my cadley cha treih!*

> Little red bird of the black turf ground,
> Where did you sleep last night?
> I slept last night on the top of the briar,
> And oh! what a wretched sleep!

> *

> 2 *Ushag veg ruy ny moanee doo*
> *C'raad chaddil oo riyr syn oie?*
> *Chaddil mish riyr er baare y crouw,*[6]
> *As ugh my cadley cha treih!*

> Little red bird of the black turf ground,
> Where did you sleep last night?
> I slept last night on the top of the bush,
> And oh! what a wretched sleep!

> 3 *Ushag veg ruy ny moanee doo*
> *C'raad chaddil oo riyr syn oie?*

---

4 There are some other bits of weather Folk-Lore which have become proverbial, and will be found under the heading of Proverbs.

5 The first and the third lines in the first three verses are repeated three times, but in the last verse the first line is only repeated.

6 *Crouw*, "a bunch growing on one stem or stalk."— *Cregeen.*

Chaddil mish riyr er baare y thooane,[1]
As ugh my cadley cha treih!

Little red bird of the black turf ground,
Where did you sleep last night?
I slept last night on the ridge of the roof,
And oh! what a wretched sleep!

*

4   *Ushag veg ruy ny moanee doo*
C'raad chaddil oo riyr syn oie?
Chaddil nish riyr eddyr daa guillag,
Myr yinnagh yn oikan[2] *eddyr daa lhuishag,*
As o my cadley cha kiune!

Little red bird of the black turf ground,
Where did you sleep last night?
I slept last night between two leaves
As a babe 'twixt two blankets quite at ease,
And oh! what a peaceful sleep!

We have also a legend about this bird in connection with the *Lhondoo*, or Black-bird:—

It is said that once upon a time the haunts of the *Lhondoo* were confined to the mountains, and those of the *Ushag-reaisht* to the lowlands. One day, however, the two birds met on the border of their respective territories, and, after some conversation, it was arranged to change places for a while, the *Ushag-reaisht* remaining in the mountains, till the *Lhondoo* should return. The *Lhondoo*, finding the new quarters much more congenial than the old, conveniently forgot his promise to go back. Consequently the poor *Ushag-reaisht* was left to bewail his folly in making the exchange, and has ever since been giving expression to his woes in the following plaintive querulous pipe: *Lhondoo vel oo cheet, vel oo cheet?* "Black-bird

---

1 *Thooane*, "a rib or lath on the roof of a house, under the scraws."— *Cregeen.*

2 *Oikan*, "The gradations from infancy to manhood are marked by a copious variety of terms: *Oikan, Lhanoo, Paitchey, Poinnar, Stuggy, Scollag, Dooiney*."— *Rev. W. Gill. Oikan* is the first stage of all.

are you coming, are you coming?" The Lhondoo, now plump and flourishing, replies—*Cha-nel dy bragh, cha-nel dy bragh!* "No never, no never!" The poor Ushag-reaisht, shivering—*Teh feer feayr. t'eh feer feayr.*[3] "It's very cold, it's very cold!"

Another form of the same story is as follows:—The *Ush-ag-reaisht* complains *giall oo dy horagh oo reesht* "you promised you would come back"; *ta'n traa liauyr, as cha vel oo ayns shoh*, "the time is long and you are not here." But the *Lhondoo* replies *Cha jig dy bragh*, "Will never come."

The following is a quaint fancy derived from the notes of the Blackbird's and Thrush's songs. The blackbird whistles *Gow* as *smook*, which is Anglo-Manx for "go and smoke." The thrush replies *Cha vel thumbaga aym* "I have no tobacco," or literally "There is no tobacco at me." To whom the blackbird again—*kionney, kionney*, "buy, buy." The thrush is then forced to confess—*Cha vel ping aym* "There is not a penny at me," and receives very bad advice *Gow er dayl*, "Go on trust," but he closes the controversy by saying, *Cha der ad dou er*, "They won't give it me!"

The following tale is told of the Herring:—

HOW THE HERRING BECAME KING OF THE SEA

Long ago the fish bethought themselves that it was time for them to choose a king in case there might be disputes among them, for they had no Deemster to tell them what was right, so they came together to choose a king. No doubt they all tried to put on their best appearance. It is said that the Fluke in particular spent so much time in putting on his red spots, that when he arrived he found the election was over and that the Herring had been made king of the sea. Upon hearing this, he curled his mouth on one side and said, "A simple fish

---

3 These words "*Teh feer feayr*" exactly represent the Plover's shrill and piteous whistle.

like the Herring, king of the sea!"; and his mouth has been on one side ever since. It is perhaps on account of this importance of the herring that the Deemsters, in their oath, swear to execute the laws of the Isle "as indifferently as the herring's back-bone doth lie in the midst of the fish."

There is a curious tradition that all the following creatures pass the winter in a torpid condition. They are seven in number, (though, as will be seen, some of the names vary), and they are consequently called *ny shiaght cadlagyn*, "the seven sleepers," having, however, no connection with the more famous seven of Ephesus. They are *Craitnag*, "the Bat"; *Cooag*, "the Cuckoo"; *Cloghan-ny-cleigh*, "the Stone-chat"; and *Gollan-geayee* "the Swallow"; which are found in all the lists; the others being *Crammag*, "the Snail"; *Doallag*, "the Dormouse"; *Foillycan*, "the Butterfly"; Shellan, "the Bee"; *Jialgheer*, "the Lizard"; and *Cadlag*, "the sleeper," a mythical animal.

We now come to the superstitions about Trees and Plants. The *Cuirn* has already been discussed. The Thorn tree also, especially when it grew to a large size, was regarded with veneration, there being a very strong prejudice against cutting it down. It was supposed to be a favourite haunt of the Fairies, and there are numerous anecdotes still current of their being seen dancing in its branches.

The Elder tree, or *Tramman*, was vulgarly supposed to have been the tree upon which Judas Iscariot hanged himself, and it was possibly on this account that great reliance was formerly placed on its sanative and mystical virtues. It was used as a charm for protecting houses and gardens from the influence of Sorcery and Witchcraft, and, even at the present time, an Elder tree may be observed growing by almost every old cottage in the Island. Its leaves, like those of the *Cuirn*, were picked on May-eve, and affixed to doors and windows to protect the house from witchcraft.

It was supposed that if you trod on the *Luss-y-chialg*,[1] "Plant of the prickle," or St. John's wort, after sunset, on St. John's Eve, a fairy horse would rise out of the earth and carry you about during the whole night, only leaving you at dawn. The *Luss-ny-tree duillag*, "Plant of three leaves," or Shamrock, was said to be a cure for tooth-ache, and the *Luss-ny-ollee*,[2] "Plant of the cattle," was efficacious for sores in the mouths of cattle, as well as for tooth-ache.

The *Luss-yn-aacheoid*, "Plant of the sickness," or Purple Meadow-button, was reckoned a preservative against the "Evil Eye."

The *Luss-y-chellan* is an herb which was said to keep milk from turning sour, and butter from being discoloured.

The *Luss-ny-kiare-duillag*, "Four-leaved clover," was efficacious against the wiles of Fairies or of Witches, and so was the *Bollan feaill-Eoin*, "John's Feast-day plant, or Mugwort."[3] This yellow weed was gathered on Midsummer-eve, and made into chaplets, which were worn on the heads of man and beast, who were then supposed to be proof against all malign influences. Of the metals, Iron was the only one invested with magical power. This notion probably took its rise from a dim tradition of the period when the people who had iron weapons overcame the earlier people of the stone and bronze ages. The Fairies, as should be noted in this connection, were always supposed to have used stone-headed arrows, the numerous flint arrow heads which are found being supposed to be their weapons. The magical power of iron, referred to above, is demonstrated in some of the legends already given about the virtues of magic swords, and it will also be remembered that an iron tongs sufficed to protect a newly-born baby from the Fairies. In the days when iron was rare,

1 Hypericum perforatum.

2 Pinguicola.

3 Artemisia Vulgaris.

it would either be an object of veneration, or be viewed with suspicion. Mysterious virtues are, in fact, attributed to it in the popular stories of many nations. Even at the present day, a horseshoe is hung up over the entrance door of a house, a stable, or a cow-house, as a protection against the powers of evil. We have already referred to the strange superstition against using an iron poker to stir the fire on Good Friday. It is remarkable, in this connection, that iron knives were never made use of by savages in their sacrificial ceremonies, because they supposed that the spirits objected to this metal. But for this very reason that the spirits objected to it, it was used, as we have already seen, as a protection against them. It is possible that the superstition against cutting a child's nails during the first year of its life may be connected with this objection of spirits to iron.

The virtues of Salt[1] as a protection against Fairies, Magicians, &c., were universally recognised. If milk were taken from a house, it was considered necessary to put a pinch of salt in it, and this must be done by the mistress to prevent the luck of the house going with it. Fishermen will not lend any salt out of their boat, as to do so is considered unlucky. Salt was also strewed about the threshold if a woman were approaching her confinement, in order to drive away the fairies. It was put into a child's mouth at birth, and laid on the breast of a corpse.

A white Stone was considered very unlucky, and nothing will induce the fishermen to use one as ballast.

SUPERSTITIONS CONNECTED WITH SACRED EDIFICES

In the first part of this chapter we have discussed the superstitions which probably originated in the primitive Nature religion, and we may now briefly refer to those which have had their origin in other religions, especially the Christian. They

---

1 See stories of "Fairy Dogs," ch. III; "Magician's Palace," ch. V; and "New Year's Eve," ch. VI.

are, for the most part, connected with churches and *keeills*, and all ancient monuments supposed to have been used for religious observances, which have always been regarded with superstitious awe. Any sacrilege against such edifices has always been considered by the Manx people as a most serious sin which would bring certain punishment on the offender.

In the words of Bishop Wilson, "They have generally hated sacrileges to such a degree that they do not think a man can wish a greater curse to a family than in these words:—*Clogh ny killagh ayns corneil dty hie mooar*," *i.e.*, "May a stone of the church be found in the corner of thy dwelling-house." Many stories might he told to illustrate this feeling, but we must content ourselves with a few specimens.

About one hundred years ago a farmer, in the parish of Jurby, during a violent storm of thunder and lightning, drove his sheep into one of the ancient *keeills*. It was afterwards observed that he lost all the lambs of that flock in the ensuing spring, and that many of them were born monstrosities.

Not long ago a small windmill was erected for driving a threshing machine, a portion of which was built of stones from an adjacent *keeill*; but immediately it was set to work it went with tremendous fury, and shook the whole of the premises, and had in consequence to be taken down. The owner of the farm on which this windmill was situate lost four head of cattle and three horses by disease within a very brief period. All these calamities were attributed to the use of the stones from the sacred edifice.

A portion of the roof of the *keeill* on the Rhyne farm in Baldwin was removed to a farm-house, but such unearthly noises resulted that it was soon restored. A somewhat similar story is told of a stone which was taken from St. Luke's Chapel in the same neighbourhood to a farm-house, but it had to be taken back, as those who lived in the house could not sleep at nights for noises, sometimes resembling a calf bleating, and at other times like a cart of stones being upset. At one time it was placed on the earthen fence of an adjoining field, but the fence would never stand, and the stone had to be removed again to the chapel.

Some years ago a farmer began levelling the *keeill* on Camlork farm, but he at once "took a pain in his arm, and had to stop work some days." Afterwards he continued his task, assisted by his wife and daughter, the consequence was the two latter died soon after, and the man became insane, and expired after living in that state for some time.

About thirty years ago a farmer put his sheep to graze in a field in which there was a stone circle, the result in the following spring being the same as in the case of the man who drove his sheep into a *keeill*. About the same period two men were employed to remove the stones from the circle at The Braid, in the parish of Braddan, in order to build a wall with them. No sooner had they commenced operations than one of them was seized with a terrible pain in one of his legs, and the other was similarly afflicted in one of his arms. They at once desisted and went home, but the leg of one and arm of the other were crippled and useless for the rest of their lives. Stories are also told of ploughs being broken without any apparent cause, when they were driven too close to one of these circles. Even to appropriate a portion of an old cist was sacrilege, as the following tale will show:—A man had been tempted to take a large stone slab that formed the top of an old cist for a lintel. No sooner had he done this than his cow sickened and a calf died, and, more curious still, one of his hens was found dead on her nest. He at once recognised that this was a just punishment for the sacrilege he had committed and restored the slab to its original position. After this, of course, all went well.

Even sacrilege of a milder kind was resented, as will appear from the following show:—Some thirty years ago the church-wardens of Maughold decided to put two steps to the communion rails of the church, instead of one, which was very high. The labourers in taking away the old steps disinterred a number of bones, which were left exposed during the time that two of them were absent at dinner. The third, who remained and took his mid-day (*munlaa*) dinner in the church, distinctly heard sounds of whispering or murmuring (*tassaneagh*) all over the church. When his fellows returned, they at once re-interred the bones, when the whispering ceased.

But in the following, on the contrary, which is of quite recent origin, there seems to be no resentment at all:—There was an old Roman Catholic Chapel at the south end of Douglas, near the Castletown-road. When this chapel was pulled down, a house was built on its site. The woman who occupied this house with her husband, and who often used to sit up waiting for him to return home till a very late hour, declared that every night when the clock struck twelve she distinctly heard the tramp of many feet entering the room where she sat. Then there was silence, and after a time the sound of feet again. Doubtless this was the arrival of the ancient worshippers at mid-night mass, and their departure from it.

As a proof of the simplicity and piety of the Manx, Vicar-General Wilks, writing in 1777, states that they do not usually reckon the time "by hours of the day, but by the *traa shirvaish*, i.e., the service time, viz., nine in the morning, or three in the evening, an hour, two hours, before service time, &c."

Other superstitions connected with religion have already been mentioned. They are the bowing of the sun on Easter Sunday morning; and the lowing of the cattle and blooming of the myrrh plant at midnight on Christmas-eve; the making of the branches of the *cuirn* into crosses on May-eve; the notions that the influence of Christ is a protection from Fairies, &c., at Christmas time, and that children were more especially liable to evil influences before baptism.

CHAPTER VIII

CUSTOMS AND SUPERSTITIONS CONNECTED WITH BIRTH, MARRIAGE, AND DEATH

IN THE ISLE OF MAN, as elsewhere, a number of curious customs and superstitions have naturally grouped themselves about the important events of Birth, Marriage, and Death.

BIRTH

From the birth of a child, till after it was baptised, it was customary to keep in the room where the woman was confined, a *peck*, or wooden hoop, about three or four inches deep, and about twenty inches in diameter, covered with a sheep's skin, and resembling the head of a drum, which was heaped with oaten cakes and cheese, of which all visitors may freely partake, and small pieces of cheese and bread, called *blithe meat*, were scattered in and about the house for the Fairies. The woman who carried the infant to church for baptism, was also supplied with bread and cheese, to give to the first person she met on the way, in order to preserve her charge from evil influences. After returning from church, the remaining part of the day, and often a great part of the night, was spent in eating and drinking, to which "the whole country round" was invited, and they, in return, gave presents to the child. If, after child-birth, a woman did not recover her usual strength as soon as expected, she was then declared to be the victim of an "Evil Eye." Some neighbour is soon suspected of having given the envenomed glance; and to counteract its malignancy, a square piece was secretly cut out of some part of her garment, and burnt immediately under the nose of the afflicted woman. This was considered an infallible cure. — *Train*.

The baby, also, was supposed to be especially liable to be affected by the "Evil Eye" before baptism, and it was considered that the best way to prevent this was to keep it constantly within the same room in which it was born. Children were also supposed to be much more liable to abduction by Fairies before the same ceremony. From the time that a woman was delivered of a child, till thanksgiving for her safe recovery was offered up by some divine, or until the consecrated candle[1]— which was kept in her room at this time—was burnt, it was deemed requisite, as a protection for herself against the power of evil spirits, that she should keep her husband's trousers beside her in the bed, to prevent her infant being carried off by the Fairies, before being secured from their grasp by baptism. A person was invariably appointed for its special protection, and when she had occasion to leave the child in the cradle she would place the tongs, which must be made of iron, across it till her return.

Another specific to ward off evil from babies was to put salt in their mouths as soon as possible after their birth. In connection with this it may be noted. that, as it was once the custom to expose infants in order that they might die, this practice may have been resorted to as a means of prevention. For, if the child had once partaken of any food, it could not be

---

1 The churching of a woman, in the Manx language, is called *lostey-chainley*, from the practice of burning a candle, in former times, during this service.

exposed. It was deemed most unlucky to cut their hair or nails before they were a year old, and, if it was done, the fragments were carefully burned. A posthumous child was supposed to have the gift of second-sight; and the seventh son of a seventh son, and a child born on Hallowe'en had powers of intercourse with the unseen world.

A child born with a caul—a thin membrane covering the head—would probably be notorious in some way. This caul was supposed to be a preventive against shipwreck and drowning, and was accordingly purchased by sailors. This idea of the value of a caul was widespread, as would appear from numerous advertisements in the newspapers. One of these, which appeared in the London *Times* in 1835, was as follows:—"A Child's Caul to be disposed of, a well-known preservative against drowning, &c., price 10 guineas." And a caul has been advertised for sale in a Liverpool paper in this year (1891).

MARRIAGE

Waldron describes a Manx Wedding in his time, 1726, as follows:—"The match is no sooner concluded than besides the banes (sic) of matrimony being publicly asked in the Church three Sundays, notice is given to all friends and relations, tho' they live ever so far distant. Not one of these, unless detained by sickness, fail coming, and bring something towards the feast; the nearest of kin, if they are able, commonly contribute most, so that they have vast quantities of fowls of all sorts. * * *

They have Bride-men, and Bride-maids, who lead the young couple, as in England, only with this difference, that the former have ozier-wands in their hands, as an emblem of superiority, they are preceded by musick, who play all the while before them the tune *The Black and the Grey*,[1] and no other ever is used at weddings. When they arrive at the Churchyard, they

---

1 This was not a popular tune in the time of Charles II, and it continued in vogue till the end of the last century.

walk three times round the Church, before they enter it. The ceremony being performed, the return home and sit down to the feast; after which they dance in the Manx fashion, and, between that and drinking, pass the remainder of the day." This Marriage-Feast was a lavish if not a sumptuous repast, and is described by the same writer as follows:—"Broth is served up in wooden piggins, every man having his portion allowed him. This they sup with shells called *sligs*, very much like our mussel shells, but larger. I have seen a dozen capons in one platter, and six or eight fat geese in another; hogs and sheep roasted whole, and oxen divided but into quarters." These customs have now fallen into disuse. But the blowing of horns, the day before and the morning of the wedding, is still continued. It was formerly usual for the lover to employ a go-between called a *dooinney-moyllee*, "a praising man," to court and win over his mistress to accept his addresses. It was also part of his duty to get the parents to consent to the match, and to arrange the marriage portion with them.

Train, writing about marriages fifty years ago, says that "when two persons agreed to become united in matrimony, and this had been proclaimed in the parish church on three several Sundays, all the relations and friends of the young people were invited to the bridal, and generally attended, bringing with them presents for the 'persons about to begin the world.' Their weddings, as in Galloway, were generally celebrated on a Tuesday or a Thursday. The bridegroom and his party proceeded to the bride's house, and thence with her party to church—the men walking first in a body and the women after them. On the bridegroom leaving his house, it was customary to throw an old shoe after him, and in like manner an old shoe after the bride on leaving her house to proceed to church, in order to ensure good luck to each respectively; and if, by stratagem, either of the bride's shoes could be taken off by any spectator on her way from church, it had to be ransomed by the bridegroom. On returning from church, the bride and bridegroom walk in front, and every man, with his sweetheart, in procession, often to the number of fifty. The expenses of the wedding dinner and drink are sometimes paid by the men individually. It was formerly the custom after the marriage had been performed for some of the most active of the young people to start off at full speed for the bridegroom's house, and for the first who reached it to receive a flask of brandy. He then returned in all haste to the wedding party, all of whom halted and formed a circle. He handed spirits first to the bridegroom, next to the bride, and then to the rest of the company in succession, each drinking to the health of the new-married couple. After this, the party moved onwards to the bridegroom's house, on their arrival at the door of which the bridecake was broken over the bride's head, and then thrown away to be scrambled for by the crowd usually attendant on such occasions. The girls present were especially anxious to secure a piece to place under their pillows, that they might dream of their future husbands, as this ceremony is supposed to strengthen the dreaming charm." The writer has heard this ceremony somewhat differently related by men still living, who have taken part in it. They say that there was a race among the young men from the church to the house, and that the first to arrive got the cake, and broke a portion of it over the bride's head when she reached the threshold.

In his notes on Customs and Superstitions in Vol. XXI of the Manx Society, William Harrison adds the following particulars to Waldron's account of Weddings, which, he says, obtained about 20 years before the time he wrote (*i.e.*, about 20 years after Train's account):—"After the ceremony, on coming out of the church, money is thrown amongst the idlers, who generally congregate about, for which they scramble. This is also done in passing any public place on the way home. On returning home, some of the most active of the young people start off at full speed for the bride's house, and he who arrives there first is considered best man, and is entitled to some peculiar privilege in consequence. Occasionally, when the wedding party is attended by their friends on horseback, some severe riding takes place, and it is well if all ends without an accident. After the feast the remainder of the day is spent with the utmost hilarity in dancing and other amusements."

DEATH

Many were the omens which preceded the solemn event of death. If the dogs howled more loudly than usual, if the deathwatch[1] was distinct in the sick person's room, if his or her wraith was seen by anyone, and if the strains of the funeral psalm were heard, then death was near. When death ensued the corpse was laid on what was called a "straightening board," a trencher with salt[2] in it and a lighted candle were placed on the breast, and the bed, on which the straightening board lay, was generally strewed with strong scented flowers. It was then waked, as we shall see, and carried to the grave, wrapped in a winding sheet and on an open bier (*carbad*, in Manx). With regard to this winding sheet, Merick, who was Bishop of Man from 1577 to 1600, and who supplied Camden with a brief account of the Isle for his *Britannia*, made the extraordinary statement that the women of the Island wore them during their lives to remind them of their mortality. This was contradicted by later historians, who pointed out that these so-called shrouds were merely the blankets, plaids, or shawls which the women habitually wore. Waldron wrote about death and funerals in Man 160 years ago as follows:—

---

1 This sound was really produced by a small wood-moth.

2 Sometimes earth as well as salt was laid on the corpse, the former being an emblem of the corruptibility of the body, the other of the incorruptibility of the soul.

"When a person dies, several of his acquaintances come and sit up with him, which they call the Wake[1] (*Farrar*, in Manx). The Clerk of the Parish is obliged to sing a Psalm, in which all the company join; and after that they begin some pastime to divert themselves, and having strong beer and tobacco allowed them in great plenty. . . . As to their Funerals, they give no invitation, but everybody, that had any acquaintance with the deceased, comes either on foot or horseback. I have seen sometimes at a Manks burial upwards of a hundred horsemen, and twice the number on foot: all these are entertained at long tables, spread with all sorts of cold provision, and rum and brandy flies about at a lavish rate. The procession of carrying the corpse to the grave is in this manner: When they come within a quarter of a mile from Church, they are met by the Parson, who walks before them singing a psalm, all the company joining with him. In every Church-yard there is a cross round which they go three times before they enter the Church. But these are the funerals of the better sort, for the poor are carried only on a bier,[2] with an old blanket round them fastened with a skewer."

There were formerly crosses on the roads leading to the Parish Churches. When funerals passed, "the corpse," says Train, "as usually set down at these stones, that all the people attending might have an opportunity of praying for the soul of the deceased." He also tells us that "one of this description was lately to be seen at Port-y-Vullin, on the wayside leading

---

1 Watching with the dead was an ancient custom of the Church. Pennant, in his *Tour of Scotland*, speaks of it as follows: "The evening after the death of any person, the relations or friends of the deceased meet at the house attended by bag-pipe or fiddle; the nearest of kin, be it wife, son, or daughter, opens a melancholy ball, dancing and greeting (*i.e.*, crying) at the same time."

2 Burial in coffins, as a universal custom, did not begin in England before the end of the seventeenth century.

from Ramsey to St. Maughold, and another near Port Erin." It would seem that before 1594, when it was forbidden by Statute, it was customary to carry bells and banners before the dead. Colonel Townley, who visited the Island towards the end of the eighteenth century, describes a funeral entertainment as follows: "The concourse of people, upon the occasion, was wonderful, and the quantity of provisions prepared. . . . was as wonderful; but not more so than the speedy mode of dispatching them; for the people of this Island (I mean the country farmers and their good wives, together with many handicraft-people) esteem a funeral attendance as one of their very first entertainments."

Lord Teignmouth, when in the Isle of Man in 1835, was informed that persons walking in the neighbour-hood of a churchyard sometimes found themselves entangled in a crowd, which suddenly vanished—a sign that foreboded a funeral. It was supposed that when the funeral hymn was sung in a low key that it was a sign of another death.

It is a practice at the present day for the relatives of the deceased to attend the parish church the next Sunday but one after the funeral and to sit down throughout the service.

SECOND-SIGHT

Closely connected with death is the curious superstition about *Second-sight*, because it is with reference to death that its visions almost always occur. It may be defined as the faculty of seeing future events by means of a spectral exhibition of the persons to whom such events relate, accompanied with signs denoting their fate. This superstition is more prevalent among Gaelic peoples than others. Dr. Johnson, when on his tour in Scotland and the Western Isles, remarks upon it as follows:—"Second sight is an impression made either by the mind upon the eye, or by the eye upon the mind, by which things distant or future are perceived and seen as if they were present. . . . Things distant are seen at the instant when they happen. This receptive faculty, for power it cannot be called, is neither voluntary nor constant. The appearances have no dependence upon choice; they cannot be summoned, detained, or recalled—the impression is sudden, and the effect often painful." People who have a hairy cross on their breasts, or whose eyebrows meet, often have the faculty of *Second-sight*, and so, as we have already seen, had those of posthumous birth. Such people if they go into a churchyard on the Eves of the New Year, of St. Mark's Day and of Midsummer Day can tell who will be buried in it during the ensuing year. A child whose eye touches water in baptism has no chance of becoming second-sighted.

The belief in the faculty of *Second-sight* was formerly very prevalent in the Island. According to Higden, it was the reputed prerogative of Manxmen, for he says, "There, ofte by daye time, men of that Islande seen men that bey dede to fore honde, byheeded or hole, and what dethe they dyde. Alyens setten there feet upon feet of the men of that londe for to see such syghts as the men of that londe doon."[1] Sacheverell, who was Governor of the Isle of Man from 1692-1696, says that this power was sometimes derived by inheritance, and transmitted from father to son, and he remarks that there were people who would attest to having seen apparitions of funeral solemnities on the large barrow called "Fairy Hill" in Rushen. He does not altogether believe in this, however, "but as to the light being generally seen at people's deaths, I have some assurances so probable, that I know not how to disbelieve them; particularly an ancient man, who has been long clerk of a parish, has affirmed to me that he almost constantly sees them upon the death of any of his own parish; and one Captain Leathes, who was chief magistrate of Belfast, and

---

1 Polychronicon, A.D., 1482, Rolls series.

reputed a man of great integrity, assured me that he was once shipwrecked on the Island, and lost the greater part of his crew; that when he came on shore the people told him he had lost thirteen of his men, for they saw so many lights going toward the church, which was the just number lost. Whether these fancies proceed from ignorance, superstition, or prejudice of education, or from any traditional or veritable magic, which is the opinion of the Scotch divines concerning second sight; or whether nature has adapted the organs of some persons for discerning of spirits, is not for me to determine." This belief is not yet extinct, for "corpse-lights" seen about the bed of the patient are still supposed to be the certain forerunners of death.[2]

Bishop Wilson gives, in his Pocket-Book, the following instance of a supernatural warning:—"Mar., 1721. Two boats of Ballaugh, being at sea, but not any distance without hearing each other, ye men in each boat heard a voice very distinctly repeating these words— "Churr hoods," a term used by fishermen to raise the anchor. They immediately did so, and well it was for them, for a violent storm arose in half-an-hour's time, so y^t as it was they had enough to save their boat and their lives. This is well attested. N.B.—Mr Corlett assured me y^t the very same thing happened once to the boat he was in, only with the addition y^t ye master of ye boat saw ye appearance of a man."[3]

It was formerly supposed, as already stated, that families had *Second-sight* by succession, and it was also supposed that the only way to be freed from it was by a man who had it marrying a woman affected in the same way. Waldron, who gives several instances of the possession of this faculty, was evidently

2 Its frequency in earlier times may be reasonably attributed to the greater prevalency of marshy ground over which such phenomena as the *ignis fatuus*, or Will-o'-the-wisp, would often be seen.

3 Manx Note Book, vol. II, p. 87.

much impressed by them, as he declared himself "positively convinced by many proofs." He stated that the Manx consider that the warnings caused by these mock funerals were the work of friendly demons, who even condescended to warn a host of the arrival of an unexpected guest, and servants of the return of a master who had not been expected. "As difficult as I found it," he says, "to give any faith to this, I have frequently been very much surprised, when, on visiting a friend, I have found the table ready spread and everything in order to receive me, and been told by the person to whom I went, that he had knowledge of my coming, or some other guest, by those good natured intelligencers. Nay, when obliged to be absent some time from home, my own servants have assured me they were informed by these means of my return, and expected me the very hour I came, though, perhaps, it was some days before I hoped it myself at my going abroad."

He then gives the following account of

MOCK FUNERALS

"The natives of this Island tell you that before any person dies, the procession of the funeral is acted by a sort of beings which, for that end, render themselves visible. I know several that, as they have been passing the road, one of these funerals has come behind them, and even laid the bier on their shoulders, as though to assist the bearers. One person, who assured me he had been served so, told me that the flesh of his shoulder had been very much bruised, and was black for many weeks after. There are few or none of them who pretend not to have seen or heard these imaginary obsequies (for I must not omit to say that they sing psalms in the same manner as those do who accompany the corpse of a dead friend), which so little differ from real ones that they are not to be known till both coffin and mourners are seen to vanish at the church doors."

CHAPTER IX

CUSTOMS FORMERLY ENFORCED BY LAW

IT MAY POSSIBLY BE CONSIDERED that the above heading is a contradiction in terms, for, as Dr. E. B. Tylor remarks, "the distinction between a law and an authoritative custom may be best drawn with reference to the manner in which Society compels obedience to it. If a judge or tribunal declares the rule, and punishes its infraction, it is a law; if it is left loosely to public opinion to practically accept the rule, and to visit those who disobey with blame, insult, and social exclusion, it is a custom."[1] But many of the following customs originated in popular usage long before there was any law to enforce them; and they could only have continued, without being enforced by law, as long as popular opinion was unanimously in their favour. When a majority only favoured them, there would have been a difficulty in compelling obedience to them without law, and, when popular opinion had pronounced against them, no law would have availed to put them

---

1 Anthropological Notes and Queries—British Association.

in force. They are now, though some of them still remain un-repealed in the Statute Book, all obsolete.

WATCH AND WARD

One of the duties most strongly enforced by law was that of keeping a look-out for the approach of enemies, or of *Watch* and *Ward*, as it was called. We find the Deemsters, in 1417, informing Sir John Stanley that it was one of the constitutions "of old time" that every man was liable to perform the duties of "Watch and Ward" upon pain of life and limb, "for whosoever fails any night in his ward forfeiteth a wether to the warden;[1] and to the warden the second night a calve; and the third night life and lymb to the Lord." In 1594 the duty of "Watch and Ward" was the subject of the following strict orders:—"Whereas the safe keeping of this Isle consisteth in the dutiful and careful observance of Watch and Ward, without which the Lord can never be well defended, nor the people live in safety; therefore, be it ordained that all Watch and Ward be kept according to the strict order of the law; and that none be sent thither but such as are of discretion, and able to deserve (sic) to be careful; and that the night watch shall come at the sun setting, and not depart before the sun rising; and that the day watch shall come at the sun rising, and not depart before the sun setting." This "Watch and Ward" was kept on various points of vantage round the coast, where the existence of watch stations is still recorded by such names as *Cronk-ny-Arrey*, "Hill of the Watch," and *Cronk-ny-Arrey Laa*, "Hill of the Day Watch."

CUSTOMS CONNECTED WITH LAND TENURE

We have already mentioned the Tenure by the presentation and custody of a Saint's Staff under St. Patrick's Day; the following customary payments are also noteworthy: An ox was

1 There were two of these officials in every parish, one for the day and the other for the night watch.

formerly exacted from the tenants of the Bishop's Barony on the installation of each Bishop, as will be seen by the following extract from the ecclesiastical records:—

"1646. At this court it was most graciouslie offered by the right Hono[ble] the Lord of the Island that for as much by antient custome the tenants of the B[ps] Lands were accustomed to pay at the change of every B[op] an oxe or fortie shillings in money out of every quarter land that now such y[e] tenants shall have twentie yeares term from y[e] death of y[e] last Lord B[op] for their payings of y[e] said dutie of one oxe or xl[s] out of every quarter land unto his L[op]. Provided that if there shall happen to bee any B[op] enstalled in this Island wth in the said tearme such their paym[ts] shall be & stand during ye life of that B[op] & his Lo[rp] & his heyres shall free them of the said duties from that B[op]. Which motion was consented unto by such of the said tenants whose names are under written that they will pay xl[s] out of every quarter." This exaction was not confined to the Barony, as there are other estates which formerly made the same payment.

A portion of the estate of Kirby, in the parish of Braddan, was formerly held on the tenure of lodging the Bishop whenever he left the Island or came to it. This was commuted about two hundred years ago for the very moderate sum of ten shillings. All rents and tithes were formerly paid in kind, the apportionment of which often occasioned considerable difficulty. An amusing case with reference to this appears in the records two hundred years ago:—A portion of a farm had been washed away by the Sulby river, and, consequently, the rent was reduced by one-fourth, which, as the report of the proceedings informs us, resulted in "great inconvenience in making allowance of the fourth part of a goose or hen." Labour rents, called *Boons*, are still legal, but are not enforced. It may be mentioned that there are traces of the *Open Field* system in Man, but the elucidation of this would be out of place in a book devoted to Folk-Lore.

JURY FOR SERVANTS

There was a rural tribunal called the "Jury for Servants," which possessed the power of compelling the service in agriculture of persons whom they considered as unemployed. In 1577, the Deemsters gave as the customary law "that, if any of the Lord his tennants be destitute of servants, and come and make his complaint to the Deemster that he can get none to occupy my Lord his land withall, then the Deemster is to send to the Coroner and to the Lockman of every parish, and then to swear four honest men in every parish to enquire first of vagrant servants." These juries were to "be impannelled all times in the yeare as often as there will be just cause for the same; and that the vagrant servants by the said jurors found be first made liable and put to service, otherwise to suffer punishment till they submitt."

CUSTOM ABOUT GIVING SERVANTS NOTICE

By customary law, servants wishing to leave their masters at the expiration of their agreement were required to give notice of their intention on a certain day; "but lest the master might happen to be from home, or might absent himself in a deceitful manner, to take advantage of the servant; in either case the servant may repair with a competent witness to the place where the master usually sits, at the hearth or at meat, and there make a nick with his knife in such master's chair; or, if the door should be shut against him, he may make a nick in the threshold, which shall be authentic in law against such master." A similar law was put on record in the Statute Book, in 1665; but without the obligation of making the "nick."

YARDING

A curious privilege, called Yarding, was conferred by an ancient customary law on the Deemsters, Moars, Coroners, and Serjeants of Baronies, which enabled them to compel people to enter into their service at a trifling fee, fixed by law. The ceremony was performed by an officer called the Sumner, who laid a straw over the shoulder of the person so required, and said, "You are hereby Yarded for the service of the Lord of Man, in the house of his Deemster, Moar, Coroner, or Serjeant of Barony;" at the same time repeating the name of the person requiring such servant. Persons refusing to comply with this requisition were committed to prison, and there kept on a daily allowance of one barley cake and a pint of water, "till they yielded obedience to perform their service." Such Yarded servants were "proclaimed and made known at the parish church or cross . . . the Sunday next after the day of Yarding aforesaid, whereby the farmers may the timelier know to provide themselves with other servants." All vicars and members of the House of Keys were allowed their "bridge and staff," which implied that their servants should not be taken from them by Yarding. It was a customary ordinance that the porridge or *sollaghyn* of Yarded servants should be so thick that the potstick would stand upright in the centre of the pot immediately before dishing the porridge; and the cakes given to them were required to be as thick as the length of a barley-corn.

The law instituting Yarding has long since been repealed.

THE DEEMSTER'S OATH

It is well known that the Celts formerly reckoned not only the night with which the week or any period began, but also the night with which it ended. A curious instance of this method of reckoning occurs in the Deemster's oath, in which the six days of creation have been made into six days and seven nights. It runs thus: "By this book, and by the holy contents thereof, and by the wonderful works that God hath miraculously wrought in heaven above and in the earth beneath in six days and seven nights, I, A.B., do swear that I will, without respect of favour or friend-ship, love or gain, consanguinity or affinity, envy or malice, execute the laws of this Isle justly, betwixt our Sovereign Lord the King, (or Lady the Queen), and his or her subjects within this Isle, and betwixt party and party, as indifferently as the herring backbone doth lie in the midst of the fish." Of late years it has been the practice to make the 'six days and seven nights' into 'six days and six nights.'

LEGAL PURGATION

By the statute of 1665 we learn that the Manx Legislators encouraged legal purgation in general, especially that form of it which is thus described in the tenth ecclesiastical customary law:—"He that enters his claim within the year and a day after the probate of the Will . . . without bill, bond or evidence, shall prove the same upon the grave of him or her from whom the debt was due, with lawful compurgators according to the ancient form; that is to say, lying on his back with the Bible on his breast, and his compurgators on either side." This compurgation seems to have been only prescribed in default of documentary evidence. In 1609 it had been denounced by the temporal authorities as "not fitting nor Christian-like," but the then bishop, Phillips, vigorously protested against this view in a letter written in that year to the Earl of Salisbury, who was then one of the guardians of the Island, in which he says—"one of our best lawes (the nature of that people considered), vizt., the oath for swearing on the grave, in case where there is not specialty he (The Governor) hath abrogated, and prescribes us some others not so convenient not with so good a conscience to be used of us, seeing they want their due allowance and forme, vizt. generall consent upon good advice and the Lord's approbation." To this the Governor and Legislature replied that "the swearing of and upon the grave of the dead was unfitting and caused much wrong to be done to poor orphanes and simplest of friends." Nevertheless the Bishop's view was to prevail for sometime longer, for we find the following case in 1616:—"M^d that Mr Christopher Younge chaplaine of the Castell of Rushen left in his last will that Mr Thomas Samsburie Demster did owe unto him The sum of sevene pounds and Mrs Jaine Samsbuerie weiff to the said Tho Samsbuerie twelve shillings neine pence. The said Thomas and Jaine came to the Grave of the forsaid Christopher and die lie upon theire backes wth ye bibel on their brest wth theire compurgatours and did sweare that they ought (sic) him nothinge when they did recken wth the Executore and immediately the same daye being the second of July Ano 1616 they did recover of the Executore vij^s ij^d after the accounte was made by me Edw Caloe Vic^r (of Malew);" and, as we have seen above, purgation was included in the ecclesiastical laws in 1665. Moreover, as we shall see below; Bishop Wilson, in the eighteenth century, approved of it and quoted Exodus xxii., 11., and Leviticus v., 1., in its favor.

THE STOCKS

The Stocks were in vogue in the Isle of Man, as elsewhere, and we find that in 1610 it was "by generall consent as afforesaid proclaimed, that as oft as any man or woman shall be found drunk hereafter, the Party soe offending, if not of ability to pay a fine, shall be for the first time punished in the Stocks, the second time to be tyed to the Whipping Stocks, and the third time to be whipped therein." By another law passed in 1655 it was enacted that, "If any servant hire more than twice, he shall be whipped at the parish church on Sunday, or at the market in the Whipping Stocks." This punishment, though long since obsolete, was not legally abolished till 1876.

THE PILLORY

The Pillory was also an Insular institution. So late as 1757 it was ordained by the Marriage Act that any stranger convicted of having solemnized marriage without licence or previous banns was to "be publickly exposed with his ears nailed to a Pillory to be erected for that Purpose at Castletown Cross upon the next Court Day of General Gaol Delivery after such conviction at twelve o'clock at noon, and there to remain for the space of one hour, when his ears are to be cut off and remain on the said Pillory," &c. This was repealed in 1849. By the 72nd ecclesiastical law "whosoever shall swear an oath (by taking the name of God in vain) shall for the first time pay 12 pence, and sit one hour in the Stocks; for the second time two shillings, and so double to be for every such offence, to be levyed by the churchwardens and afterwards disposed of by the ordinary to pious uses."

THE WOODEN HORSE

Another curious punishment was being whipped on the Wooden Horse. Thus we find among the laws passed in 1629: "Whosoever shall be found or detected to pull Horse Tayles shall be punished upon the Wooden Horse, thereon to continue for the space of two hours and to be whipped naked from the waist upwards."

BISHOP WILSON ON PECULIAR LAWS AND CUSTOMS

Bishop Wilson tells us in his History of the Isle of Man that "there are a great many laws and customs which are peculiar to this place and singular" in his time (1697-1755), and he proceeds to enumerate them as follows:—

"The eldest daughter (if there be no son) inherits, though there be more children."

"The wives, through the whole Island, have a power to make their wills (though their husbands be living) of one-half of all the goods movable or immovable; except in the six northern parishes, where the wife, if she has had children, can only dispose of a third part of the living goods; and this favour, tradition saith, the south-side women obtained above those of the north for their assisting their husbands in a day of battle." (This is said to be the battle of Stantwat, in 1098, between the north and south Manx.)

"A widow has one half of her husband's real estate, if she be iris first wife, and one-quarter if she be the second or third;

but if any widow marries, or miscarries, she loses her wid-ow-right in her husband's estate."

"When any of the tenants fell into poverty, and were not able to pay their rents and services, the sitting quest, consist-ing of four old moars or baliffs in every parish, were obliged to find such a tenant for the estates as would secure the lord's rent, &c., who, after his name was entered in the court-rolls, had an unquestionable title to the same."

"A child got before marriage shall inherit, provided the marriage follows within a year or two, and the woman was never defamed before with regard to any other man."

"Executors of spiritual men have a right to the year's prof-its if they live till after twelve of the clock on Easter Day."

"They still retain a usage (observed by the Saxons before the Conquest) that the Bishop, or some priest appointed by him, do always sit in the great court along with the Gover-nor, till sentence of death (if any) be pronounced: the Deem-ster asking the jury (instead of 'Guilty or not guilty?') *Vod fir-charree soie?* which, literally translated, is 'May the man of the chancel, or he that ministers at the altar, continue to sit?' If the foreman answers in the negative, the Bishop, or his sub-stitute, withdraws, and the sentence is then pronounced on the criminal."

"When any laws which concern the Church are to be en-acted, the Bishop and the whole clergy shall be made privy thereunto, and join with the temporal officers, and have their consents with them till the same shall be established."

"If a single woman prosecutes a single man for a rape, the ecclesiastical judges impannel a jury; and if this jury find him guilty, he is so returned to the temporal court, where, if he be found guilty, the Deemster delivers to the woman a rope, a sword, and a ring, and she has it in her choice to have him hanged or beheaded, or to marry him."

"If a man get a farmer's daughter with child, he shall be compelled to marry her, or endow her with such a portion as her father would have given her. No man could dispose of his estate unless he fell into poverty; and, at this day, a man must have the approbation of the Governor and Officers before he can alienate."

"The manner of calling any person before a magistrate, spiritual or temporal, is pretty singular: The magistrate, upon a piece of thin slate or stone, makes a mark, generally the first letters of his christian or surname. This is given to the proper officer, the summoner, if it be before an ecclesiastical magistrate; or the lockman, if before a temporal, with twopence, who shows it to the person to be charged, with the time when he is to appear, and at whose suit; which, if he refuses to obey, he is fined or committed to prison, until he give bonds to appear and pay costs."

Bishop Gibson (1695)[1] says that "This stone, so marked is called a *Token*, which, being given to the plaintiff, he delivereth it to the Coroner of the place where the defendant resides, and the defendant, having received it, is bound to appear and answer. It has been an ancient custom in that Island, that if the plaintiff find his adversary present in the Court while the Court is sitting, he may take him by the arm, and bring him before the Governor, and set his foot upon his adversary's foot, and there plead his cause against him without the formality of summoning him with a token."

The following laws, taken from the Statute Book, may also be mentioned: All goats belonged to the Queen of Man. In case of people removing from one parish to another, "if the cock crow trice, they remaining there three nights and three days after removing, that then the person departed shall pay all spirituall dutyes to that same Church within the same parish he doth remove to." One of the duties of the Sumner was to stand at the chancel door of his Parish Church "at time of service, to whip and beat all the doggs."

1 In Camden's Britannia.

"All Scotts avoid the land with the next vessell that goeth into Scotland, upon paine of forfeiture of his goods, and his body to prison."

"That whensoever any theef shall be found to steal either mutton, sheep, lambe, goate, kidd, swine, or pigg, the same shall be found to be Fellony in like manner to death, without valuing the same."

"That the stealing and cutting of bee-hives in gardens shall be Fellony in like manner to death, without valuing the same."

The Manx Ecclesiastical Law is also responsible for many curious enactments, by which the Church enforced its discipline. Bishop Wilson writes of this ecclesiastical discipline as follows:—"There is nothing more commendable than the discipline of this church. . . . Offenders of all conditions, without distinction, are obliged to submit to the censures appointed by the church, whether for correction or example (commutation of penances being abolished by a late law), and they generally do it patiently. Such as do not submit (which have hitherto been but few) are either imprisoned or excommunicated; under which sentence if they continue more than forty days, they are delivered over to the Lord of the Isle, both body and goods. . . The manner of doing penance is primitive and edifying. The penitent, clothed in a sheet, &c., is brought into the church immediately before the Litany; and there continues till the sermon be ended; after which, and a proper exhortation, the congregation are desired to pray for him in a form provided for that purpose; and thus he is dealt with, till by his behaviour he has given some satisfaction that all this is not feigned, which being certified to the bishop, he orders him to be received by a very solemn form for receiving penitents into the peace of the church. But if offenders, after having once done public penance, relapse into the same or other scandalous vice, they are not presently permitted to do penance again, though they should desire it ever so earnestly, till they shall have given better proofs of their resolution to amend their lives; during which time they are not permitted to go into any church in time of divine service, but stand at the church door, until their pastor and other grave persons are convinced by their conversation that there are hopes of a lasting reformation, and certify the same to the bishop. There is here one very wholesome branch of church discipline . . . namely, the injoining offenders' purgation by their own oaths, and the oaths of compurgators (if need be) of known reputation, where the fame is common, the crime is scandalous, and yet not proof enough to convict them; and this is far from being complained of as a grievance: for if common fame has injured any person, he has an opportunity of being restored to his good name (unless upon trial the Court find just cause to refuse it), and a severe penalty is laid upon any that, after this, revive the scandal. On the other hand, if a man will not swear to his own innocency, or cannot prevail with others to believe him, it is fit he should be treated as guilty, and the scandal removed by a proper censure."[1]

EXCOMMUNICATION

The following was the form of Excommunication:—"For as much as your crimes have been so great repeated and continued in so long as to give offence to all sober Christians, and even to cry to Heaven for vengeance. And you having had sufficient time given you to consider of the consequence of continuing in them without any visible or sincere remorse or probability of a future reformation. Therefore, in the name of our Lord Christ and before this Congregation, we pronounce and declare you, A.B., Excommunicate and shut out of the Communion of all faithful Christians. And may Almighty God who by His Holy Spirit has appointed this sentence for

---

1 History of the Isle of Man. Manx Society, vol. XVIII., pp. 113-14.

removing of scandal and offence out of the Church and for reducing of sinners to a sense of their sins and danger make this censure to all the good ends for which it was ordained. And that your Heart may be filled with fear and dread that you may be recovered out of the same and power of the Devil and your Soul may be saved, and that others may be warned by your sad example not to sin nor continue in sin so presumptuously."

By the 3rd accustomed law of the Church "excommunicated persons persisting irregularly are to be imprisoned and delivered over, body and goods, to the Lord's mercy."

By the 20th ecclesiastical law any one "that strikes a minister shall be excommunicated (*ipso facto*) and to do penance and after satisfaction given to the Law to receive absolution, and to be received at the church stile into the church by the minister's reading before him the 51st Psalm and before the congregation to repeat his schedule after the minister."

PENANCE

The penalty of Penance was inflicted for a variety of offences. It consisted in standing in a sheet at the Parish Church, or several Parish Churches, on Sunday during service, or at the Market Cross on Saturdays during market time. The number of days' penance was regulated by the seriousness of the offence. According to an entry in the Episcopal Records, dated 1623, a malicious slanderer was "to remain a Lyer of Record, and do open penance . . . . putting his finger on his mouth, and confessing a Lye in saying 'Tongue, thou Lyed,' and so publickly to ask the party offended forgiveness." By the 23rd accustomed law "Whosoever commits Fornication shall make three Sundays' pennance, and if they marry that they go from the Sheet to the Ring;" and by the 34th "All offenders censured to Pennance are to perform their censures and satisfy the Law before they be admitted to the Holy Communion, and to pay 3d to the minister for every day's Penance for writing

certificates, and to the Sumner 2d, and if the offender bring
not a sheet he is to pay the Sumner 4d for furnishing him,
and no appeal be from the Church, and none offending be
privileged from censures." The 5th ecclesiastical constitution,
passed under the superintendence of Bishop Wilson in 1703,
makes the punishment of Penance and Excommunication still
more severe. It runs as follows: "For the more effectual dis-
couragement of Vice, if any Person shall incurr the censures of
the Church, and, having done Penance, shall afterwards incurr
the same Censures, he shall not be permitted to do Penance
again (as has been formerly accustomed) untill the Church be
fully satisfied of his sincere repentance; during which time he
shall not presume to come within the Church, but be obliged
to stand in a decent manner at the Church Door every Sunday and Holy Day the whole time of morning and evening
service, untill by his penitent behaviour, and other instances
of sober living, he deserves and procures a certificate from the
Minister, Churchwardens, and some of the soberest Men of
the Parish, to the satisfaction of the Ordinary, which if he does
not so deserve and procure within three months, the Church
shall proceed to Excommunication; and that during these proceedings the Governor shall be applied to not to permit him
to leave the Island; and this being a matter of very great importance, the Ministers and Church-wardens shall see it duly
performed, under penalty of the severest Ecclesiasticall Censures; and whenever any daring offender shall be and continue
so obstinate as to incurr Excommunication, the Pastor shall
affectionately exhort his Parishioners not to converse with
him upon peril of being a partaker with him in his Sin and
Punishment." In 1737 the following civil law was passed with
reference to excommunicated persons: "Be it further ordained
and enacted . . . . that the custome and practice of delivering
over persons excommunicated in the Spirituall Court, body
and goods to the Lord of the Isle, shall entirely cease, and that

such persons excommunicated continuing obstinate for the space of three months under censure, shall, upon application by the Governor to the said Court, be confined three months in one of the Castles, instead of the rigorous Punishment and forfeiture aforesaid: But this shall not be construed or understood to take off his censure, any Law, Custome, or Usage to the contrary notwithstanding."

The following is a story about a Penance which the Nuns of St. Bridget's Nunnery, near Douglas, were said to have been compelled to perform:—

THE NUN'S CHAIRS

Over a place called The How of Douglas there is a rock, vastly high and steep, about the middle of which is a hollow not very different from the fashion of an elbow chair, and near the top another very much like the former. Whether these are made by art or nature I cannot pretend to determine, nor did I ever hear; but, on the slightest accusation, the poor nun was brought to the foot of this rock, when the sea was out, and obliged to climb to the first chair, where she sat till the tide had twice ebbed and flowed. Those who had given greater cause for suspicion, went up to the second chair, and sat the same space of time. Those who endured this trial, and descended unhurt, were cleared of the aspersion thrown upon them; but the number of fortunate could not be great, for besides the danger of climbing the ragged and steep rock (which now very few men can do above 30 or 40 paces), the extreme cold when you come to any height, the horror of being exposed alone to all the fury of the elements, and the horrid prospect of the sea, roaring through a thousand cavities and foaming round you on every side, is enough to stagger the firmest resolution and courage, and without all question has been the destruction of many of those unhappy wretches. — *Waldron*.

Penance was done in Ballaugh Church 55 years ago, in Parson Stowell's time, according to information given by a man now living, who was one of the chapter-quest at the time. During the time he was in office two men and two women were brought to church for this purpose. They stood in the "alley" of the church, and the Sumner threw white sheets over them. This was for the first three Sundays; but on the fourth they stood inside the chancel railing, and were addressed by the parson, who "made them feel thoroughly ashamed of themselves." A similar penance was seen about the year 1825, also by a man now living, in the parish church of Lezayre.

THE BRIDLE

Among the accustomed unwritten laws of the Manx Church was the following:—"That he or she that call a man a Dog or a woman a Bitch shall wear the Bridle at the Market Cross or make 7 Sundays penance in several Parish Church-es." This ordinance was freely put in force by Bishop Wilson, who wrote in June, 1714, "I ordered a bridle to be made, as a terror to people of evil tongues; and it is now brought about the circuit by the General Sumner, and lodged in his hands for the time to come."

Waldron remarks upon this:—"If any person be convict-ed of uttering a scandalous report, and cannot make good the assertion, instead of being fined or imprisoned, they are sentenced to stand in the Market-place on a sort of scaffold erected for that purpose, with their tongue in a noose of leath-er, which they call a bridle, and having been thus exposed to the view of the people for some time, on the taking off this machine they are obliged to say three times, *Tongue thou hast lied.*" A somewhat similar instrument was used in various parts of England; it was called "the bridle" or "the branks." In Scot-land, too, it was used for the correction of scolds and gossips. It was made of thin iron, passing over and round the head, and fastened behind by a padlock. The bit was a flat piece of iron, about two inches long and one broad, which went into the mouth and kept the tongue down by its pressure. A specimen of the "Bishop's brank" is sketched and noticed in the Abbotsford Edition of *The Monastery*.

THE PUNISHMENT OF BEING DRAGGED AFTER A BOAT

The 26th ecclesiastical law was to the effect "that common w—h—r—s be drawn after a boat in the sea during the Ordinaries appointment." This barbarous punishment was put in force by Bishop Wilson in at least one case. The most notorious of which, that of Kathrine Kinred, is copied from the Episcopal Registry, dated March 15th, 1713, *in extenso*, as follows:—"Forasmuch as neither Christian advice or gentle methods of punishments are found to have any effect on Kath: Kinred, of kk Christ, a notorious str—m—p—t, who has brought forth illegitimate children, and still continues to *strowl* about the country, and to lead a most vicious and scandalous life on other accounts. All such tending to the great dishonour of the Christian name, and to her own utter destruction, without a timely and *thorow* reformation. It is, therefore, hereby order'd (as well for the further punishment of the said delinquent, as for the example of others) that the said Kath. Kinred he dragged after a boat in the sea, at Peeltown, on Wednesday, the 17th instant (being the fair of Saint Patrick), at the height of the market. To which end a boat and boat crew are to be charged by the General Sumner. And the constable and souldiers of ye garrison are, by the Governor's order, to be aiding and assisting in seeing this censure performed. And in case any owner, master, or crew of any boat are found refractory, by neglecting or refusing to perform this service for the restraining of vice, their names are to be forthwith given in by the Sumner-General, to the end that they may be severely fin'd for their contempt, as the Governor's order directs. Dated at

Bishop's Court, this 17th day of March, 1713." Signed, "Tho, Sodor and Man, Wm. Walker."

The above is endorsed as follows:—"St. Patrick's Day being *soe* stormy and tempestuous that *noe* boate could performe the within censure; upon St. German's Day (July 13th), about the height of the market, the within Kath. Kinred was dragged after a boat in the sea, according to the written order, which is humbly certified by me." Signed, "Thomas Corlett, Generall-Sumner."

Bishop Wilson has been the object of much obloquy for the severity of his ecclesiastical discipline, and the above has been frequently quoted to prove this reproach; but it must be remembered that this was an exceptional case, and also that Bishop Wilson only administered a law which he found in existence; and a reference to the records will show how often he intervened to mitigate these punishments, which were, on the whole, more severe before his episcopacy than during it.

BOWING TO THE ALTAR

There was an ancient custom, long retained in the Island, of bowing to the altar. The Manx people of two centuries ago, seem to have been what would now be called "ritualists" in some of their acts of worship. Indeed, there seems to have been but little change at the time of the Reformation, and whatever changes took place afterwards were gradual till the arrival of Wesley. With reference to this custom, Bishop Wilson gives the following, among other instructions which he received from Archdeacon Hewestone: That he should be careful "to make obeisance at coming into and going out of the church, and at going up to and coming down from the altar. All ancient, commendable, and devout usages, and which thousands of good people of our Church practice at this day."

OBSERVATION OF SUNDAY

The observation of Sunday was strictly enforced by civil as well as ecclesiastical law. By the Statute of 1610, no one was "admitted to fish from Saturday morning till Sunday at night, after sun-set, upon pain of forfeiture of his boat and netts." In 1690, this period, by the influence of Bishop Levinz, was extended till Monday morning. As a consequence of this legislation and their custom of not going to sea on Friday, the fishermen were formerly idle for three days out of seven. It would appear, both from the above Statute, and from a number of fines and other punishments recorded between 1600 and 1750, that "Sunday" was the period from sunset on Saturday to sunset on Sunday. For we find that, if those who were presented were able to prove that, they had done after sunset on Sunday what would have been breaking the Sabbath before it, they were not punished. Similar offences on Saturday night after sunset were severely punished till 1690, when, by order in Convocation, Bishop Levinz extended Saturday till midnight. For he ordained that "noe milner do suffer his milne to grind from 12 of the clock on Saturday at night till nightfall on Sunday," under penalty of "14 dayes imprisonm[t] in St. German's prison and penance in every church of the Island for the first offence, and for every relaps double punishment and £4 fine to the Lo: use without mittigacon." He did not, however, as we have already seen, permit the fishermen to set sail till Monday morning. There is no legislation on record against other occupations on Saturday evening, but it was the almost universal practice to avoid any work then, as it was supposed to be displeasing to the Fairies, though doubtless this idleness had originally the sanction of customary law.

THE THREE RELIQUES

Among "the constitucons of the ould tyme," to be observed by the Lord of the Isle at the Tinwald, was, according to

the Sloane M.S., of the Acts of Sir John Stanley, in the British Museum, that "the 3 Reliques of Man" should be borne
before him by three "Clarkes . . . in their surplesses." We
nowhere learn what these "Reliques" were, but possibly two
of them might be the "hand" and the "bishop's head," which
were among the silver plate belonging to Rushen Abbey, sold
by the Earl of Derby to the Crown after the dissolution of that
Monastery. This "hand" and "head" seem to have been silver
reliquaries which perhaps enclosed reputed relics of some early
Bishop of the See.

GAMES, ETC.

There is nothing peculiar about the outdoor games of either young or grown-up Manxmen or Manxwomen, and they
are, therefore, of little interest from the Folk-Lorist's point of
view. Waldron remarks: "In their sports they retain something
of Arcadian simplicity. Dancing, if I may call it so, jumping and
turning round at least, to the fiddle and base-viol, is their great
diversion. In summer they have it in the fields, and in winter
in the barns." Of the indoor games, at Hollantide, Christmas,
and Twelfth Night, we have already treated in Chapter VI.

Horse racing and shooting with the bow and arrow seem
to have been the chief amusements of the Manx. Prizes for
these were given by the 7th and later Earls of Derby, the first
race under their patronage, of which we have any record,
having been in 1627. The racecourse was on the peninsula of
Langness, and the races took place on the 28th of July, being
the birthday of the 7th Earl. During the time of the Commonwealth they fell into disuse, but they were continued after the
Restoration, as will be seen by the following order given by
the 8th Earl—"It is my good will and pleasure y^t ye two prizes
formerly granted (by me) for hors running and shouting shall
continue as they did, to be run, or shot for, and so continue
dureing my good will and pleasure.—Given under my hand

att Lathom ye 12 of July, 1669." The following were the chief conditions under which the race was run for a plate of the value of five pounds:—"No horse, or gelding, or mair shall be admitted to run for the said plate, but such as was foaled within the said Island, or in the Calfe of Mann. That every horse, gelding, or mair that is designed to run shall be entered before the 8th day of July, with his master's name and his ovine, if he be generally knowne by any, or else his colour, and whether horse, mair, or gelding . . . . That every person that puts in either horse, mair, or gelding, shall at the time of their entering depositt the sume of five shill a piece into the hands of the cleark of the rolls, which is to goe towards the augmenting of the plate for the year following, besides one shill a piece to be given by them to the said cleark of the rolls for entering their names . . . . That every horse, mair, or gelding shall carry horseman's weight, that is to say, ten stone weight, at fourteen pounds to each stone, besides saddle and bridle."

As to the shooting, for which prizes were also given, Waldron tells us that "the young men were great shooters with bowe and arrows. They had shooting matches frequently, parish against parish, and wagers were laid which side would have the better." There are records of these matches having taken place at the end of the last century.

The only indigenous outdoor game, properly so-called, is *cam mag*, a sort of hockey.

There is a strange superstition among the Manx fishermen about being in the third boat to go out of harbour, which is considered most unlucky. After the first two boats have gone out, a number will follow as nearly as possible in line, so that no one in particular can be said to be the third. No reason is assigned for this curious notion.

CHAPTER X

PROVERBS AND SAYINGS

N O ACCOUNT OF THE CUSTOMS AND SUPERSTITIONS of the Manx would be complete without touching upon their proverbs and characteristic sayings. For nothing shows the peculiarities in the character and prevailing habits of thought of a people more vividly than its proverbs. Any one reading the Manx proverbs would at once say that many of them were similar to those of other peoples, but this does not necessarily show that they are not of native origin. It is, indeed, a well-known fact that there is a remarkable similarity in the proverbs of all peoples, *e.g.*, our comparative philologists tell us of the likeness between the proverbs of the Zulu and the Finn. Yet this simply proves that human thought runs in a common groove, and does not disprove the separate origin of the thoughts of each people. In fact the proverbs of different peoples, which may be defined as the result of their common-sense welded into trite sayings, are similar, because their ordinary ideas and wants are sure to be much the same. Still, national characteristics do appear in proverbs, and, as will he seen from those which follow, the special Manx attribute, that of caution, is no exception to this rule. These proverbs, which appear in the various forms of Maxims, Axioms, or Precepts, are, for convenience, classified under the following headings:— (I) Proverbs relating to General Truths; (2) Proverbs inculcating Caution, Contentment, Thrift, Independence, Industry, and Charity; (3) Proverbial Weather-Lore; (4) Miscellaneous Proverbs and Sayings.

The following Proverbs are summary, statements of *General Truths*:—

Cha jagh moylley ghooinney hene rieau foddey voish e ghorrys.
"A man's praise of himself never went far from his door"—
i.e., "Self praise is no recommendation."

Boayl nagh vel aggle cha vel grayse.
"Where there is no fear there is no grace."

Eshyn nagh gow rish briw erbee t'eh deyrey eh hene.
"He who will acknowledge no judge condemns himself."

Ta bee eeit jarroodit.
"Eaten food is forgotten."

Cha vel fer erbee cha bouyr, as eshyn nagh jean clashtyn.
"There is no man so deaf as he who will not hear."
Gowee bleb rish voylley, as gowee dooinney creeney rish foill.
"A fool will receive praise, and a rich man will receive blame."

Ta fuill ny s'chee na ushtey.
"Blood is thicker than water."

Ta scuirrys y laue dy choyrt, scuirrys yn veeal dy voylley.
"When the hand ceases to give, the mouth ceases to praise."
James, the 7th Earl of Derby, made use of this proverb, in complaining of the ingratitude of Captain Edmund Christian, whom he had made Governor of the Island, and upon whom he had conferred many benefits.

Caghlaa obbyr aash.
"Change of work is rest"—a very notable and true proverb.

Ta ynsagh coamrey stoamey yn dooinney berchagh; as t'eh berchys yn dooinney boght.
"Learning is fine clothes of the rich man, and it is riches of the poor man"—*i.e.*, It is of some value in the one case, but of much more value in the other. The following Italian proverb conveys a similar idea—"Knowledge is silver among the poor, gold among the nobles, and a jewel among princes."

Myr sniessey d'an chraue s'miljey yn eill.
"The nearer the bone the sweeter the flesh."

Ta drogh hammag ny share na magher foshlit.
"A miserable bush is better than an open field." This is similar to the Scotch proverb, "a wee bush is better than nae bield." This imagery can be well appreciated in a country so swept by the wind as the Isle of Man. The meaning is, in effect, "Half a loaf is better than no bread."

Cha dooar rieau drogh veaynee corran mie.
"A bad reaper never got a good sickle"—*i.e.*, "A bad workman quarrels with his tools."

Cha deinee rieau yn soogh y shang.
"The greedy will never feel for the hungry."

Un eam gys bee, as jees gys obbyr.
"One call to meat, and two to work."

Obbyr dyn sharrey, obbyr dyn booise.
"Work without desire, work without thanks"—*i.e.*, "Proffered service stinks."

Sooree ghiare, yn tooree share.
"Short courting, the best courting."

Boayl to gioee ta keck, as boayl to mraane ta pleat.

"Where there are geese there is dirt, and where there are women there is talking."

De ve aashagh 'syn oie, monney shibber nagh ee, er nonney nee oo plaiynt er laccal dty laynt.

"To be easy in the night much supper don't eat, or else thoul't complain at wanting thy health."

Myr sniessey da'n oie, slhee mitchooryn.
"The nearer to the night, the more rogues."

Cha row rieau cooid chebbit mie.
"Never were offered wares good."

T'an yeean myr e ghooie my vel clooie er y chione.
"The chicken is like its kind before down is on its head."

Ta fys ec dy chooilley ghooinney c'raad t'an vraag gortagh eh.
"Every man knows where the shoe hurts him."

Oie mooie as oie elley sthie,
Olk son cabbil, agh son kirree mie.
"One night out and another in,
Bad for horses, but good for sheep."

Ta greim ayns traa cooie, sauail nuy.
"A stitch in due time saves nine."

Foddeee fastyr grianagh ve ec moghrey bodjalagh.
"A sunny evening may follow a cloudy morning"—*i.e.,*
Nil desperandum.

My to keim 'sy laair, bee keim 'sy lhiy.
"If there's an amble in the mare, it will be in the colt."
Though,
Ta boa vie ny gha agh drogh lheiy ee.
"Many a good cow hath but a bad calf."

Keeuyl chionnit, yn cheeayl share,
Mannagh vel ee kionnit ro ghayr.
"Bought wit, the best wit,

If it he not bought too dear."

The following are especially connected with *Morality*:—
T'an aghaue veg shuyr da'n aghaue vooar.
"The little hemlock is sister to the great hemlock"—*i.e.*,
"The little sin is sister to the great sin."

Ta cree dooie ny share na kione croutagh.
"A kind heart is better than a crafty (knotty) head."

Ta dooinney creeney mennick jannoo carrey jeh e noid.
"A wise man often makes a friend of his enemy."

Eshyn ghuirrys skeealley hayrtys skeealley.
"He who hatches tales shall be caught by tales."

Ta chengey ny host ny share na olk y ghra.
"The silent tongue is better than evil speaking."

Eshyn lhieys marish moddee, irrys eh marish jarganyn.
"He who will lie down with the dogs will rise up with the fleas"—*i.e.*, "Evil communications corrupt good manners."

Yiow moyrn lhieggy.
"Pride will have a fall."

Cha vel eh cheet jesh da moyrn dy jannoo red erbee ta laccal leshtal.
"It does not become pride to do what needs an apology."

Cha bee breagery credjit ga dy ninsh eh y n'irriney.
"A liar will not be believed tho' he speaks the truth."

Cha nee tra ta'n cheyrrey gee yn ouw to cheet r'ee.
"It is not when the sheep eats the march-penny it tells a tale" (literally, "it comes to her")—*i.e.*, The result of evil-doing is not always apparent at first. The *ouw* is a slow poison.

Tasht prughag, as ee lughag.
"Store miser, and eat mouse."

Ta un cheyrrey screebagh mhilley yn slane shioltane.

"One scabby sheep infects (or injures) the whole flock."

Ta keeayll ommidjys ny sloo my t'ee ec dooinney creeney dy reayll.

"Wisdom is folly unless a wise man keeps it."

S' mie ve daaney, agh s'olk ve ro ghaaney.

"How good to be forward, but how bad to be too forward."

The following Proverbs appear to inculcate *Selfishness*:—

Faggys ta my lheiney, agh ny sniessey to my crackan.

"Near is my shirt, but nearer is my skin."

Cha stamp rieau yn dow doo er e chass.

"The black ox never stamped on his own foot."

Dy chooilley ghooinney er e hon hene, as Yee son ain ooilley.

"Every man for himself, and God for us all."

Baase y derrey voddey, bioys y voddey elley.

"The death of one dog is the life of another."

Ceau craue ayns beeall drogh voddey.

"Throw a bone into a bad dog's mouth"—*i.e.*, Give a sop to any one who annoys you, though he does not deserve it.

Sniessey yn ullin na yn cloan.

"Nearer the barn than the children"—*i.e.*, Our own welfare is more important than our children's.

Slaa sahll er toinn muck roauyr.

"Daub grease upon the rump of a fat pig"—*i.e.*, Flatter the prosperous.

The following Proverbs illustrate one of the chief characteristics of Manxmen, *i.e.*, *Caution*:—

Ta aile meeley jannoo bry millish.

"Slow fire makes sweet malt"—*i.e.*, Don't be in a hurry. Don't jump to a conclusion.

Foddee yn moddey s'jerree tayrtyn y mwaagh.

"Perhaps the last dog may catch the hare"—This enforces precisely the same conclusion as the previous proverb.

Lurg roayrt hig contraie.
"After spring tide will come neap"—*i.e.*, Don't be elevated by present good fortune, a reverse may come.

Coonley ny hein roish ta ny hoohyn guirl.
"Counting the chickens before the eggs are hatched."

Myr smoo siyr, smoo cumrail.
"The greater hurry, the greater hindrance."

Leah appee, leah lhoau.
"Soon ripe, soon rotten."—This seems to carry much the same idea as "Slow and steady wins the race."

Moyll y droghad myr heu harrish.
"Praise the bridge as thou wilt go over it"—*i.e.*, Don't be in a hurry to praise a thing before you try it.

Eddyr daa stoyl to toinn er laare.
"Between two stools the bottom is on the floor"—or, you will fall on the floor.

Tra s'reagh yn chloie, share faagail jeh.
"When the play is merriest it is better to leave off."

Stiark keayrt ta dooinney siyragh ass seaghyn.
"Seldom is the time that a hasty man is out of trouble."

Cha jean un ghollan-geayee sourey,
My un chellagh-keylley geurey.
"One swallow will not make summer,
Nor one woodcock winter."

Mollee yn molteyr oo my odays eh
Share yn olk shione dooin, na yn olk nagh nhione dooin.
"Better the evil we know than the evil we do not know."
Tra ta thie dty naboo er aile gow cairail jeh dty hie hene.
"When thy neighbour's house is on fire take care of thine

own house."

Ta ashag 'sy laue chammah as jees 'sy thammag.
"A bird in the hand is as well as two in the bush."

Ta lane eddyr raa as janno.
"There's much between saying and doing."

Ta lane caillit eddyr y lane as y veeal.
"There's much lost between the hand and the mouth"—
i.e., "There's many a slip 'twixt the cup and the lip."

Ec shibber Oie Ynnyd my vees dty volg lane,
My jig Laa Caisht yiow traisht son shen.
"At Shrove Tuesday if thy belly be-full,
Before Easter Day thou mayst fast for that."

Eaisht lesh dagh cleaysh, eisht jean briwnys.
"Listen with each ear, then do judgment."

The following may also be put under the heading of cautious proverbs as their moral is "Do not be deceived by appearances":—

Cha nee yn woa smoo eieys smoo vlieaunys.
"It is not the cow which lows the most will milk the most."

Siyn follym smoo sheean nee.
"Empty vessels will make the most noise."

The following seem to inculcate virtues of *Contentment* and *Kindness*:—

Tra hig yn laa, hig yn coyrle lesh.
"When the day comes, its counsel will come with it"—
i.e., "Sufficient for the day is the evil thereof."

Shegin goaill ny eairkyn marish y cheh.
"We must take the horns with the hide."

Cha nee eshyn ta red beg echey ta boght.
Agh eshyn ta geearree smoo.
"'Tis not the man who has little that's poor,

But he that desires more."

Eshyn nagh bee mie rish e gharran,
Shegin dan phollan y cur-lesh er e vooin.
"He who will not be kind to his nag must bring the saddle on his own back"—*i.e.*, Kindness is the best policy.

The following inculcate the virtue of *Thrift*:—

Millish dy ghoaill, agh sharroo dy eeck.
"Sweet to take but bitter to pay"—*i.e.*, When you are enjoying yourself and spending money remember you will have to pay for it.

Hig daill gys eeck.
"Credit will come to pay."

Roshee daill y dorrys.
"Credit will stretch the door."

Ta fooiliagh naareydagh ny s'messey na ee scammyltagh.
"Shameful leaving is worse than shameful eating."

Cha daink lesh y gheay, nagh ragh lesh yn ushtey.
"What did not come with the wind would not go with the water."

Dhaa ghrogh eeck t'ayn, geeck rolaue, as dyn eeck eedyr.
"There are two bad pays—pay beforehand, and no pay at all."

Share goll dy lie fegooish shibber na girree ayns lhiastynys.
"Better to go to bed supperless than to get up in debt."

Taa aaa pharick[1] jannoo un ghimmagh.
"Two small lobsters make a big one"—*i.e.*, "Many a little makes a mickle."

Cha vel sonnys gonnys.
"Store is no sore."

Soddag cham, bolg jeeragh.

---

1 "Patricks," a slang word for a lobster.

"Crooked bannock, straight belly."

The meaning of this is probably that spare living will make strong, able men.

The dignity of *Independence* is the moral of the following:—

Lhig dy chooilley ushag guirr e hoohyn hene.
"Let every bird hatch its own eggs."

Lhig dy chooilley vuck reuyrey jeh hene.
"Let every pig dig for itself."

Ta dty lhiasagh dty ghoarn.
"Thy recompense is thine own hand."
A similar idea is conveyed by
Lhiat myr hoilloo.
"To thee as thou deservest."

The following proverbs inculcate *Industry, Promptitude,* and *Thorough Work*:—

Litcheragh goll dy lie, litcheragh dy irree,
As litcheragh dy goll dys y cheeill Je-doonee.
"Lazy to go to bed, lazy to rise,
And lazy to go to church on Sunday."

Cha vow laue ny haaue veg.
"The idle hand gets nothing."

Cadley ny moddee tra ta ny mraane creearey.
"Dogs sleep when the women are sifting"—*i.e.*, sifting meal at the mill.

Bwoaill choud as ta'n yiarn cheh.
"Strike as long as the iron's hot."
Jean traagh choud as ta'n grian soilshean.
"Make hay as long as the sun shines."

Lhig da'n innagh lhie er y chione s'jerree.
"Let the weft rest upon the last end."—*i.e.*, Finish your work. Do what you have to do thoroughly.

The following charitable saying seems to be peculiar to the Isle of Man:—

Tra ta un dooinney boght cooney lesh dooinney boght elley, ta Jee hene garaghtee.

"When one poor man helps another poor man, God Himself laughs."

The poor in the Isle of Man are remarkably kind and helpful to each other.

The following proverb would seem to be a caution against permitting the abuse of charity by unworthy objects:—

Cur meer d'an feeagh, as hig eh reesht.
"Give a piece to the raven, and he'll come again."

WEATHER PROVERBS AND SAYINGS

These are for the most part in connection with the seasons and certain days, and have been given in Chapter VI; but there are a few of more general application, as follows:—

Yn chiuney smoo erbee geay jiass sniessey jee.
"The greater the calm the nearer the south wind."

A great calm is an almost certain token of coming storm. The worst storms in the Isle of Man usually commence by blowing from the S.E. or S., and take off when they reach the N.W.

Glare sheear, liauyr shiar.
"Short west, long east."

Alluding to the wind. The west winds are much the most common in the Isle of Man, but when the east winds set in they last longer.

My ta'n grian jiarg tra girree eh,
Foddee shiu jerkal rish fliaghey.
"If the sun is red when he rises, you may expect rain."

A bright clear day coming in unsettled weather is called "a fox day," as it is not to be depended upon. Throughout the southern part of the Island a cloud on South Barrule Mountain is considered a sure sign of coming rain.

MISCELLANEOUS PROVERBS AND SAYINGS

Myr sloo yn cheshaght share yn ayrn
Myr smoo yn cheshaght s'raie yn chloie.
"The smaller the company, the bigger the share,
The larger the company, the better the sport (or cheer)."

Cronk ghlass foddey voym; lhome, lhome tra roshym eh.
"A green hill far from me; bare, bare when I reach it."
This would seem to mean that expectation is much better than the reality. "Distance lends enchantment to the view." Things toiled for that seemed most desirable in the distance are found of little worth when attained.

The following fine manly saying seems to be of purely native origin:—

Nagh insh dou cre va mee, agh insh dou cre ta mee.
"Don't tell me what I was, but tell me what I am"—*i.e.*, Take a man for what he is himself worth. Don't consider his origin.

Fuirree yn mwaagh rish e heshey.
"The hare will stop for its mate."

Brishys accyrys trooid voallaghyn cloae.
"Hunger will break through stone walls."

Raad ta jees to reih,
As raad ta troor ta teiy.
"Where there are two there is a choice,
But where there are three there is a pick."

Cha vel y Vanninagh dy bragh creeney dys y laa lurg y vargee.
"The Manxman is never wise till the day after the market" (or after the fair).

Cha jinnagh dooinney to coyrt dy ve ry-akin dy bragh jeirk 'sy dorraghys.

"A man that doth not give to be seen always give in the dark."

Yn oghe gyllagh 'toyn losht' da'n aiee.

"The oven crying 'burnt bottom' to the kiln"—*i.e.*, "The pot calling the kettle black."

Goll thie yn ghoayr dy hirrey ollan.

"Going to the goat's house to seek for wool"—*i.e.*, Going on a fool's errand.

Myr s'doo yn feagh yiow eh sheshey.

"Black as is the raven, he'll get a partner."

Ta sheshey chammah as ayrn.

"A companion is as good as a share."

Guilley smuggagh, dooinney glen,
Inneen smuggagh, trowse dy ven.

"Snotty boy, clean man;
Snotty girl, slut of a woman."

The notion seems to that a dirty girl will never improve, as she is wanting in proper pride in her appearance, but that a dirty boy will probably improve, as a boy who is too much concerned with his appearance is not likely to do much good in after life.

Stroshey yn theay na yn Chiarn.

"The Commons are stronger than the Lord"—*i.e.*, The Lord of the Isle. The Manx have always been noted for their ability to maintain their independence when it was threatened.

Share farkiaght er baare faarkey, ny er keim rullickey.

"It is better to be waiting on the top of wave than on the church-yard stile"—*i.e.*, "A live dog is better than a dead lion."

Bioys da dooinney as baase da eeast.

"Life to man, and death to fish."

This was a regular toast at public dinners. Its meaning being of course an abundant fishing, without loss of life to those engaged in it.

Yn raad mooar Ree Goree.

"The great road of King Oree"; or, the Milky Way.

Tradition has it that when King Oree landed in Man he was asked whence he came, upon which, pointing to the Milky Way, he said, "That is the road to my country." Hence the Manx name for it.

Kione mooar er y veggan cheayley, as kione beg gyn veg eddyr.

"A great head with little wit, and a little head without any." It is said that as some farmers were cutting their yearly stock of turf on the mountain side near Snaefell, they came upon a large block of stone on which was engraved—

Chyndaa us mish, as yiow us choyrle.

"Turn thou me, and thou shall get advice."

On turning it after much labour, they found on the other side—

Ta brolt cheh boggagh arran croie,
Chyndaa us mish myr va roie.

"Hot broth softens hard bread,
Turn thou me as I was before."—

i.e., "A soft answer turneth away wrath."

Ny poosee eirey-inneen ny ta'n ayr eck er ny ve craghit.

"Do not marry an heiress unless her father has been hanged." She is sure to be proud and difficult to manage.

Mannagh vow cliaghtey cliaghtey, nee cliaghtey coe.

"If custom be not indulged with custom, custom will weep." Manxmen are very conservative and tenacious of old customs.

Kiangle myr void, as yiow myr carrey.

"Bind as an enemy, and you shall have as a friend."

Cre yiow jeh'n chayt agh y chrackan.

"What wilt thou get of the cat but the skin?"

Ta lhane klinkyn ayns car-y-phoosee.

"There are many twists in the nuptial song"—*i.e.*, Matrimony has its hazards.

Traa-dy-liooar!—"Time enough"—is a phrase often on a Manxmen's lips. They are noted procrastinators. Gossips and tale-hearers are said "To go about like a brewing pan," because, as one brewing pan usually served a whole neighbourhood, in the days when beer was home-brewed, it went about constantly from house to house. Those who were wont to "draw the long-bow" were said to be "Playing *Fodjeeaght.*" (*Fodjeeaght*, according to Cregeen, being "the distance of the furthest arrow shot in archery.")

Tra ta'n, gheay sy villey yiow shiu yn Guilley-glass—"When the wind is in the tree you will get the Lockman." There is no apparent connection between the Lockman, who is a sort of under-Coroner, and the wind in the tree, but possibly some of our readers may be able to explain it.

Ta airh er cushagyn ayns shen.
"There is gold on cushags there."

Cushag is the Manx name of the weed, Ragwort, which grows luxuriantly in Man. The expression is an ironical one, and was used when people spoke disparagingly of the Island, and boastingly of other places.

"No herring, no wedding."

For, if the herring fishing was to fail, the young men would not be rich enough to marry. The Manx were formerly largely dependent on the fishing for subsistence, as Blundell remarked in 1648, "The sea feedeth more of the Manksmen than the soil." It was in recognition of this that a special clause was inserted in the Litany by Bishop Wilson, *i.e.*, "That it may please thee to give and preserve to our use the kindly fruits of the earth, *and to restore and continue to us the blessings of the seas*, so as in due time we may enjoy them."

The Manx language abounds in quaint figurative *Sayings,*

of which the following will serve as illustrations:—

The Zodiac is called *Cassan-ny-greiney*—"The footpath of the sun." The Rainbow *Goll twoaie*—"Going north." The expression for "The perfect" in the Bible is *Feallagh ny firri-nys*—"People of the truth." Of a man who prospers it is said *Te cheet lesh*—"It comes with him." When a man is advised to rely on his own understanding he is told *Shass er e chione hene*—"To stand on his own head." A person who is failing in health is said to be *Goll sheese ny liargagh*—"Going down the slope." Beggars are said to be *Shooyll ny thieyn*—"Walking (or, going) on the houses." For "the water is boiling," they say *Ta'n ushtey cloie*—"The water is playing." Remorse is expressed by the phrase *Craue beg 'sy chleeau*—"A little bone in the breast." An impudent person is compared to a white stone, thus: *T'ou cha daaney myr clagh vane*—"Thou art as impudent as a white stone." The white quartz stones are very conspicuous objects on the hill sides. An inconstant person is said to be *Lhi-am-lhiat*—"With me, with thee" or *Chengey lhiam, Chengey lhiat*—"Tongue with me, tongue with thee"—*i.e.*, "Blowing hot and cold." A Manxman calls his walking-stick *Bock-Yuan-Fannee*—"John the Flayer's pony," be pause this John is said to have flayed his pony, and to have been consequently obliged to travel on foot.

SUGGESTED FURTHER READING

Cumming, Joseph George. *The Isle of Man: Its History, Physical, Ecclesiastical, Civil, and Legendary*. London: John van Voorst, 1848.

Cumming, Joseph George. *The Story of Rushen Castle and Rushen Abbey, in the Isle of Man*. Forgotten Books, 2018.

Elleray, Robert. I*sle of Man: A Pictorial History*. The History Press, 1989.

Evans-Wentz, W.Y. T*he Fairy-Faith in Celtic Countries*. London: H. Frowde, Oxford University Press, 1911.

Keightley, Thomas. T*he Fairy Mythology*, vol. 1. London: William Harrison Ainsworth, 1828.

Keightley, Thomas. *The Fairy Mythology: Illustrative of the Romance and Superstition of Various Countries*, vol. 2. London: H.G. Bohn, 1851.

Leney, I.H (Mrs. J. W. Russell). *Shadowland in Ellan Vannin; or, Folk-Tales of the Isle of Man*. London: Elliot Stock, 1890.

Mcdonald, Neil. *Isle of Man, A Megalithic Journey*. 2012.

Morrison, Sophia. *Manx Fairy Tales*. London: David Nutt, 1911.

Rhys, John. *Celtic Folklore: Welsh and Manx*, vols. 1 and 2. Oxford: Clarendon Press, 1901.

Waldron, George. *A Description of the Isle of Man with Some Useful and Entertaining Reflections on the Laws, Customs, and Manners of the Inhabitants*. 1831.

www.ingramcontent.com/pod-product-compliance
Lightning Source LLC
Chambersburg PA
CBHW031124090426
42738CB00008B/959